ANCIENT COINS at the Elvehjem Museum of Art

Herbert M. Howe
Emeritus Professor of Classics
University of Wisconsin–Madison

Elvehjem Museum of Art
University of Wisconsin–Madison
2000

Cover illustration: A set of coins showing on the reverse the nine muses and Heracles as leader of the muses. Gift of Mr. and Mrs. Arthur J. Frank, 1979.250–260.

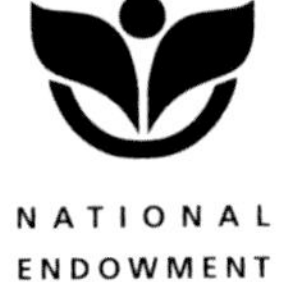

NATIONAL
ENDOWMENT
FOR THE ARTS

Library of Congress Cataloging-in-Publication Data
Elvehjem Museum of Art.
Ancient coins at the Elvehejm Musem of Art / Herbert M. Howe.
p. cm.
Includes bibliographical references.
ISBN 0-932900-48-8 (pbk.)
1. Coins, Ancient--Catalogs. 2. Coins, Greek--Catalogs. 3. Coins, Roman--Catalogs. 4. Coins--Wisconsin--Madison--Catalogs. 5. Elvehjem Musuem of Art--Catalogs. I. Howe, Herbert M. (Herbert Marshall), 1912- II. Title.

CJ215.U62 M344 2000
737.4--dc21

00-037591

Table of Contents

FOREWORD

It is with great pleasure that we publish this fourth in the series of handbooks of the Elvehjem's permanent collection.

Coins, because of their abundance and intimate connections to the ruling elite of the ancient Greco-Roman world, offer a unique insight into the historical events of their time and into the social history of power and propaganda. The Elvehjem's excellent collection of ancient coins represents an invaluable teaching resource to the various departments at the UW–Madison for which that part of the world and those fertile times in its history are the focus of intellectual investigation and analysis. The personages portrayed on the coins and the wonderfully exquisite aesthetic qualities they possess are also a source of great enjoyment for those of us who like simply to wonder every now and then about what life was like back in those distant days.

In all, thanks to a few generous benefactors, the Elvehjem Museum of Art owns 3,746 ancient coins. Of this number, 2,899 comprise a hoard of bronze Roman imperial coins, mostly of the fourth and fifth centuries A.D. and minted in the Greek Eastern Empire. The remaining 847 coins include examples from the ancient Near East, Greece, and Rome and range in date from the sixth century B.C. to the end of the fourth century A.D. The present publication, intended as an introduction to ancient coinage for Elvehjem visitors, includes 174 representative coins drawn from the latter group. The selected coins, combined with sixteen coins on permanent loan to the Elvehjem from the State Historical Society of Wisconsin and four coins from local private collectors offer a good overview of coinage in the ancient world. We do hope that the loans will eventually find a permanent home here. Coins from the hoard, donated to the museum in the late 1970s by Paul and Jon Holtzman, being somewhat homogenous in type, were excluded because they did not add to the specific purpose of this publication; for our audiences, the value of the hoard lies primarily in the fact that it is a hoard and as such offers the opportunity to make studied comparisons of the various contemporary mints represented. We would encourage numismatists and students to undertake such a study in the near future.

We are very grateful to Professor Herbert Howe who so graciously researched and wrote the current catalogue. Retired from teaching classics at the UW–Madison in 1982 after a long and distinguished scholarly career, Professor Howe has been both an advocate of and a key contributor to the Elvehjem's educational mission. Since the museum opened in 1970 Professor Howe has given generously of his knowledge and experience mission to this museum. In the fall of 1999, the Elvehjem introduced a display of coins with text and labels written by Herbert Howe to make the material more readily accessible to many visitors. But we are able to present a much greater selection with more extensive text in this catalogue, with coins selected and text written by Professor Howe.

The Elvehjem's collection of ancient coins has been donated over the years by these generous benefactors: Mr. and Mrs. Arthur J. Frank, Mr. and Mrs. Ellis E. Jensen, Mr. Jon Holtzman, Mr. Paul Holtzman, and Professor Herbert M. Howe.

We are grateful for the support of the National Endowment for the Arts and Brittingham Fund, Inc. for making this publication possible.

Russell Panczenko
Director

ANCIENT COINS

Herbert M. Howe

Coins are bits of metal whose weight is guaranteed by some governmental authority and which are accepted as equivalent to goods for which they can be exchanged. They first appear in the early sixth century B.C. in Lydia, in western Asia Minor. There may have been earlier attempts to establish means of exchange; the gold "button" of Iran (cat. no. 1) of about 1500 B.C. is an example, as are the copper ingots found in shipwrecks of a somewhat later period, neither of which has any indication of authority. Many early coins were of **electrum**, a natural alloy of gold and silver in Asian river sands, but gold or silver generally replaced it. Bronze (copper alloyed with tin) was the usual metal of Italy.

The precious metals were **struck**: a bar would be sawn into blanks of approximately the right weight. One of these would be heated and placed on an **obverse** (heads) die set in an anvil. A **reverse** (tails) die would be placed on top to be struck with a hammer. The obverse die was a bit of hardened bronze with a design cut into it, while the reverse die, more apt to slip, was at first little more than a metal bar with a pattern of teeth on its end. Early Roman bronze coins, such as cat. nos. 68, 69, 70, 71, were **cast**.

These early coins have no inscriptions, although the invention of the Greek alphabet is usually dated to the eighth century B.C., a couple of centuries before the earliest coins. We have little information about how many people could read at any time, but they all could recognize the badges of cities—the turtle of Aegina, the head of Athena of Athens. When eventually inscriptions appeared, they were no more than abbreviations, like Ϙ for Corinth or ΑΘΕ for Athens. Early inscriptions might read either left to right or right to left.

Any system of coinage needs several **denominations**, and, if more than one metal is in use, some sort of equivalence must be enforced. For example, today twenty-five copper cents can be exchanged for five nickels, five-cent pieces. We see in catalogue numbers 10 through 17 a series of Greek silver pieces, fractions and multiples of the drachma.

Ancient coins differ in many ways from modern coins. Their edges are only more or less circular, and they were not "milled," given a cogwheellike edge to prevent people from trimming off a bit of metal. They rarely have rims at the edge or the very low relief which make it possible to stack modern coins, but which force the designer to think in pictorial rather than sculptural terms. Dates were not placed on ancient coins until about 300 B.C. and not regularly then: the portrait of a ruler would change, but if he was on the throne for twenty years that would not precisely identify the year a coin was struck. Some, but by no means all, Roman emperors give annual dates. Finally, ancient coins were changed far more frequently than modern coins; in this they are more like our postage stamps.

Coins, which are peculiarly difficult to display, are shown in this catalogue all at approximately 1 1/2 inches diameter to provide magnification. Some are so badly worn that inscriptions are nearly illegible. But even with these difficulties, coins can be rewarding to the student of art and to the historian.

Note

Gold coins (aurum) are designated AU
Electrum coins are designated EL
Silver coins (argentum) are designated AR
Bronze coins (aes) are designated AE
The front or face of the coin is called the obverse; the back of the coin is called the reverse.

Abbreviations for references found on page 79.

EARLY COINAGE TECHNIQUES

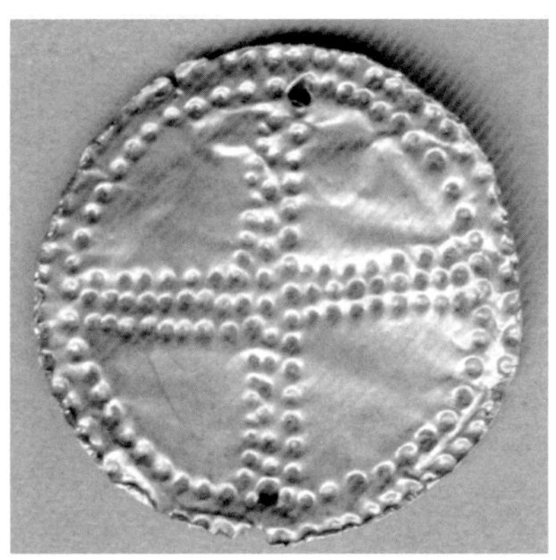

1.
AU "button," 20.6 mm
Iran, Amlash period, ca. 1500 B.C.
Uniface, dotted cross
Gift of Mr. and Mrs. Ellis E. Jensen, 69.11.1

This early example was possibly used as a medium of exchange.

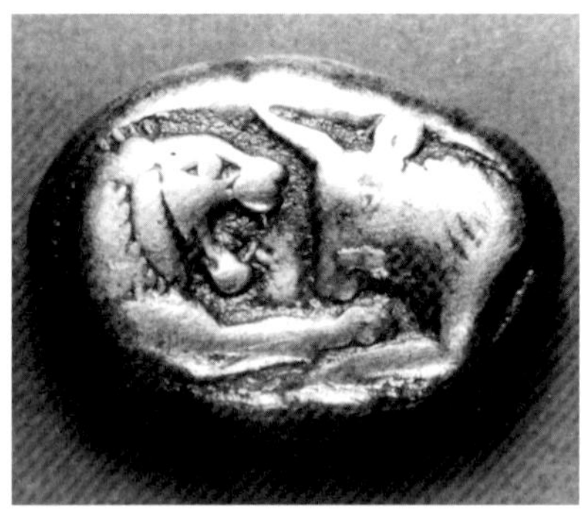

2.
AR didrachm, 22.2 mm, 10.50 g
Mint: Lydia
Croesus, ca. 550 B.C.
Obverse: lion and bull facing each other
Reverse: two incuse (punched-in) squares
Ref. BM Lydia I, 17, Lockett 2980
Gift of Mr. and Mrs. Arthur J. Frank, 1977.255

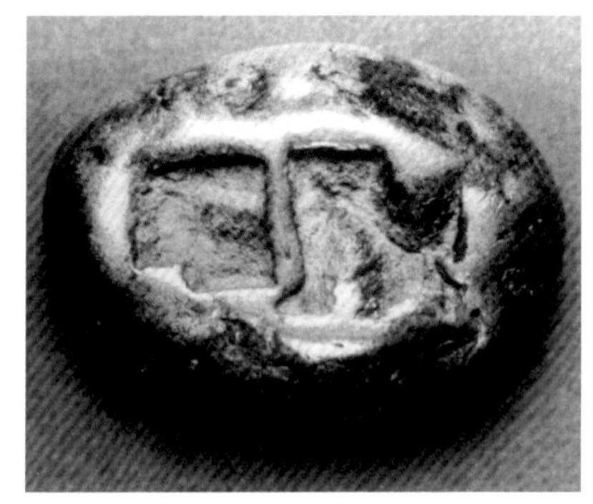

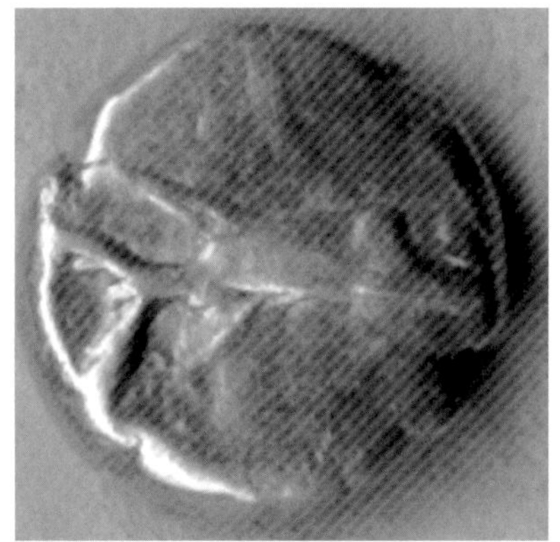

3.
EL 1/24 stater, 7.9 mm
Mint: Cyzicus (Mysia), ca. 600 B.C.
Obverse: tunny fish
Reverse: incuse square
Ref. BM Mysia III, 21
Lent by Emily Howe Wilson, 4.1991.1

So small a coin, of valuable metal and easily lost, would not circulate much; rather, it would be hoarded.

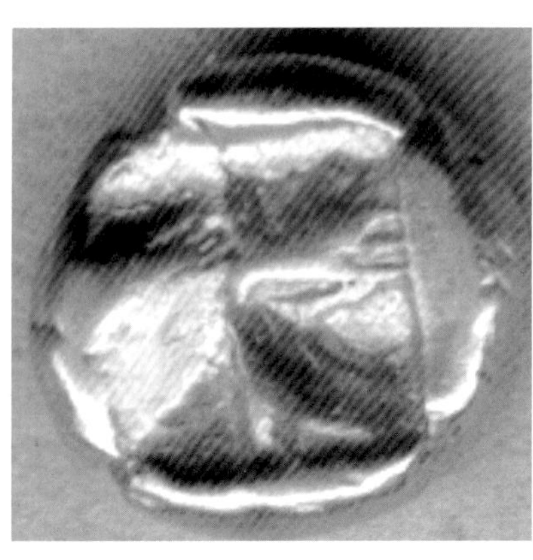

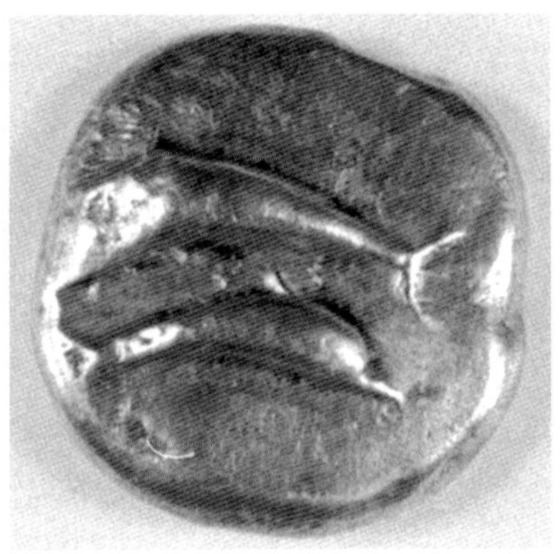

4.
AR stater, 20.6 mm, 12.37 g
Mint: Thera, ca. 575 B.C.
Obverse: two dolphins
Reverse: incuse square divided into four triangular parts
Ref. BM B 62, 17
Gift of Mr. and Mrs. Arthur J. Frank, 1978.315

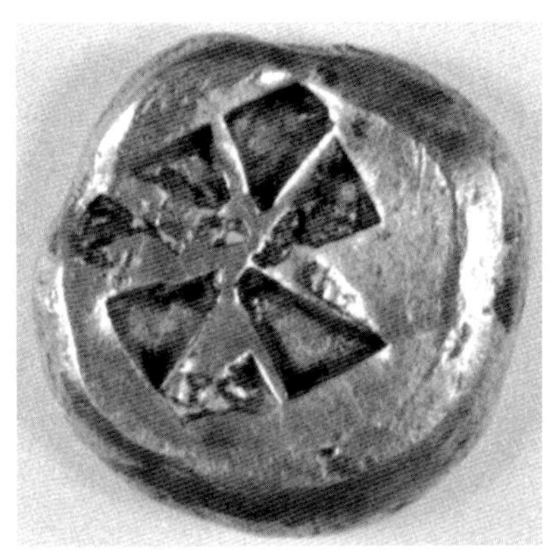

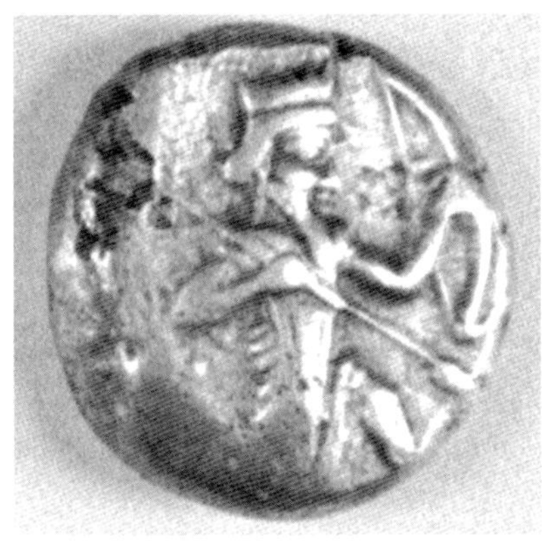

5.
AR siglos, 14.3 mm, 5.55 g
Mint: Persia
Darius I, ca. 500 B.C.
Obverse: king kneeling, to left, holding spear and bow, wearing tiara
Reverse: irregular incuse
Gift of Mr. and Mrs. Arthur J. Frank, 1979.226

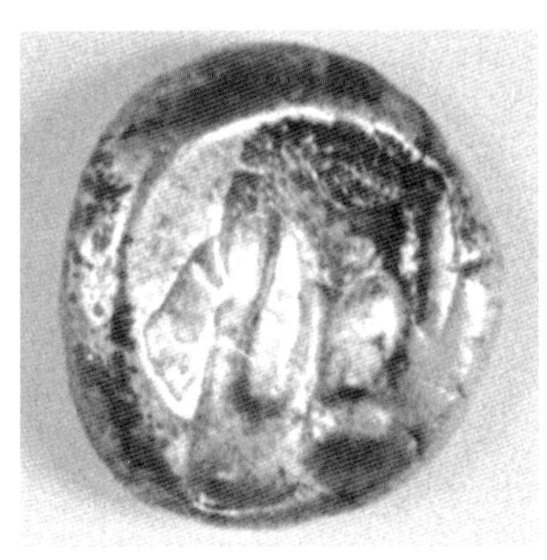

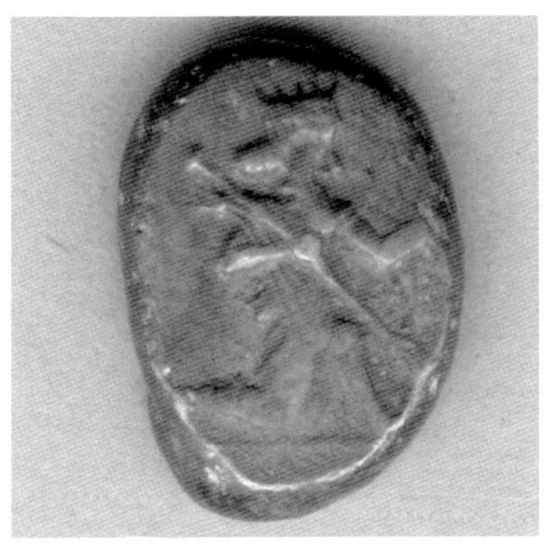

6.
AR siglos, 14.3 mm, 5.35 g
Mint: Persia
Darius I, ca. 500 B.C.
Obverse: king kneeling, to left, holding spear and bow, wearing tiara
Reverse: irregular incuse
Gift of Mr. and Mrs. Ellis E. Jensen, 69.11.2

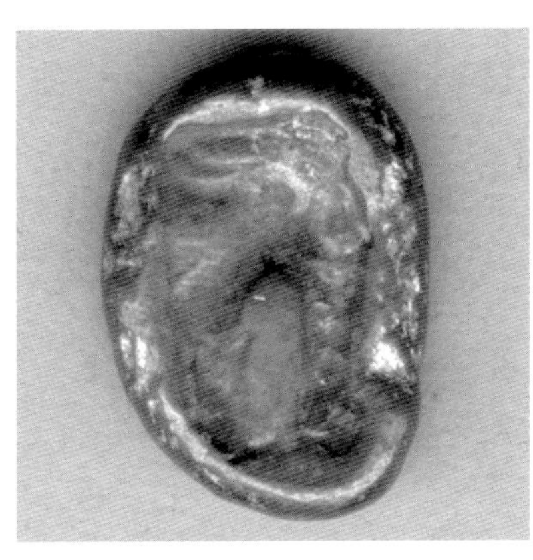

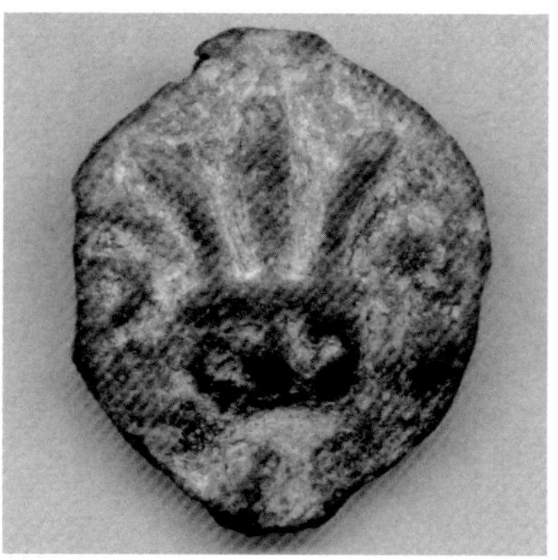

7.
AE sextans, cast, 25 mm, 15.54 g
Mint: Tuder (Umbria), ca. 290 B.C.
Obverse: ornamental trident; at left, TV (Tuder, modern Todi); at right, two pellets
Reverse: locust; on either side, pellet
Ref. BMC Italy 33.5
Gift of Herbert M. Howe, 1980.485

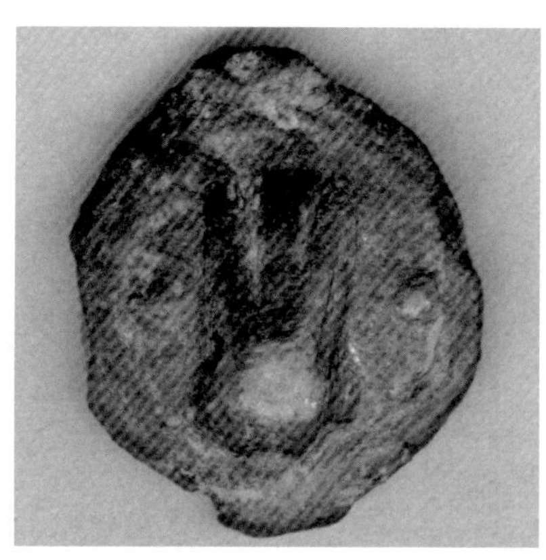

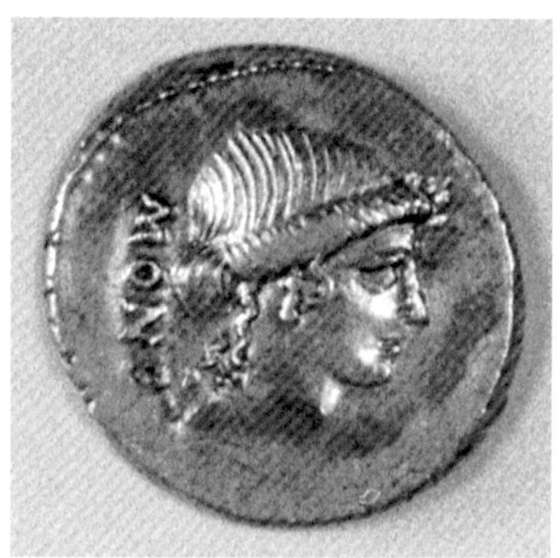

8.
AR denarius, 19.1 mm
Mint: Rome, T. Carisius, 46–45 B.C.
Obverse: head of Juno Moneta, to right; behind, MONETA
Reverse: instruments for making coins: the anvil and die for obverse, with reverse die above; on left, tongs; on right, hammer; above, T CARISIVS
Ref. BMC 4057; CRR 982a
Gift of Mr. and Mrs. Arthur J. Frank, 1979.269

Moneta, in whose temple precinct money was struck, is translated "She who gives warning." In 390 B.C. the Gauls attacked Rome and tried to seize the capitol by night. The garrison, however, was warned by the honking of the faithful geese of the goddess—hence her name.

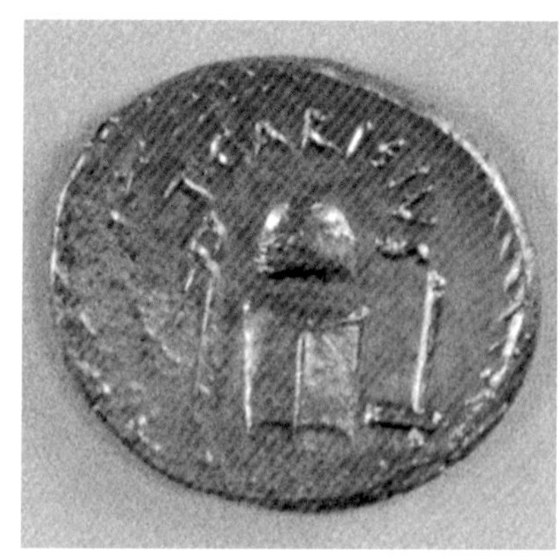

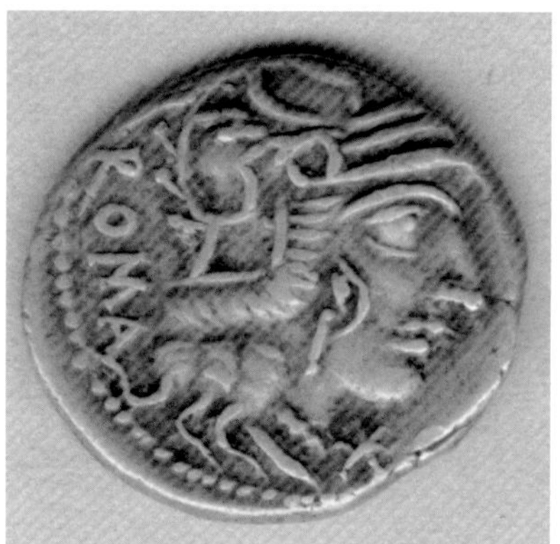

9.
AR denarius, 19.1 mm
Mint: Rome, M. Calidius, Q. Metellus, Cn. Fulvius, 117–116 B.C.
Obverse: head of Roma right; behind, ROMA
Reverse: Victory in chariot at right, holding wreath
Ref. Crawford 284.1b; CRR 539a; BMC Italy 477
Gift of Herbert M. Howe, 1980.214

This coin illustrates the sort of slip possible in hand-made coins. The moneyers struck a coin, which stuck to the reverse die. The next blank they struck had a real "heads" impression, from the obverse die, and a ghostly one, from the "heads" of the coin just struck.

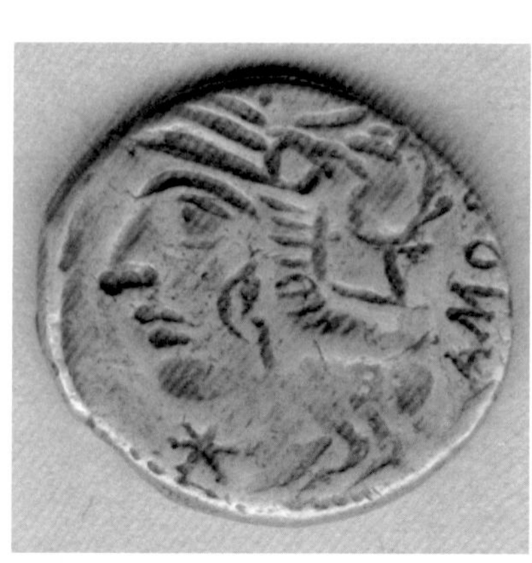

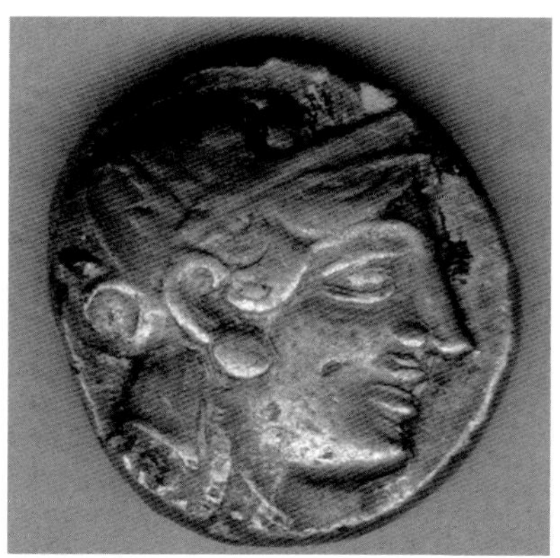

10.
AR plated tetradrachm, 23 mm, 13.79 g
Mint: Athens, 406–393 B.C.
Obverse: head of Athena, to right
Reverse: owl standing, to right, head facing front
Gift of Mr. and Mrs. Arthur J. Frank, 1979.220

At the end of the Peloponnesian War, silver ran short, and to save metal the Athenians were forced to issue copper cores dipped in molten silver, producing a "coinage of necessity." The reverse plainly shows places where silver has worn off.

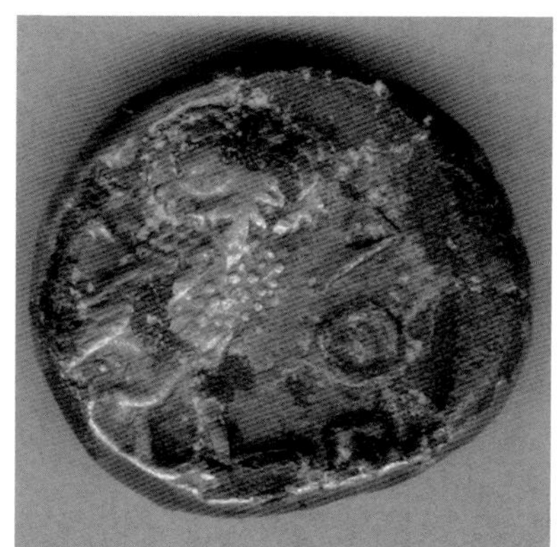

Weights And Denominations

Throughout history many names of coins have been derived from the names of weights: the English pound, from Latin *pondus* (weight); the Spanish onza, from Latin *uncia* (ounce); the Italian lira, from Latin *libra* (pound), used first for copper, and then in the Greek form, *litra*, for a weight of silver of equivalent value. The Greeks used several standards, notably that of the *stater*. But the most important standard was that of Athens, shown here, based on the drachma of about 4.4 grams of silver, which equaled 6 obols. There was a tradition of an older iron coinage elsewhere in Greece, in the form of rods or "spits" (*obeloi*); six of these made a "handful" (*drachma*). The names passed over to silver coinage.

Most Athenian coins have a head of Athena on the obverse and an owl, the sacred bird of Athena, on the reverse.

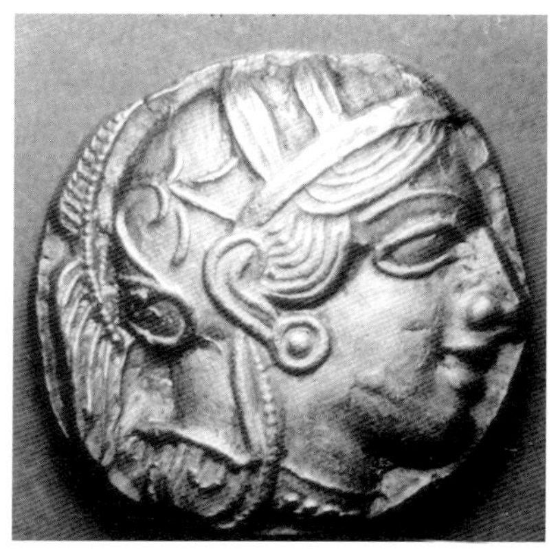

11.
AR tetradrachm, 24 mm, 17.18 g
Mint: Athens, ca. 430 B.C.
Obverse: helmeted head of Athena, facing right
Reverse: owl, spray of olive leaves, crescent moon; ΑΘΕ, all in incuse square
Gift of Mr. and Mrs. Arthur J. Frank, 1977.248

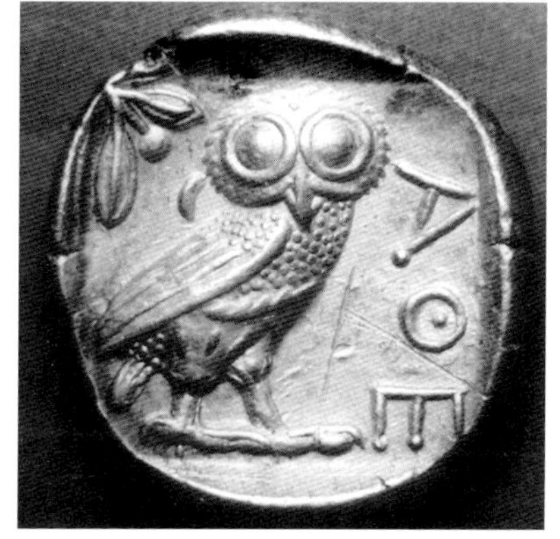

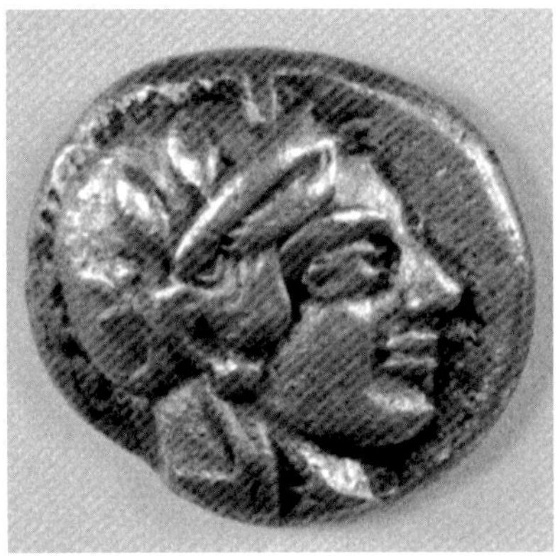

12.
AR drachma, 126 mm, 4.15 g
Mint: Athens, ca. 450 B.C.
Obverse: helmeted head of Athena, facing right
Reverse: owl with olive spray and crescent moon; ΑΘΕ, all in incuse square
Gift of Mr. and Mrs. Arthur J. Frank, 1977.249

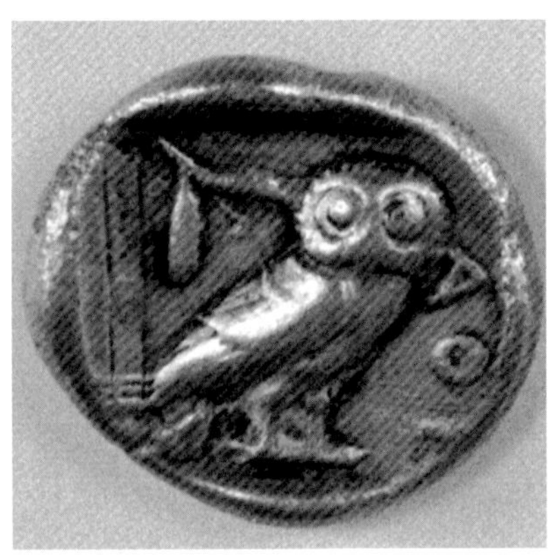

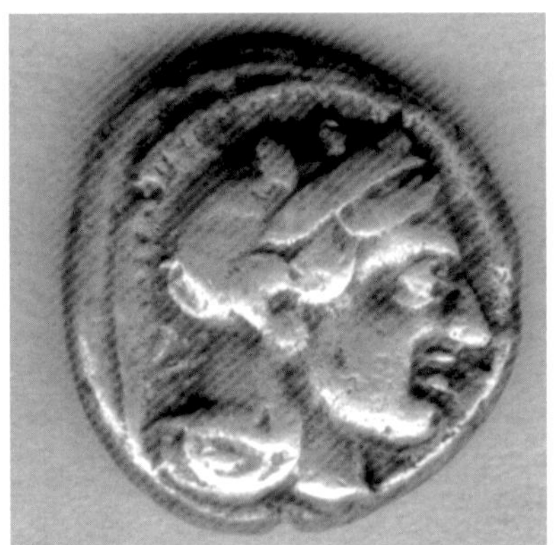

13.
AR triobol (hemidrachm), 12.70 mm, 2.04 g
Mint: Athens, ca. 450 B.C.
Obverse: helmeted head of Athena, facing right
Reverse: full-face owl, wings closed; olive leaves, no moon, ΑΘΕ
Gift of Mr. and Mrs. Arthur J. Frank, 1977.250

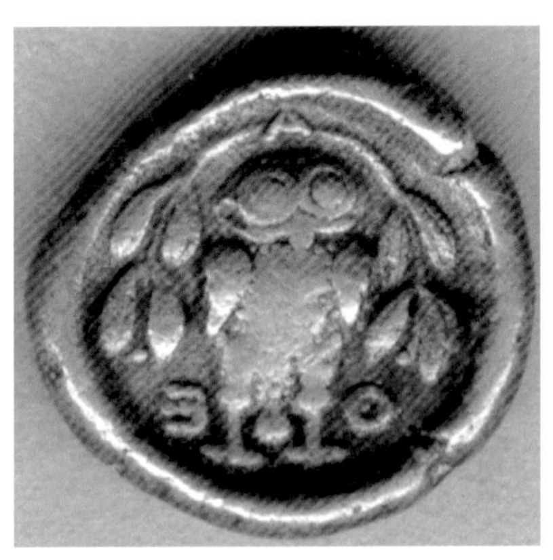

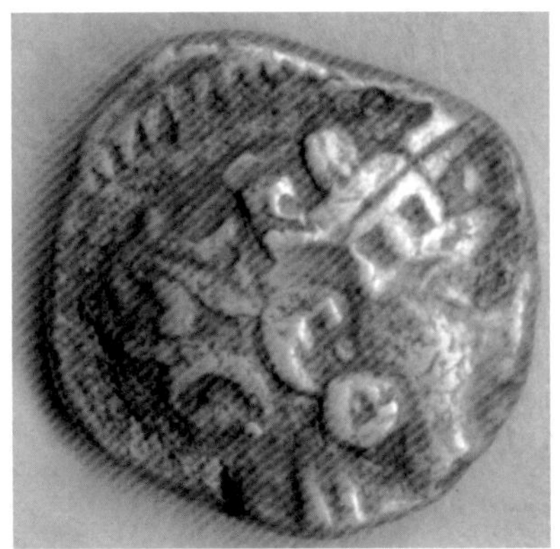

14.
AR diobol, 11.1 mm, 1.30 g
Mint: Athens, ca. 380 B.C.
Obverse: helmeted head of Athena, facing right
Reverse: owl with two bodies and only one head, with wings open; olive sprig at either side
Ref. BM Attica 17.77
Gift of Herbert M. Howe, 1980.86

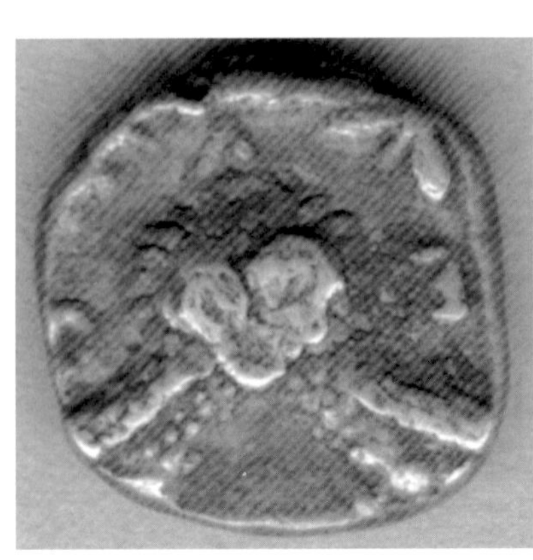

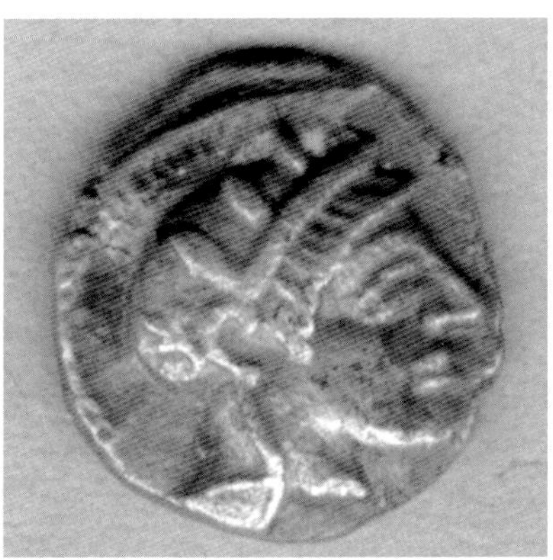

15.
AR obol, 9.5 mm, 0.67 g
Mint: Athens, ca. 450 B.C.
Obverse: helmeted head of Athena, facing right
Reverse: owl standing sideways, head facing front; one olive leaf and berry, ΑΘΕ in incuse square
Gift of Mr. and Mrs. Arthur J. Frank, 1977.251

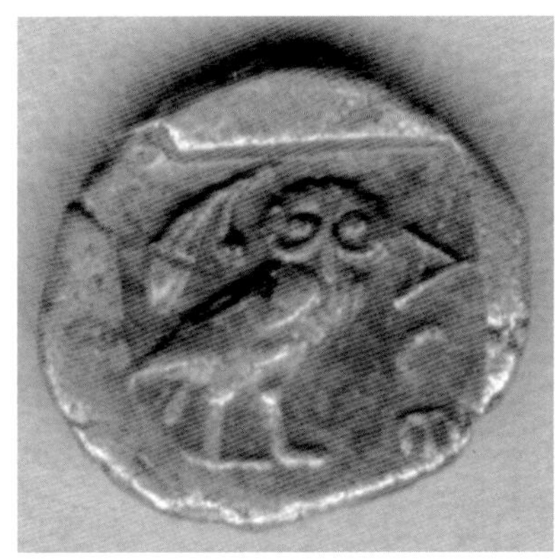

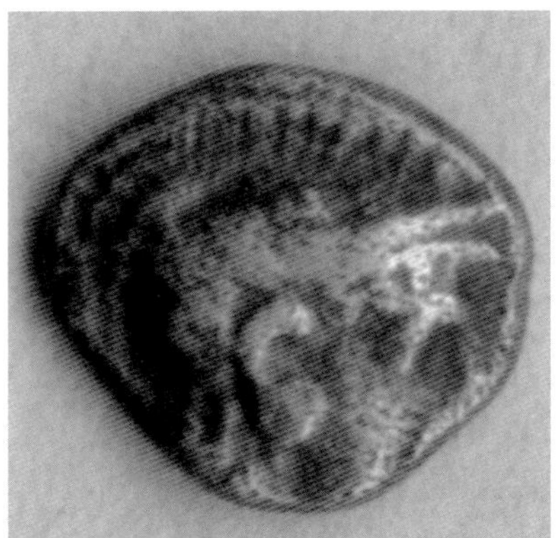

16.
AR tritartemorion, 7.9 mm, 0.50 g
Mint: Athens, ca. 380 B.C.
Obverse: helmeted head of Athena, facing right
Reverse: three crescents with horns turned in, ΑΘΕ
Ref. BM Attica 18.187
Gift of Herbert M. Howe, 1980.93

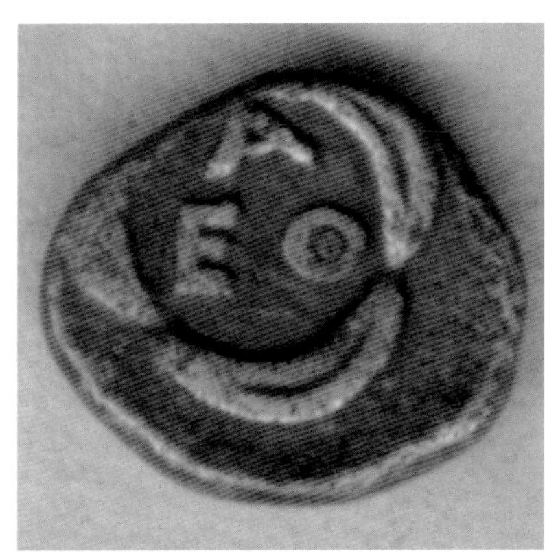

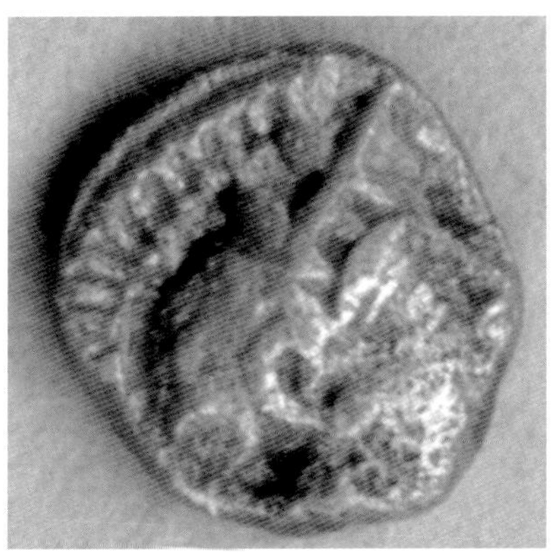

17.
AR hemiobol, 6.4 mm, 0.335 g
Mint: Athens, ca. 380 B.C.
Obverse: helmeted head of Athena, facing right
Reverse: owl standing with olive leaf, in incuse square; no inscription
Gift of Mr. and Mrs. Arthur J. Frank, 1977.252

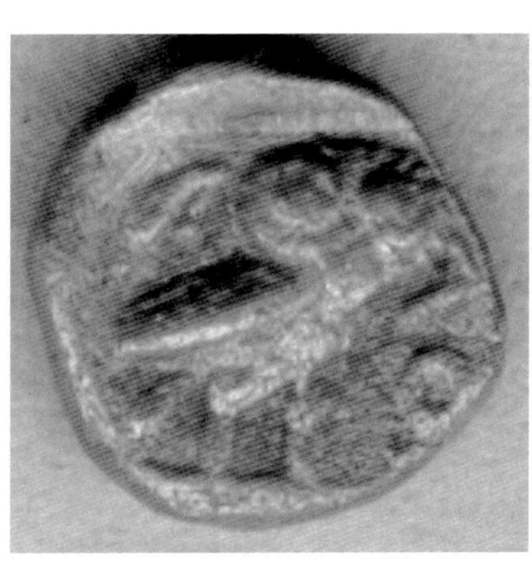

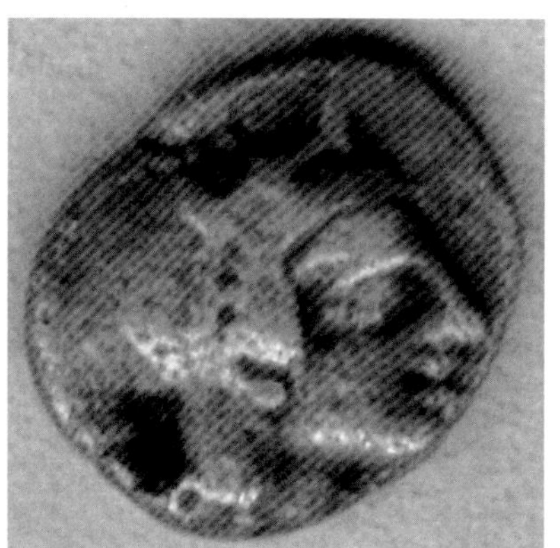

18.
AR tetartemorion, 6.4 mm, 0.16 g
Mint: Athens, ca. 420 B.C.
Obverse: helmeted head of Athena, facing right
Reverse: crescent with horns up; above, ΑΘΕ
Ref. BM Attica 1.197–206
Gift of Herbert M. Howe, 1980.85

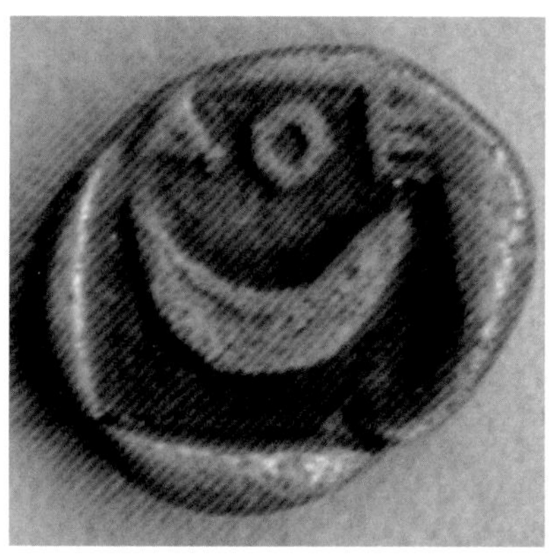

Coin Types of Greek Cities

Until the late fourth century B.C., when the portraits of rulers appeared, Greek cities generally kept the same types on their coins year after year. The types shown here, with little attention to chronology, are some of the best known and most important examples, but they are only a few of the several hundred known. A group of Athenian tetradrachms shows the evolution over about three centuries.

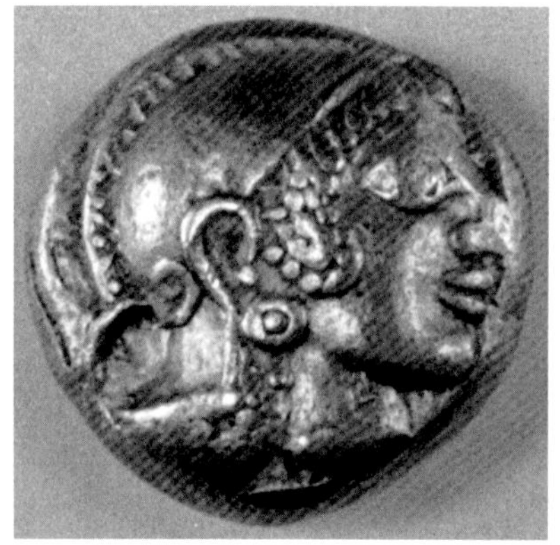

19.
AR tetradrachm, 20.6 mm, 17.32 g
Mint: Athens, ca. 500 B.C.
Obverse: head with bulbous full-face eye and smiling mouth (all conventions of the archaic style)
Reverse: owl, standing upright to right, head facing front; olive sprig behind all in shallow incuse square; |Α|ΘΕ
Ref. Seltman 49, pl. II.
Gift of Mr. and Mrs. Arthur J. Frank, 1979.218

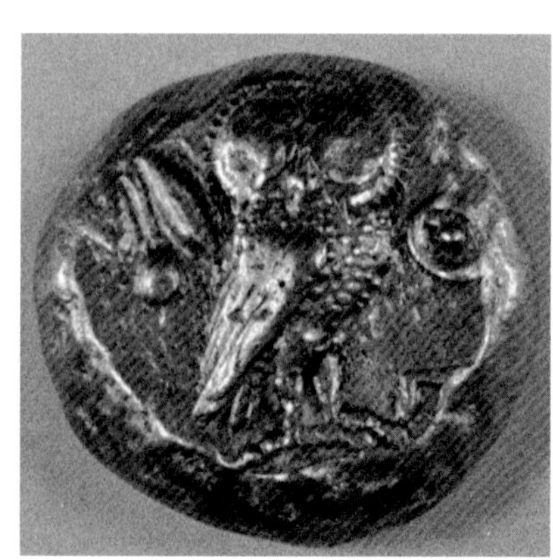

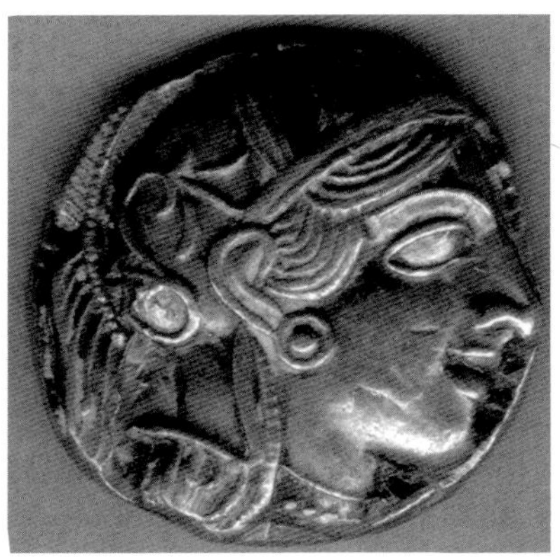

20.
AR tetradrachm, 25 mm, 17.18 g
Mint: Athens, ca. 450 B.C.
Obverse: Athena helmeted
Reverse: owl, with olive spray and crescent moon, ΑΘΕ
Gift of Mr. and Mrs. Arthur J. Frank, 1977.247

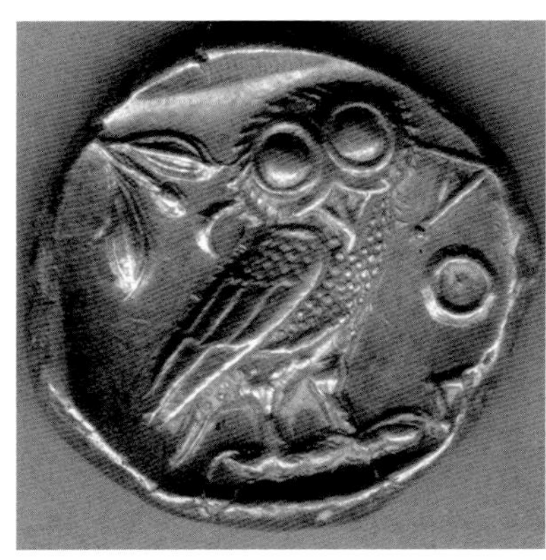

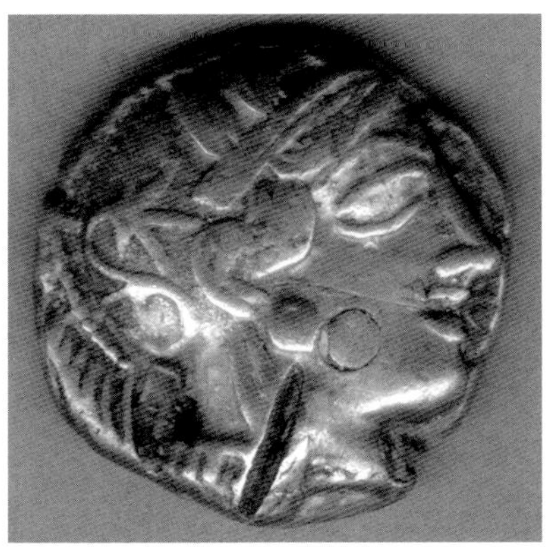

21.
AR tetradrachm, 23.8 mm, 17.00 g
Mint: Athens, ca. 410 B.C.
Obverse: Athena
Reverse: owl, head facing front, standing right, ΑΘΕ
Gift of Mr. and Mrs. Arthur J. Frank, 1979.219

Test cuts on owl's cheek and Athena's neck.

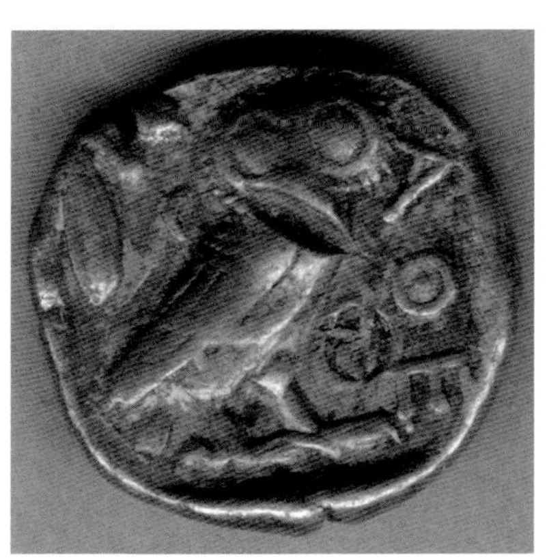

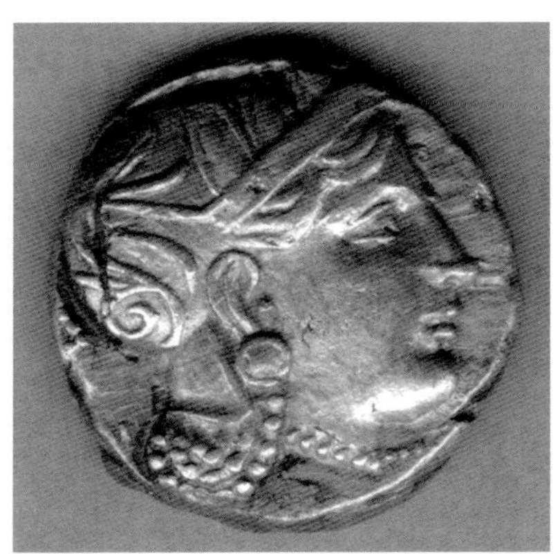

22.
AR tetradrachm, 22.2 mm, 16.76 g
Mint: Athens, 336–323 B.C.
Obverse: head of Athena, to right, with helmet, profile eye
Reverse: owl, standing right, facing head, olive sprig and waning moon, ΑΘΕ
Ref. Svor. Pl 20, 34
Gift of Mr. and Mrs. Arthur J. Frank, 1979.221

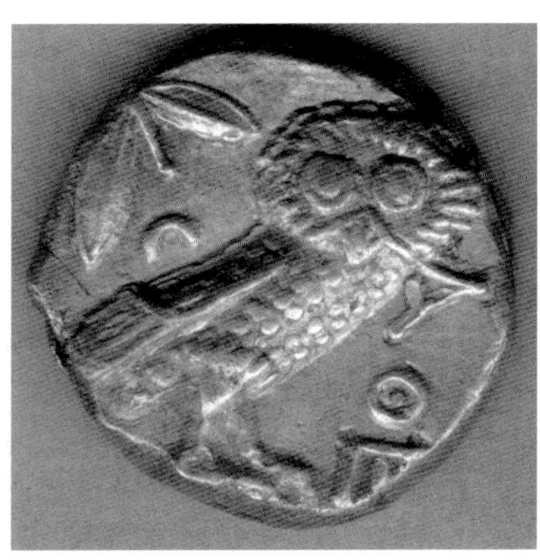

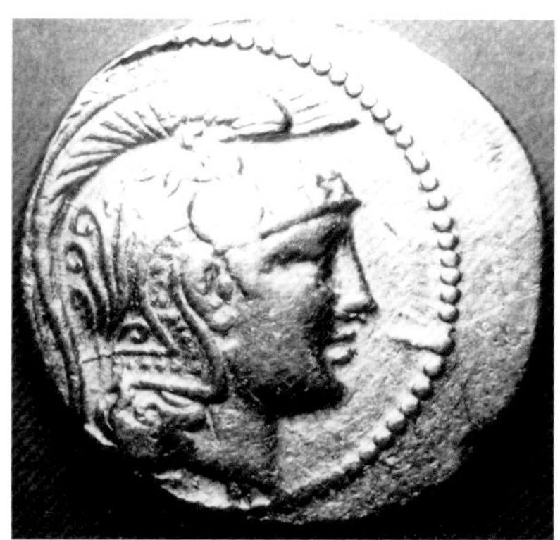

23.
AR tetradrachm, 31 mm, 16.70 g
Mint: Athens, 167 B.C.
Obverse: head of Athena in triple-crested helmet adorned with flying Pegasus
Reverse: owl, to right facing, wings closed, standing on amphora that lies on side; ΜΕΝΕΔ ΕΠΙΓΕΝΟ ΛΥΣΑΝ
Gift of Mr. and Mrs. Arthur J. Frank, 1977.253

This image is in the "new style," dating from 196–87 B.C.

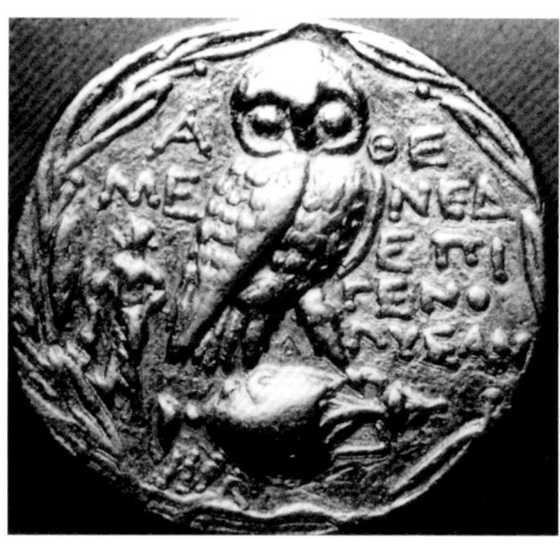

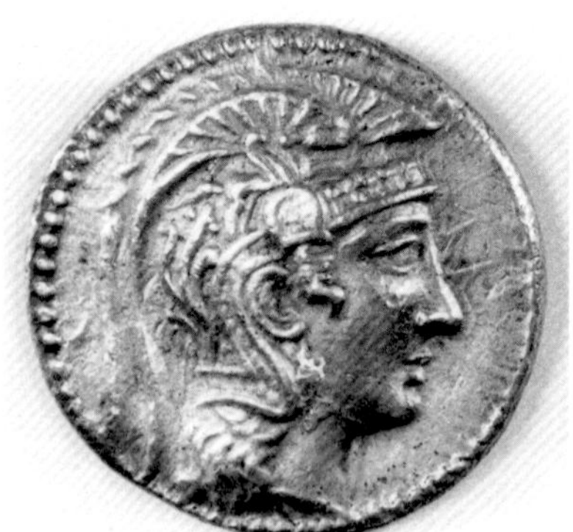

24.
AR tetradrachm, 31 mm, 16.70 g
Mint: Athens, 159 B.C.
Obverse: Athena Parthenos, to right, wearing triple-crested helmet with flying Pegasus
Reverse: owl, to right, head facing front, wings closed; above ΑΘΕ, to left and right ΛΥΣΑΝ ΓΛΑΥΚΟΣ ΑΘΗΝΟΒΙ
Gift of Mr. and Mrs. Arthur J. Frank, 1977.254

This reverse is similar to cat. no. 23. The names inscribed on both coins—here Lysander, Glaukos, Athenobios—are those of annual moneyers.

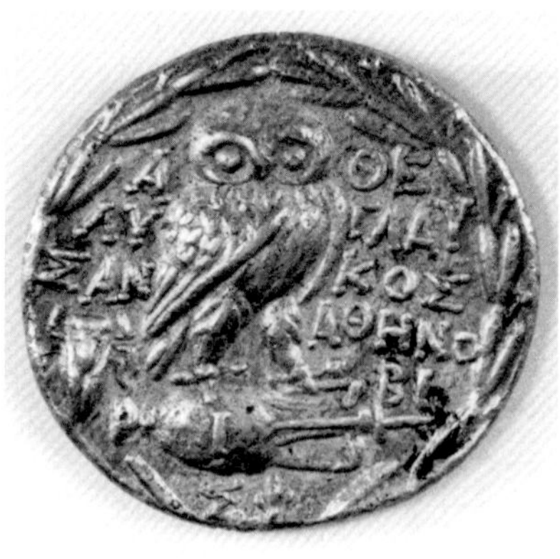

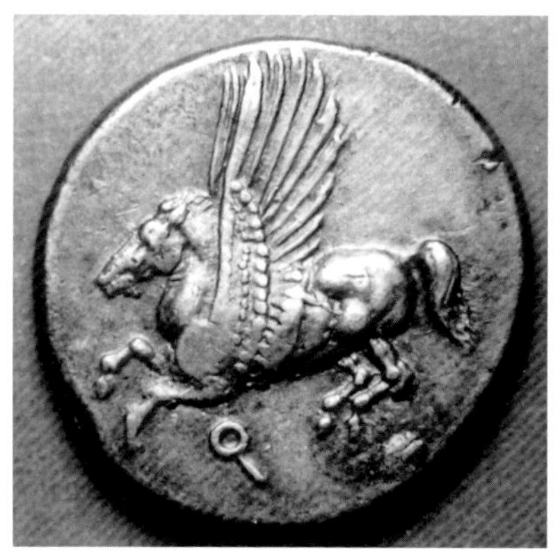

25.
AR stater, 22.2 mm, 8.60 g
Mint: Corinth, fifth-fourth centuries B.C.
Obverse: Pegasus flying to left; beneath, Q
Reverse: helmeted head of Athena, to left, wreath with bird to right
Gift of Mr. and Mrs. Arthur J. Frank, 1977.244

Except on coins, the letter Q disappeared from the Greek alphabet but was kept in the Roman.

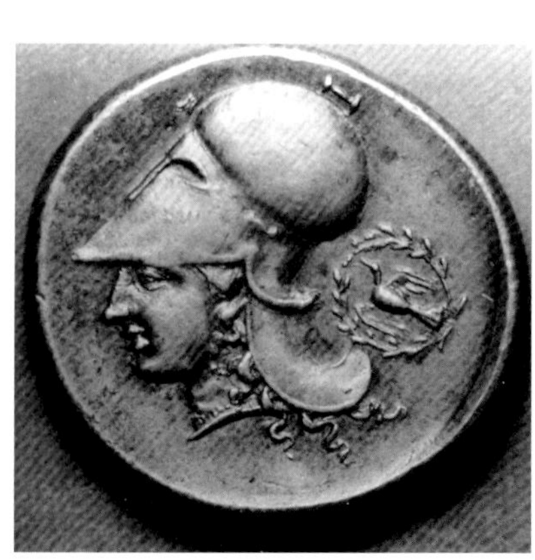

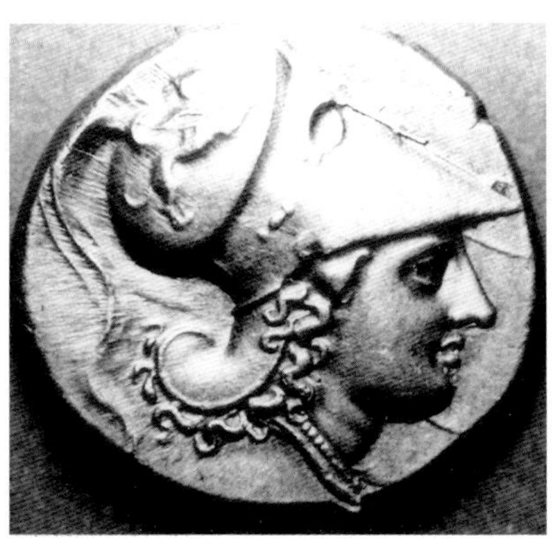

26.
AR stater, 22.2 mm, 8.38 g
Mint: Syracuse, Corinthian type, 317–316 B.C.
Obverse: head of Athena, to right, with griffin on helmet
Reverse: Pegasus flying to left; below triskeles (three legs, joined at the top, radiating, later the emblem of Sicily), ΣΥΡΑΚΟΣΙΩΝ
Ref. BM Corinth 9
Gift of Mr. and Mrs. Arthur J. Frank, 1977.230

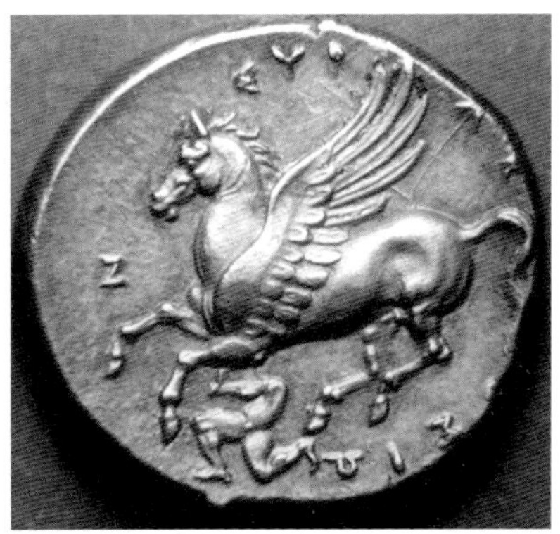

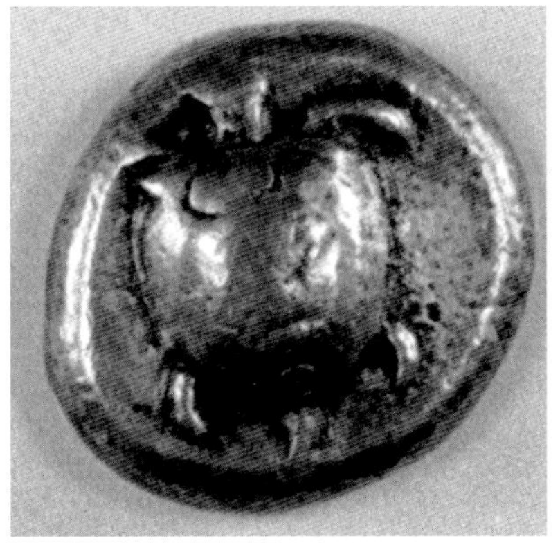

27.
AR stater, 19.1 mm
Mint: Aegina, ca. 480 B.C.
Obverse: smooth-shelled sea turtle
Reverse: incuse square divided into triangles
Gift of Mr. and Mrs. Arthur J. Frank, 1977.245

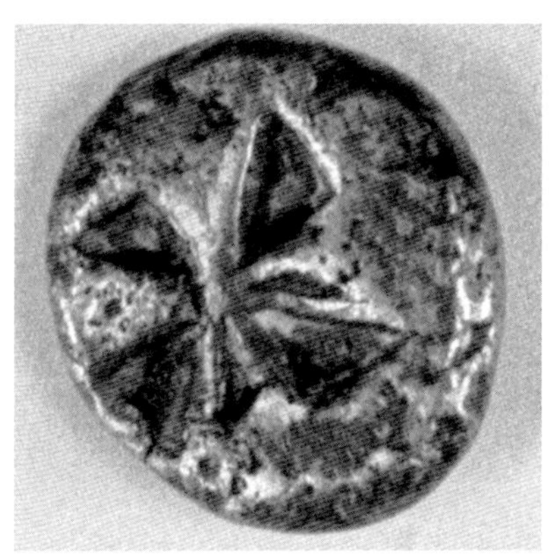

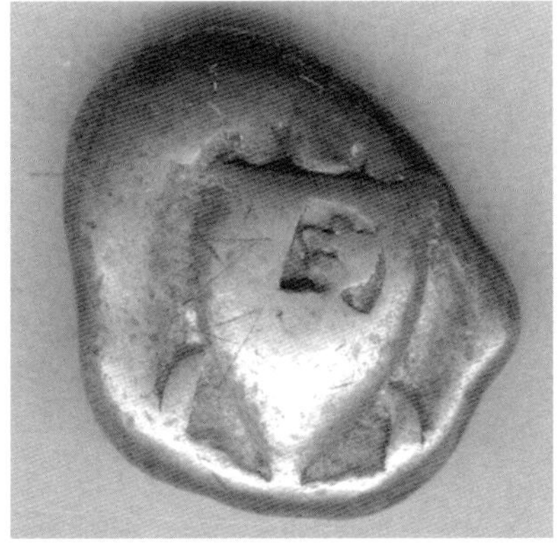

28.
AR stater, 15.9 mm, 12.15 g
Mint: Aegina, ca. 500 B.C.
Obverse: smooth-shelled sea turtle
Reverse: incuse square divided into triangles
Ref. BM Attica 133.95 ff.
Gift of Herbert M. Howe, 1980.72

From the earliest coins of the sixth century until about 456, Aegina used the sea turtle with its smooth back marked by a row of dots; from about 456 through the fourth century the coins are marked with a land tortoise, with its distinctive pattern of plates.

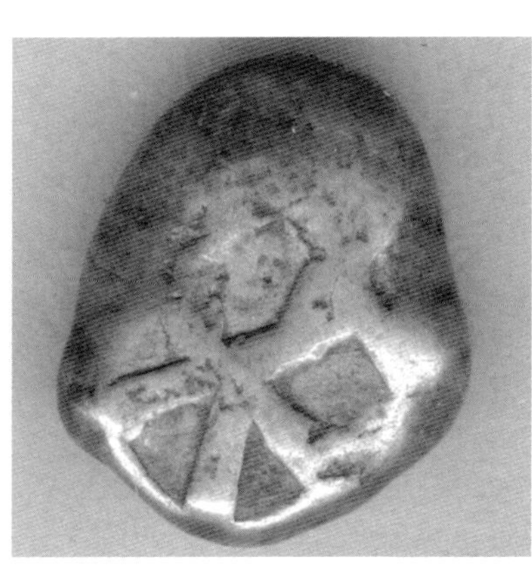

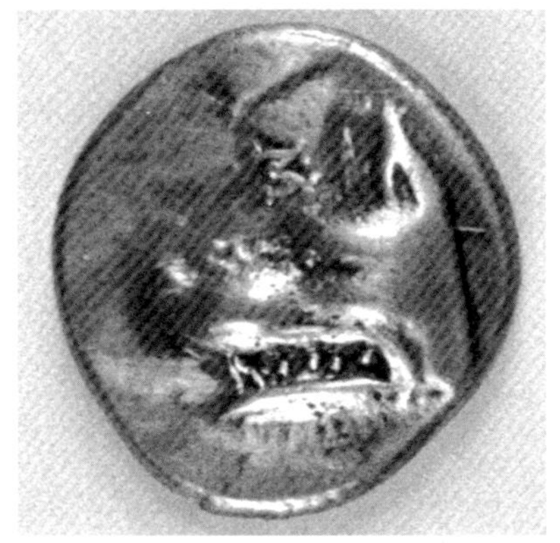

29.
AR obol, 11.1 mm, 0.85 g
Mint: Argos, before 332–229 B.C.
Obverse: protome (front half) of wolf
Reverse: letter A in incuse square
Ref. Grose, 231, 26
Gift of Mr. and Mrs. Arthur J. Frank, 1978.314

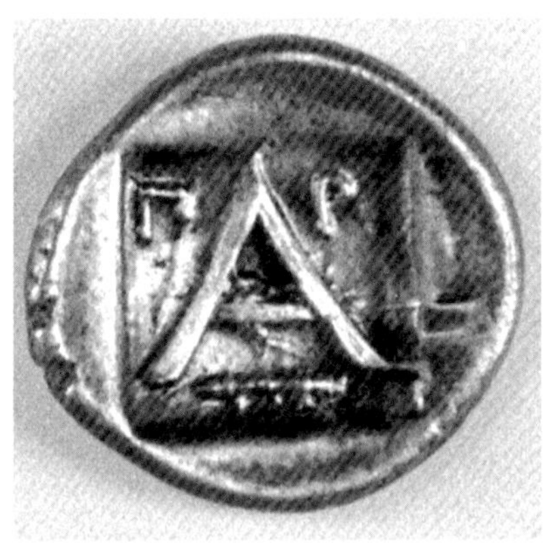

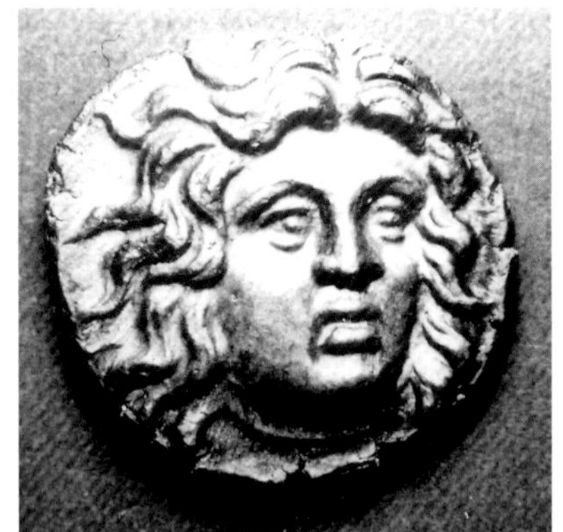

30.
AR drachma, 14.3 mm, 2.59 g
Mint: Rhodes, 304–166 B.C.
Obverse: 3/4 facing head of Helius, the sun god
Reverse: rose with bud; moneyer's name, ΓΟΡΓΟΣ ; mint mark, bow in case
Ref. BM 166
Gift of Mr. and Mrs. Arthur J. Frank, 1977.257

Like many Greek towns, Rhodes used a punning type of image on its coinage a rose (ΡΟΔΟΣ, *rodos*). Similarly Melos employed an apple (in Greek, ΜΕΛΟΣ, *melos*) and Leontini a lion (ΛΕΟΝ, *leon*).

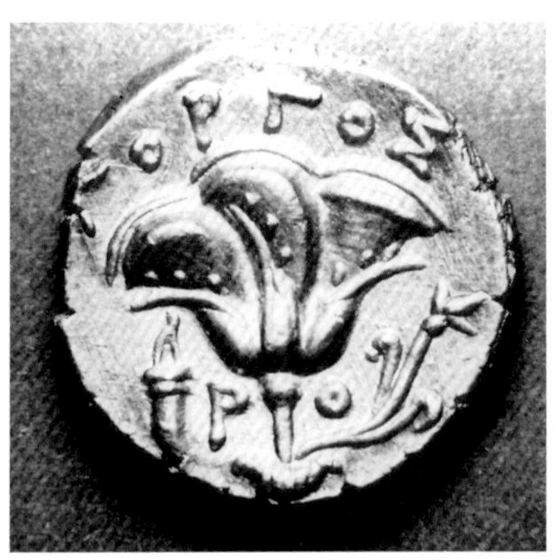

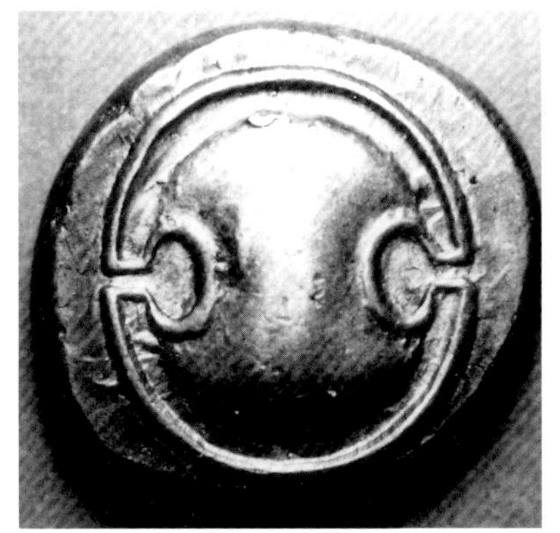

31.
AR stater, 20.6 mm, 12.42 g
Mint: Thebes, 378–338 B.C.
Obverse: Boeotian shield
Reverse: amphora (wine jar); at sides, ΔΑ ΜΩ (moneyer's name); above, club and ivy branch on left handle of jar
Gift of Mr. and Mrs. Arthur J. Frank, 1977.243

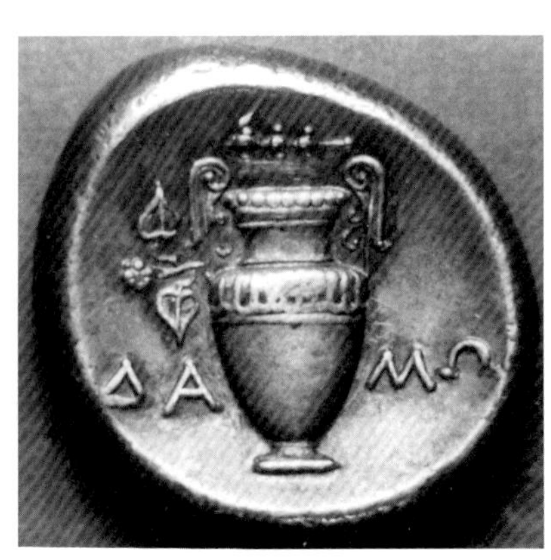

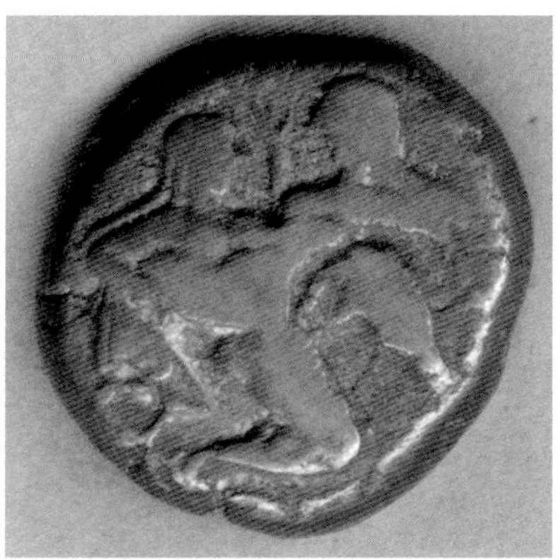

32.
AR stater, 17.5 mm
Mint: Thasos, 550–465 B.C.
Obverse: ithyphallic satyr carrying off nymph in long chiton
Reverse: quadripartite incuse square
Ref. BM Thrace 216.3
Gift of Herbert M. Howe, 1980.151

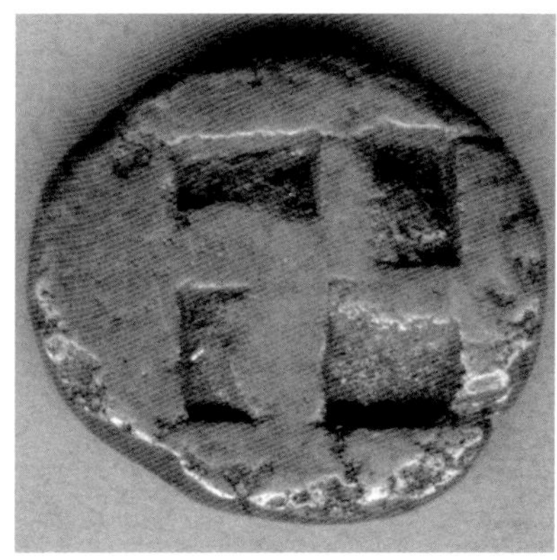

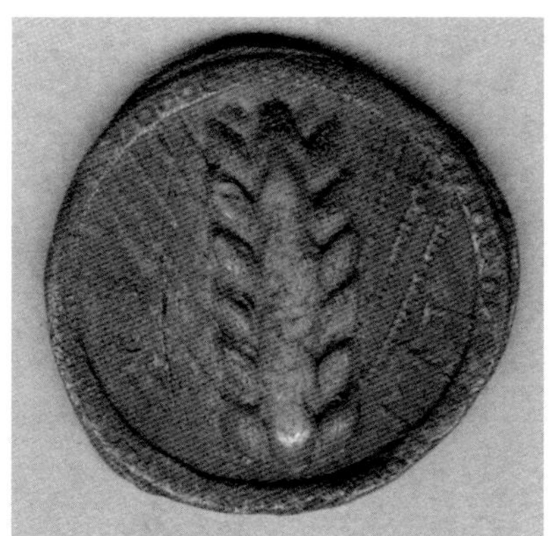

33.
AR didrachm, 25 mm, 7.50 g
Mint: Metapontum (South Italy), 550–480 B.C.
Obverse: ear of barley; to the right, META; border of dots between lines
Reverse: same as obverse, but incuse; no inscription
Ref. BM Italy 238.3
Gift of Herbert M. Howe, 1980.123

Note the curvature of this scyphate (cup-shaped) coin.

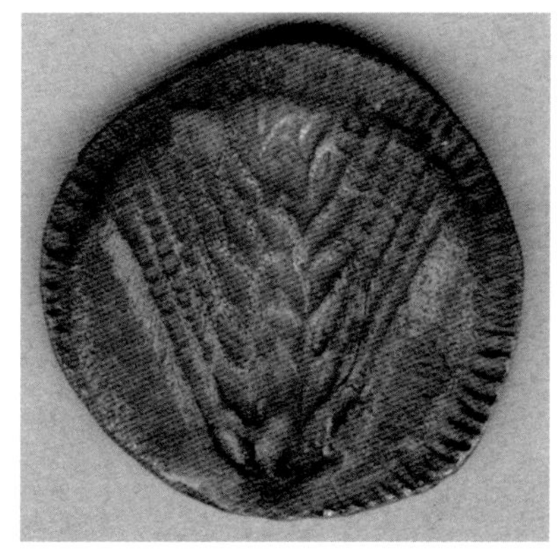

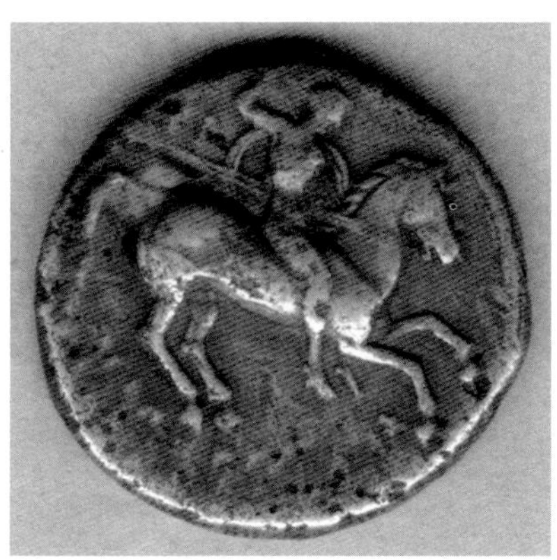

34.
AR stater, 20.6 mm
Mint: Tarentum (South Italy), before 282 B.C.
Obverse: naked horseman cantering to right
Reverse: naked Taras, legendary founder of the city, riding dolphin to left
Ref. BM Italy 194.253
Gift of Herbert M. Howe, 1980.148

According to legend, when Taras was shipwrecked, he was picked up by a friendly dolphin and carried ashore.

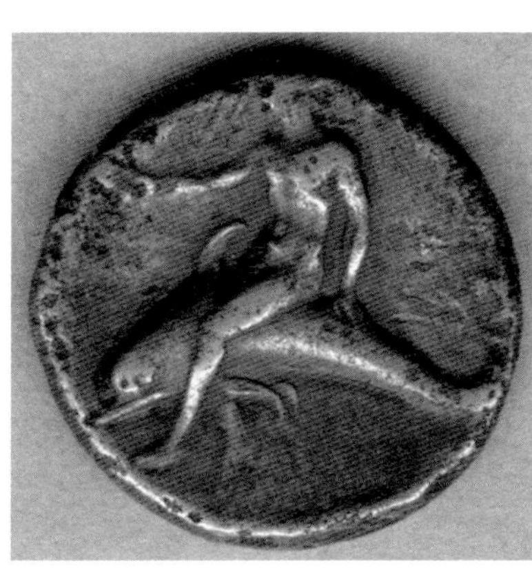

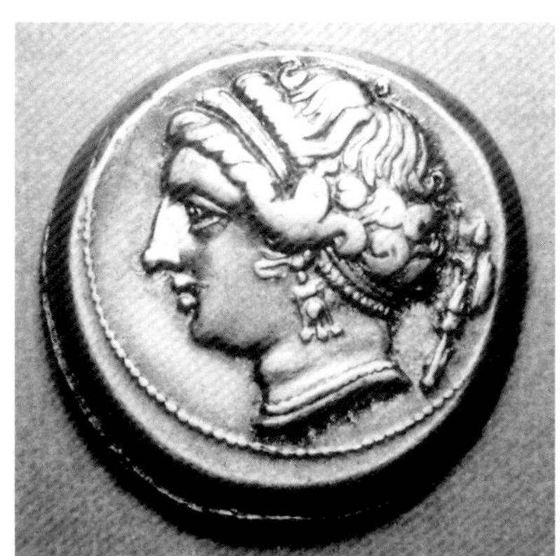

35.
AR didrachm, 20.6 mm, 7.44 g
Mint: Neapolis (Naples), 300–241 B.C.
Obverse: diademed head of water nymph Parthenope, to left; behind, trophy
Reverse: Nike (Victory), flying to right, crowning man-headed bull; below in exergue, ΝΕΟΠΟΛΙΤΩΝ (of the people of Neapolis)
Ref. BMC Italy 130
Gift of Mr. and Mrs. Arthur J. Frank, 1979.211

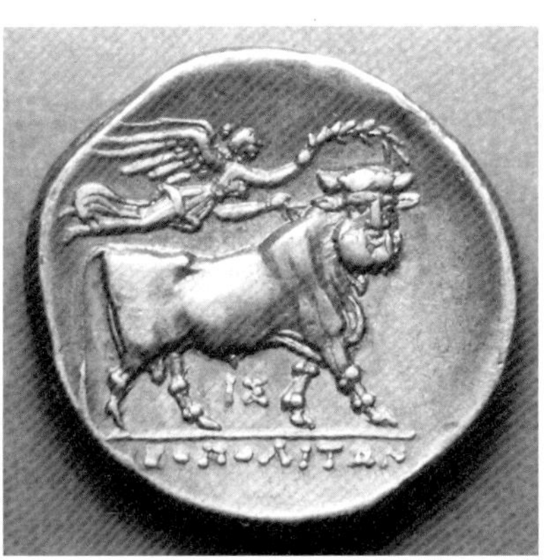

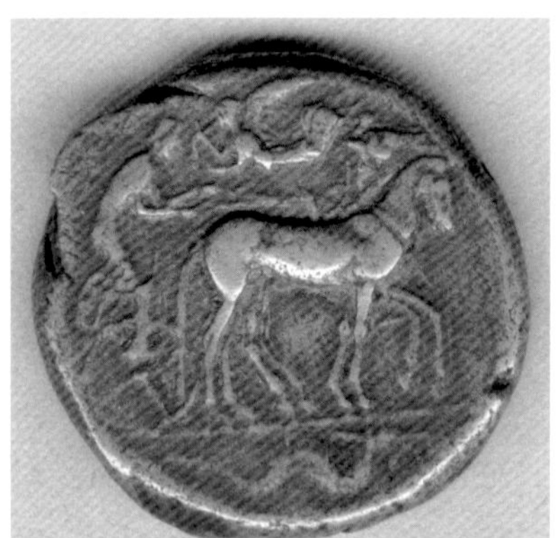

36.
AR tetradrachm, 25 mm
Mint: Syracuse (Sicily), 478–440 B.C.
Obverse: chariot at right; above, flying Nike (Victory)
Reverse: head of nymph Arethusa, to right; around, four dolphins; ΣΥΡΑΚΟΣΙΩΝ (of the people of Syracuse)
Lent by State Historical Society of Wisconsin, 1.1990.2

If this head on the reverse is Demarete, wife of Gelon, ruler of the city, this is the earliest coin portrait known.

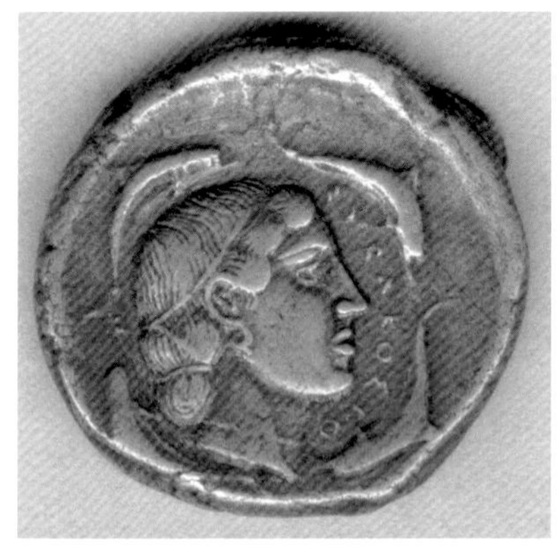

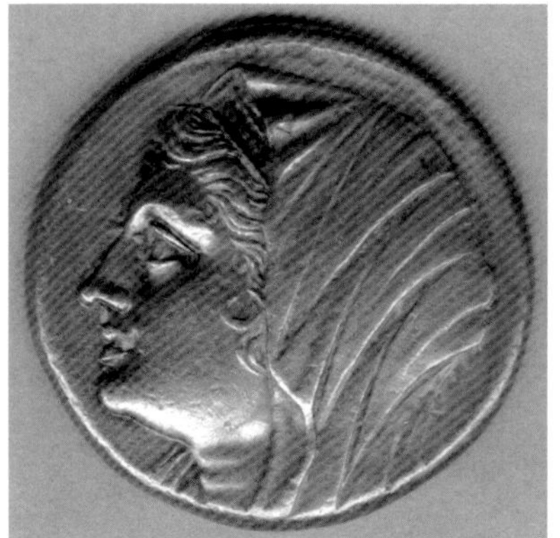

37.
AR 16 litrae, 26 mm
Mint: Syracuse, 274–216 B.C.
Obverse: veiled head of Queen Philistis (wife of Hieron), to left
Reverse: quadriga, to right; ΒΑΣΙΛΙΣΣΑΣ ΦΙΛΙΣΤΙΔΟΣ (of Queen Philistis)
Ref. Head 184, fig. 108; comp. BM 214.554
Gift of Mr. and Mrs. Arthur J. Frank, 1977.231

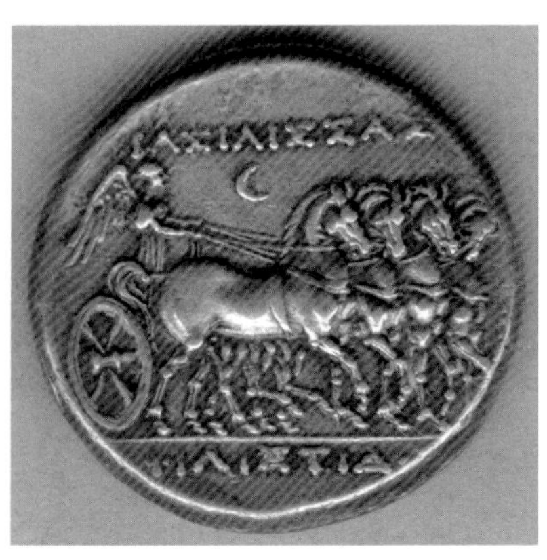

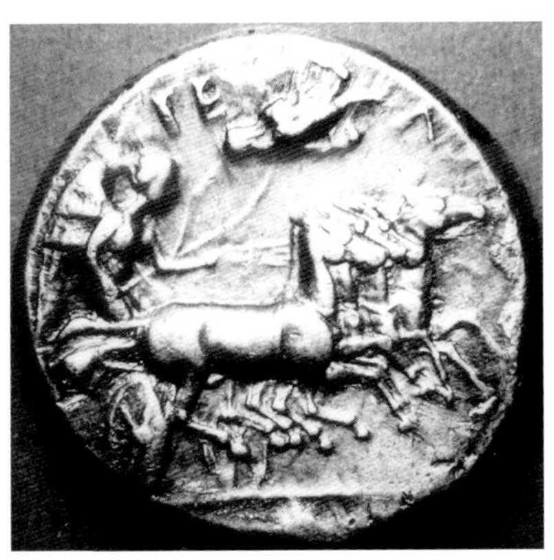

38.
AR tetradrachm, 26 mm, 16.31 g
Mint: Gela (Sicily), ca. 415 B.C., die carver, the Corn Master
Obverse: quadriga galloping to right, with standing Nike
Reverse: protome (front half) of river-god Gelas swimming to right; above, kernel of corn, ΓΕΛΑΣ
Ref. BM Sicily 57
Gift of Mr. and Mrs. Arthur J. Frank, 1978.263

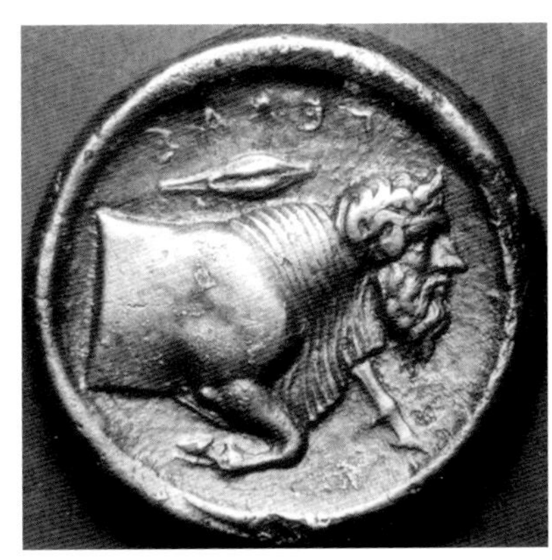

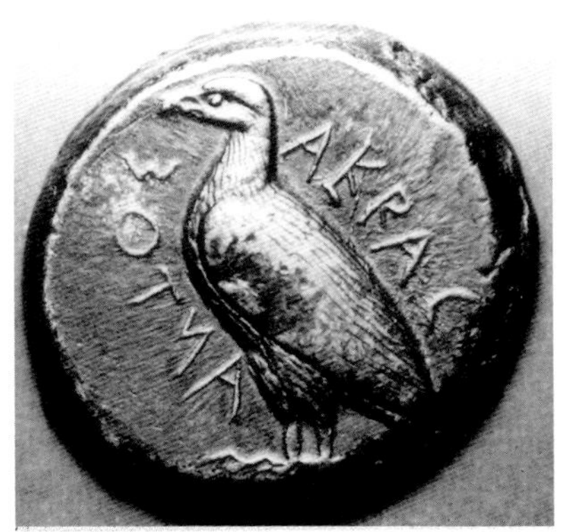

39.
AR tetradrachm, 26 mm, 17.33 g
Mint: Acragas (Sicily), ca. 450 B.C.
Obverse: eagle standing, facing left, on wavy line; ΑΚΡΑΓ ΑΝΤΩΣ
Reverse: crab
Ref. Syll. Lloyd 800
Gift of Mr. and Mrs. Arthur J. Frank, 1977.228

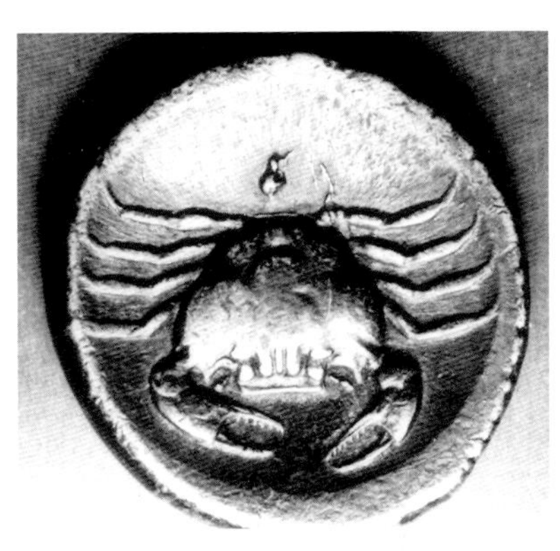

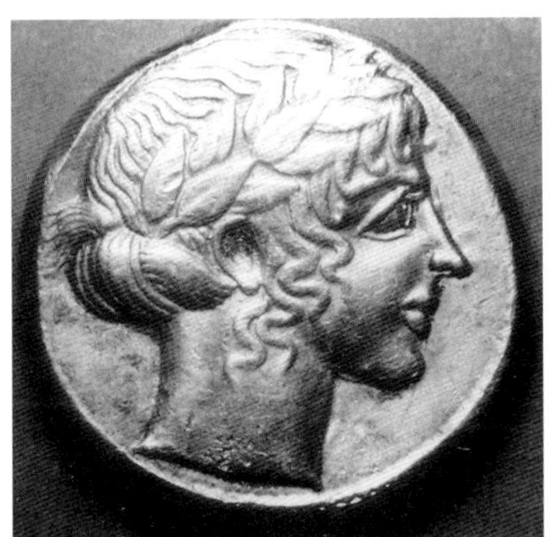

40.
AR tetradrachm, 25 mm, 17.24 g
Mint: Leontini (Sicily), ca. 445 B.C.
Obverse: laureate head of Apollo, to right
Reverse: head of lion with open jaw facing right, with four grains of barley; around, ΛΕΟΝΤΙΝΟΝ (of the people of Leontini)
Gift of Mr. and Mrs. Arthur J. Frank, 1977.227

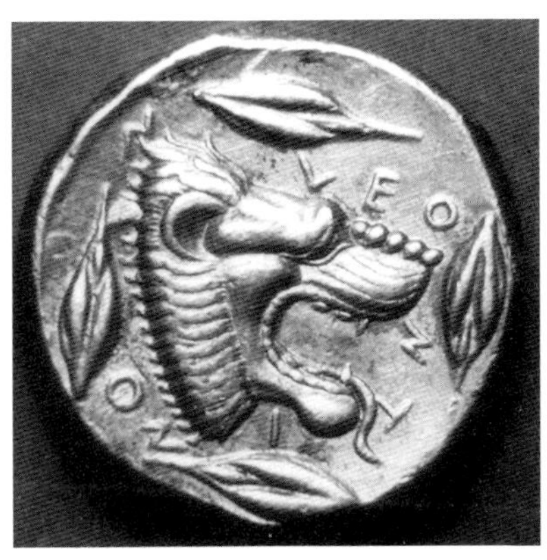

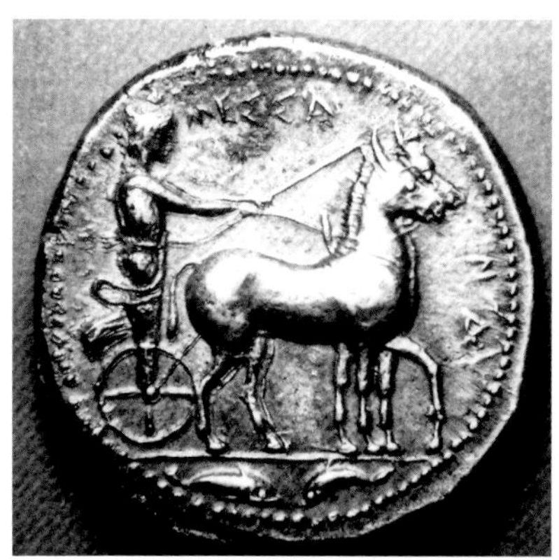

41.
AR tetradrachm, 23.8 mm, 17.11 g
Mint: Messana (Sicily), ca. 430 B.C.
Obverse: nymph Messana in biga of two mules; in exergue, two dolphins; around, ΜΕΣΣΑΝΑ
Reverse: hare; below, dolphin; around, ΜΕΣΣΑΝΙΩΝ (of the people of Messana)
Ref. Head 154
Gift of Mr. and Mrs. Arthur J. Frank, 1978.264

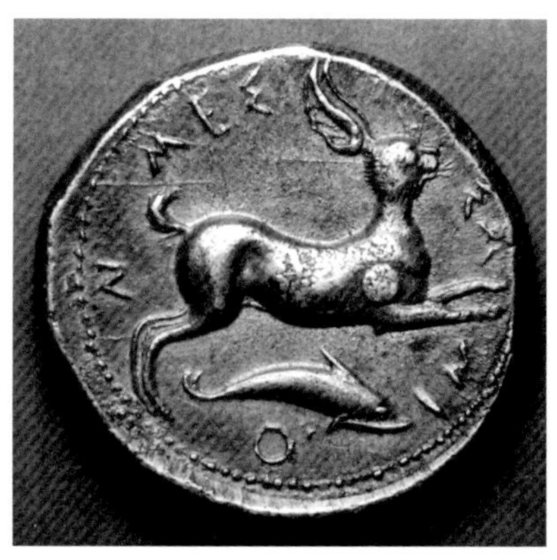

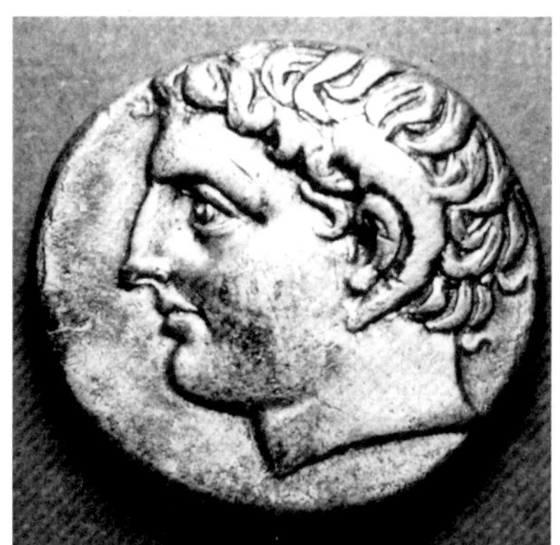

42.
AR didrachm, 20.6 mm, 7.47 g
Mint: Cyrene (North Africa), ca. 310 B.C.
Obverse: young head of Apollo Carneius facing left, with ram's horn
Reverse: silphium plant with three sets of leaves; above, ΚΥΡΑ
Ref. BM 251
Gift of Mr. and Mrs. Arthur J. Frank, 1979.239

Silphium, the spicy plant that was the chief export of Cyrene, was used as a condiment.

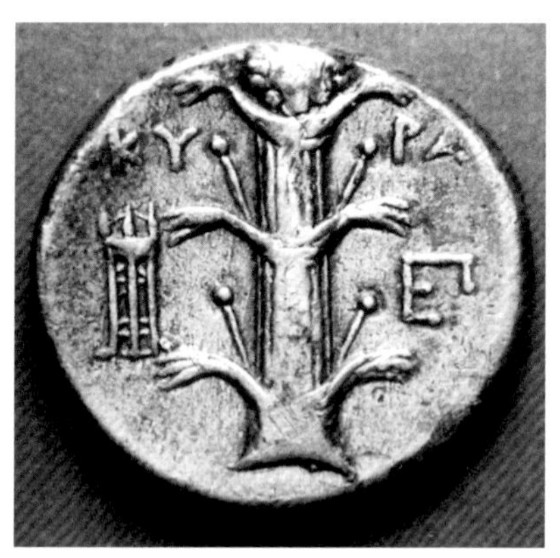

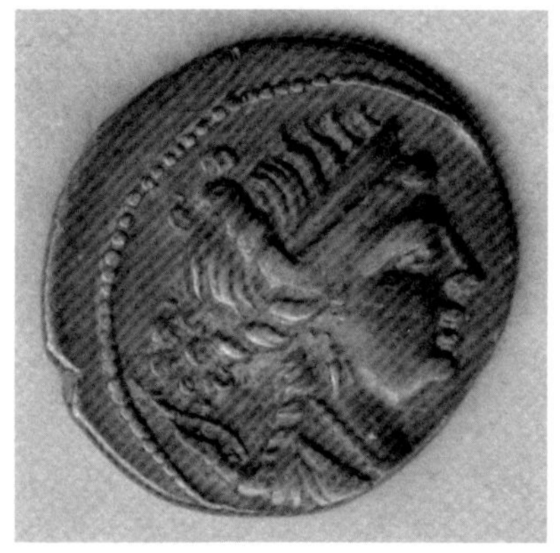

43.
AR drachma, 17.5 mm
Mint: Massalia (Marseilles), ca. 200 B.C.
Obverse: head of Artemis, to right
Reverse: lion, to right; ΜΑΣΣΑ ΛΙΑΤΩΝ
Gift of Mr. and Mrs. Ellis E. Jensen, 69.11.12

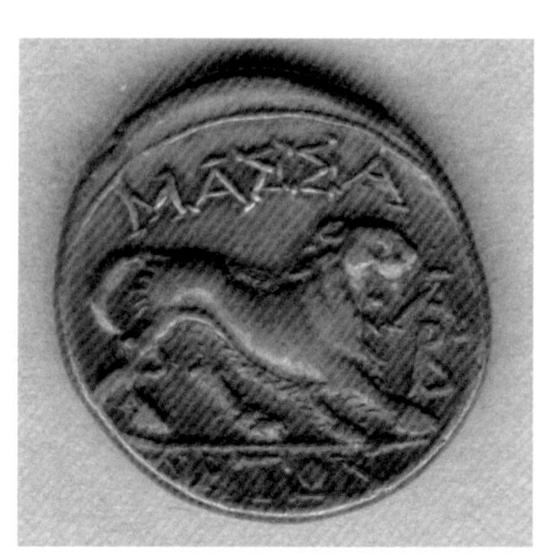

Non-Greek Coins Influenced By Those Of The Greeks

We have already seen one coin struck by non-Greek people, the siglos of Persia (cat. nos. 5–6), the state that overthrew Lydia, where coinage had been invented. There were many non-Greek coins, sometimes struck because of the convenience of common standards, sometimes because their issuers traded with Greeks; they were occasionally struck by Greek military colonists. Emphasizing place of origin and the wide influence of Greek sources, we have made little attempt to follow chronological order in this section.

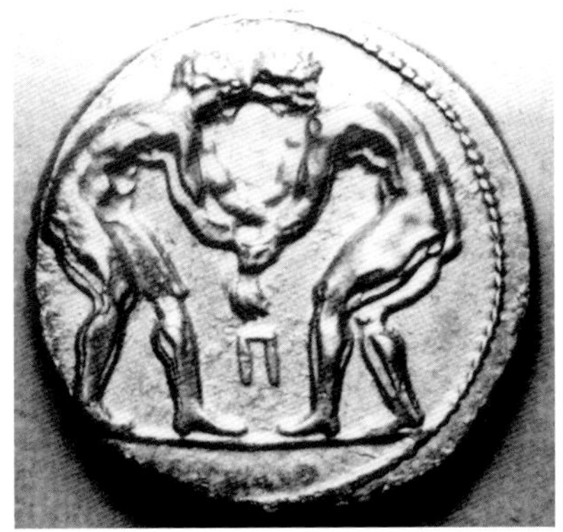

44.
AR stater, 22.2 mm, 10.73 g
Mint: Aspendus (Pamphylia, central Asia Minor), 400–300 B.C.
Obverse: two wrestlers grappling
Reverse: Incuse square with slinger throwing, to right; in field, to right a triskeles; ΕΣΤFΕΔIIVΣ (ASPENDIOS)
Ref. Head 700
Gift of Mr. and Mrs. Arthur J. Frank, 1979.225, ex col. President John Adams

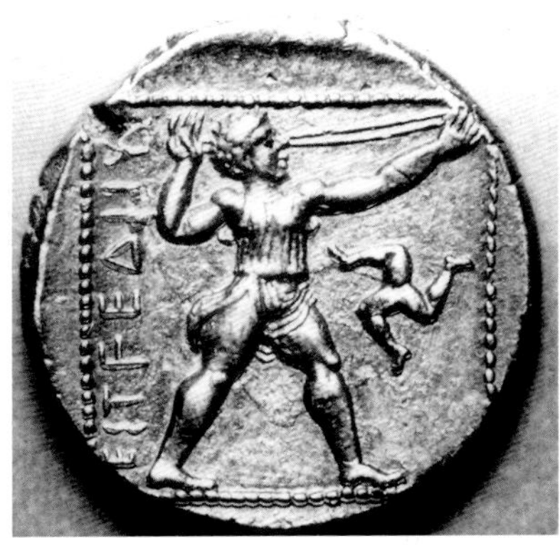

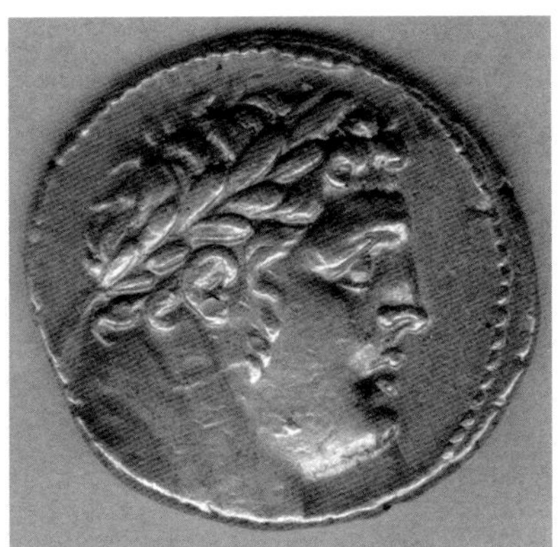

45.
AR shekel, 20.7 mm, 14.0 g
Mint: Tyre (Phoenicia), 122–121 B.C.
Obverse: head of god Melkarth facing right
Reverse: eagle on thunderbolt; in front, club; ΤΥΡΟΥ ΙΕΡΑΣ ΚΑΙ ΑΣΥΛΟΥ (of Tyre, holy and inviolable). The Punic (Carthaginian) inscription LE refers to "year 5" of the ruler
Ref. BM 55
Gift of Mr. and Mrs. Arthur J. Frank, 1977.259

Melkarth was identified with Heracles. This type is often regarded, for no clear reason, as that of the thirty pieces of silver paid Judas for the betrayal of Jesus.

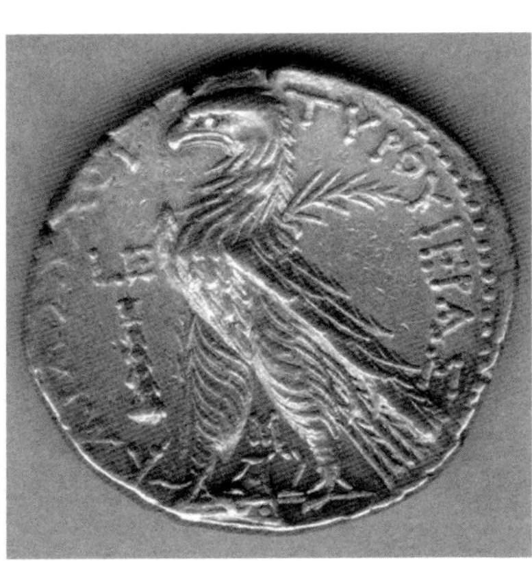

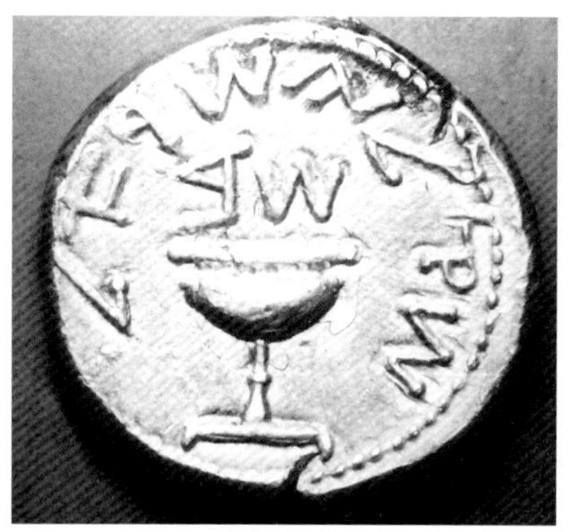

46.
AR shekel, 22.2 mm, 14.40 g
Mint: Judaea, 68 C.E.
Obverse: chalice with pearled rim; around, "Shekel of Israel" in Hebrew in Aramaic script; above the chalice, Sh B(year 2)
Reverse: three pomegranates on a stem; around (Jerusalem the Holy)
Gift of Mr. and Mrs. Arthur J. Frank, 1980.23

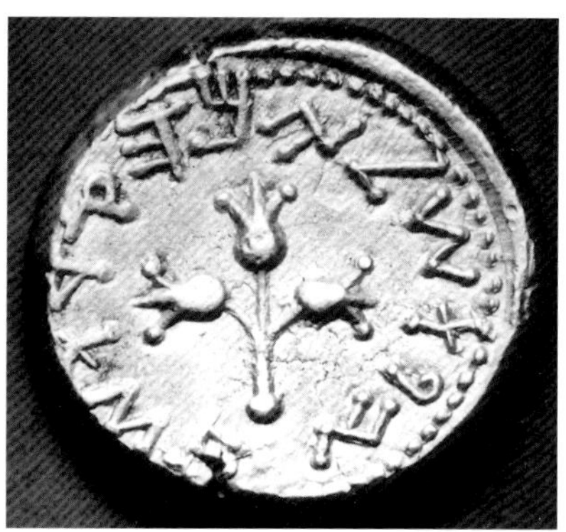

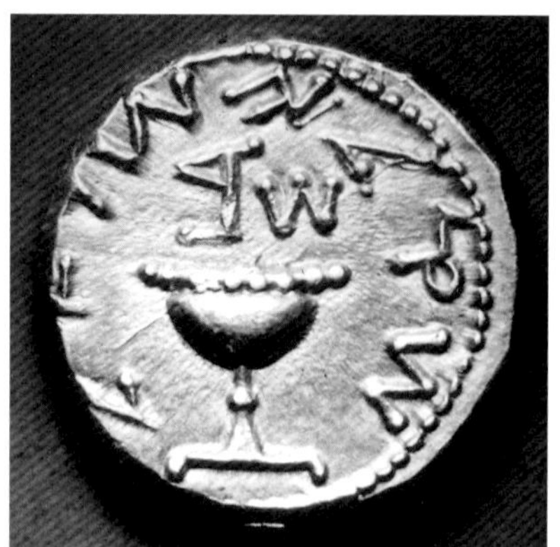

47.
AR shekel, 22.2 mm, 13.92 g
Mint: Judaea, 68 C.E.
Obverse: chalice with pearled rim; around, "Shekel of Israel" in Hebrew in Aramaic script; above the chalice, Sh B(year 2)
Reverse: three pomegranates on a stem; around (Jerusalem the Holy)
Gift of Mr. and Mrs. Arthur J. Frank, 1980.22

These coins were struck in the First Revolt (66–70 C.E.) against the Romans, which ended with the fall of Jerusalem and capture of Masada. Jewish coins following scripture showed no pictures of animals or men, only inanimate objects.

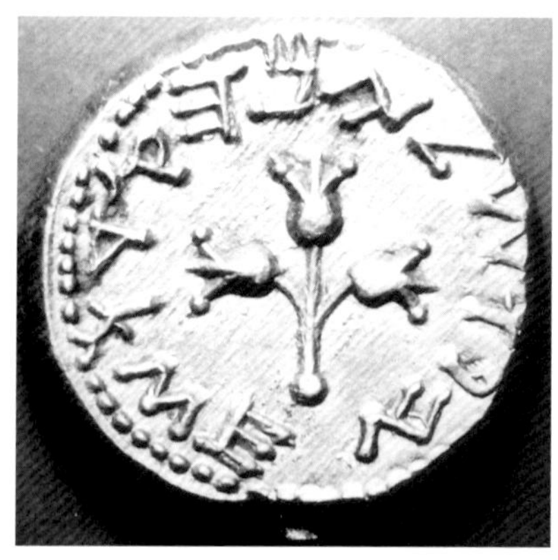

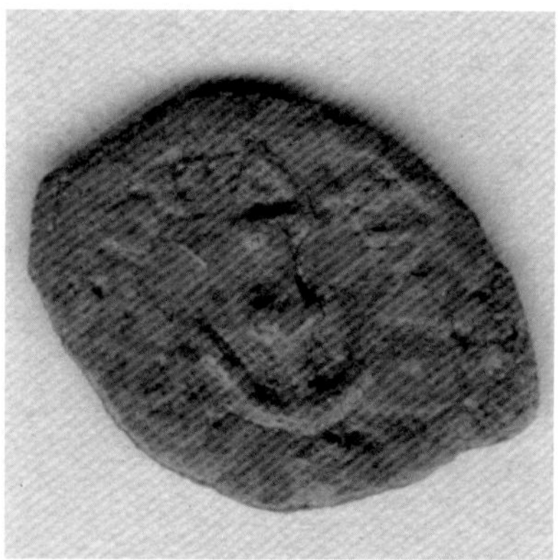

48.
AE prutah, 15.9 mm
Mint: Judaea
Herod the Great, 40–4 B.C.E.
Obverse: anchor
Reverse: crossed cornucopias
Lent by the State Historical Society of Wisconsin, L.1990.3

This is an example of the biblical "widow's mite" mentioned in Mark 12.42; Luke 21.2.

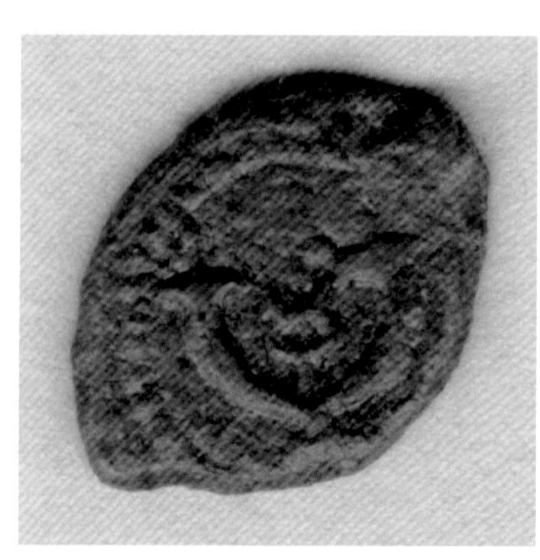

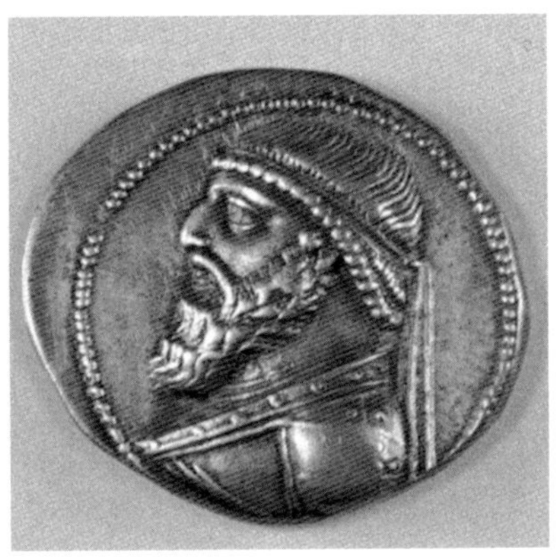

49.
AR tetradrachm, 30 mm, 16.0 g
Parthia, Mithradates II, 123–88 B.C.
Obverse: diademed bust of king, to left; border of dots
Reverse: archer seated, facing right; around,
ΒΑΣΙΛΕΩΣ ΜΕΓΑΛΟΥ ΑΡΣΑΚΟΥ ΕΠΙΦΑΝΟΥΣ
(of the great King Arsaces, the visible god)
Ref. Sellwood 24/2
Gift of Mr. and Mrs. Arthur J. Frank, 1979.228

The Arsacid dynasty ruled Iran from the decay of the Seleucid empire to the mid-third century A.D.

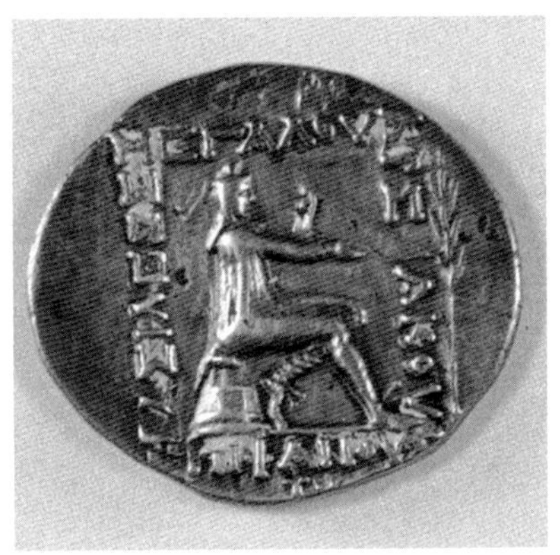

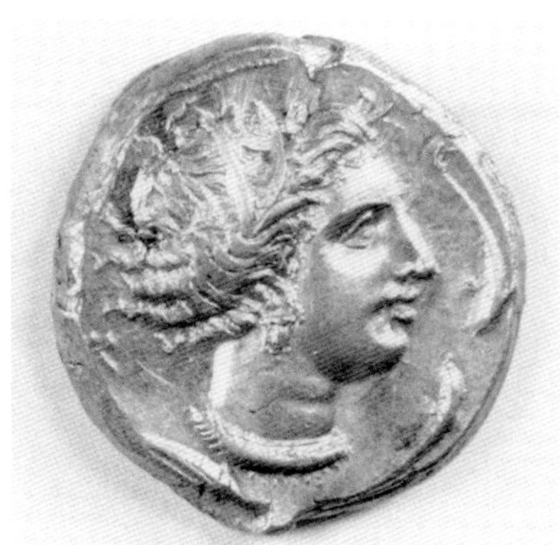

50.
AR tetradrachm, 26 mm, 17.02 g
Mint: Sicily
Carthage, Siculo-Punic, ca. 350 B.C.
Obverse: head of Punic deity Tanit, facing right; around, three dolphins
Reverse: horse standing right, before palm tree, to right a kerykeion
Gift of Mr. and Mrs. Arthur J. Frank, 1978.266

For several hundred years Carthage maintained a foothold in Sicily and copied Greek techniques of coinage.

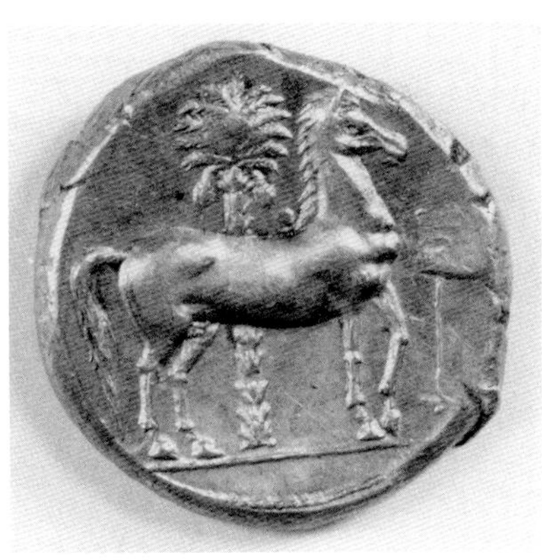

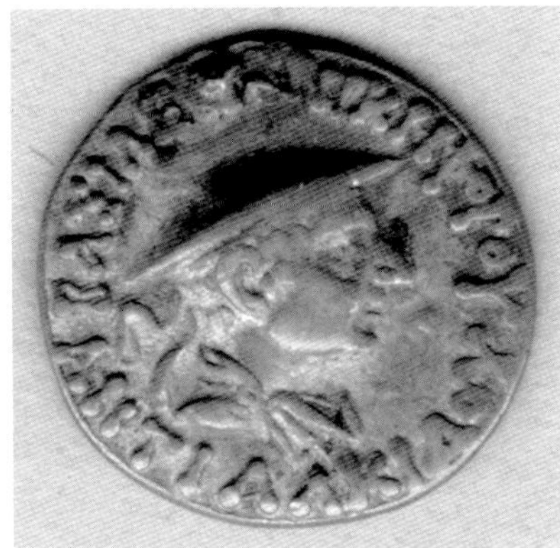

51.
AR drachma, 15.9 mm, 2.05 g
Mint: Bactria
Antialcidas, 125–95 B.C.
Obverse: head of Antialcidas, to right, wearing causia (flat hat); above (of the victorious king); below (of Antialcidas)
Reverse: Zeus enthroned, to left, holding Nike; around, Kharoshti (an Indian language) MAHARAJASA JAYADHARASA ANTIALKITASA (of Antialcidas the great king, the victorious).
Gift of Herbert M. Howe, 1980.90

Alexander the Great (r. 336–323 B.C.) marched all the way east to India. On the way he founded cities ruled by his men, including many disabled veterans. The Graeco-Bactrian kingdom they formed lasted into the first century A.D.

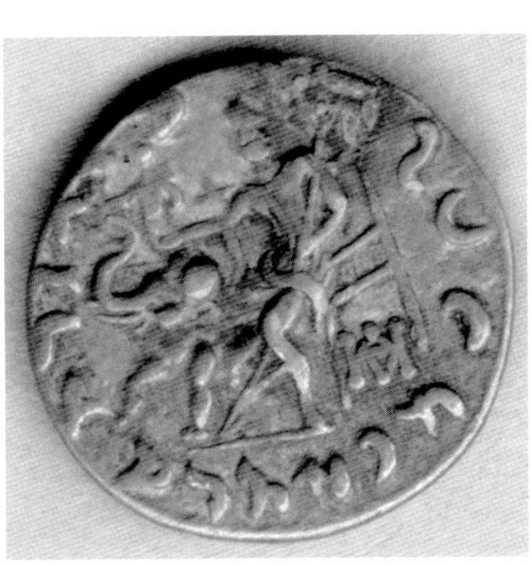

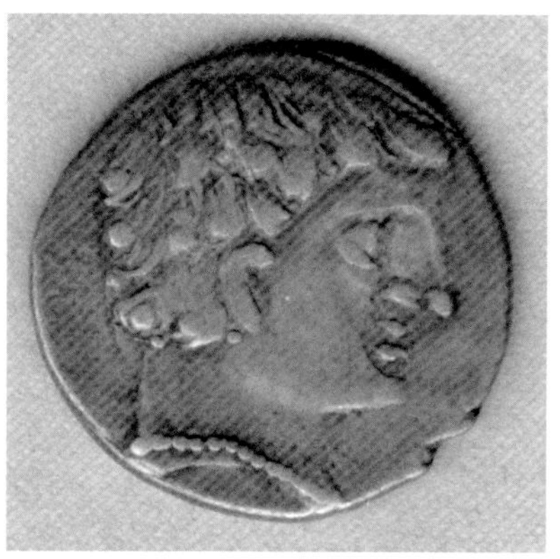

52.
AR denarius, 19.1 mm, 3.80 g
Mint: Calagurris (Spain), 206–146 B.C.
Obverse: head of a local chief, to right
Reverse: Dioscuri riding, to left
Gift of Mr. and Mrs. Ellis E. Jensen, 69.11.13

The Romans gained possession of northeastern Spain in 207 B.C. and soon demanded tribute in coined silver from this mineral-rich region. The general design of this coin is that of a Roman denarius, but the style is very different.

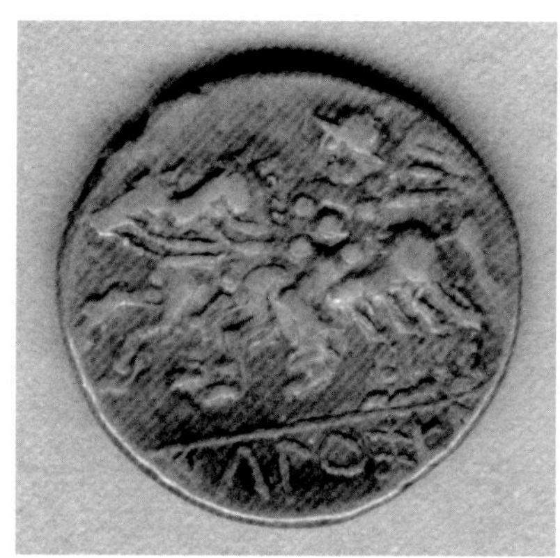

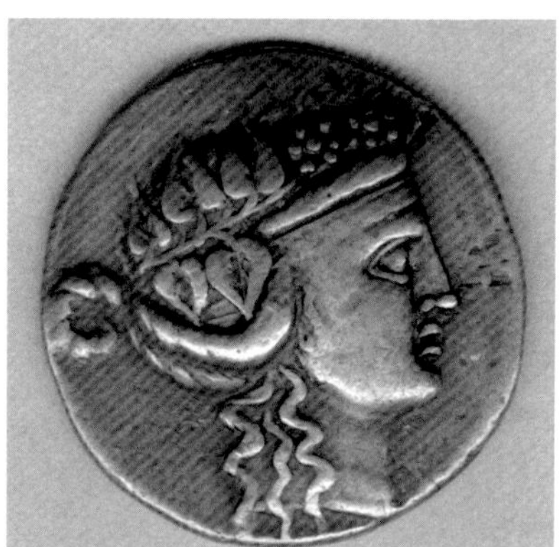

53.
AR tetradrachm, 28 mm
Mint: Thasos, probably after 146 B.C.
Obverse: head of Dionysus, to right.
Reverse: nude Heracles standing, to left, leaning on club, lion skin over left arm; to right, left, and beneath, ΗΡΑΚΛΕΟΥΣ ΣΩΤΗΡΟΣ ΘΑΣΙΩΝ (of Heracles, the savior of the Thasians)
Ref. BM Thrace 222.67–71
Gift of Herbert M. Howe, 1980.150

Compare the image and inscription on this example with those of cat. no. 54.

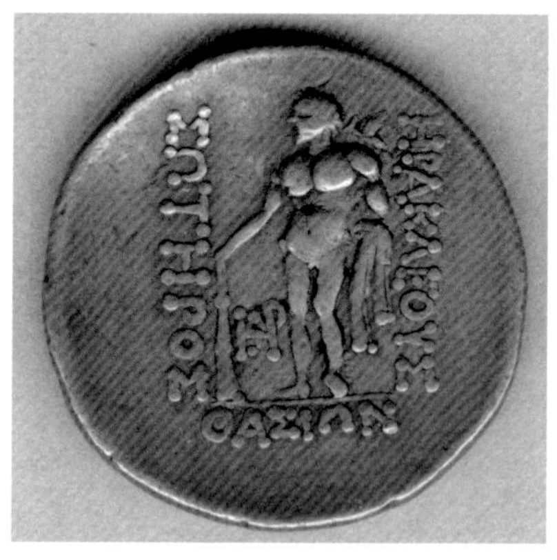

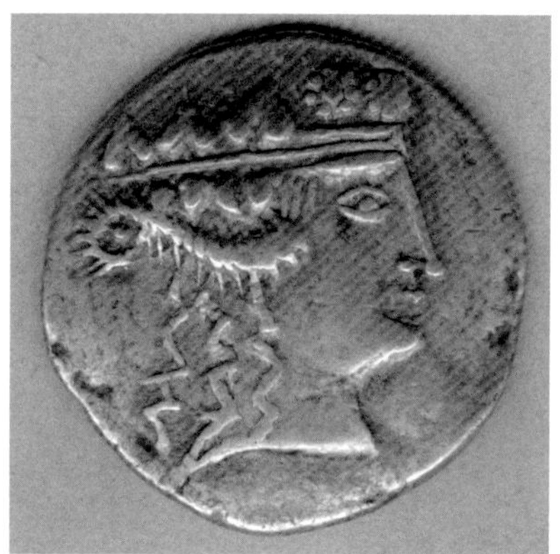

54.
AR tetradrachm, 28 mm
Mint: Danube
Western Celts, after 146 B.C.
Obverse: head of Dionysus, to right, wearing ivy crown
Reverse: Heracles standing, to left, leaning on club made of dots, all in a double border of dots
Ref. BM Thrace 224.89
Gift of Herbert M. Howe, 1980.153

This imitation of cat. no. 53 was made for people who could not read Greek; the letters of the inscription have been replaced by a line of dots. Greek coin types, carried by traders, were imitated in more and more stylized form as far west as Gaul and Britain.

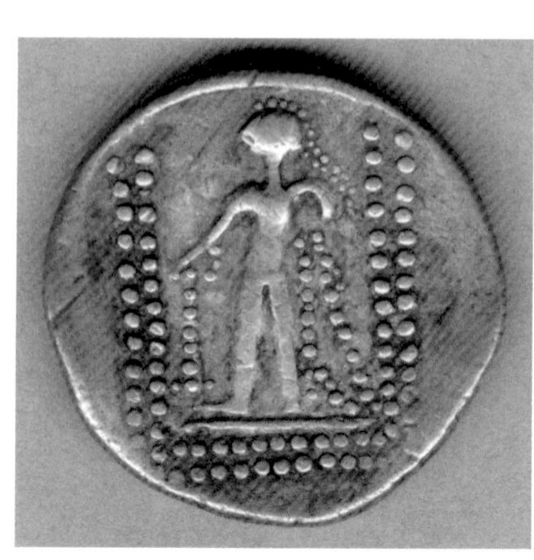

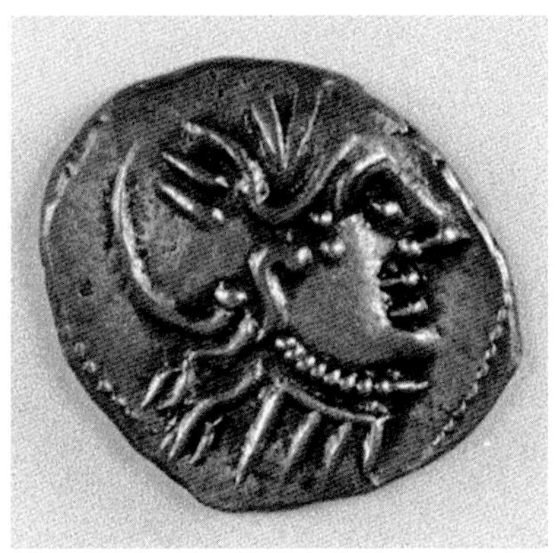

55.
AR drachma, 17.5 mm, 2.17 g
Mint: Vocontii (Gaul), 118–50 B.C.
Obverse: helmeted head of Roma, to right
Reverse: horseman with spear, galloping right, COMA
Ref. BN 5871; Blanchet, p. 263, 15
Gift of Mr. and Mrs. Arthur J. Frank, 1979.210, ex col. Changarnier

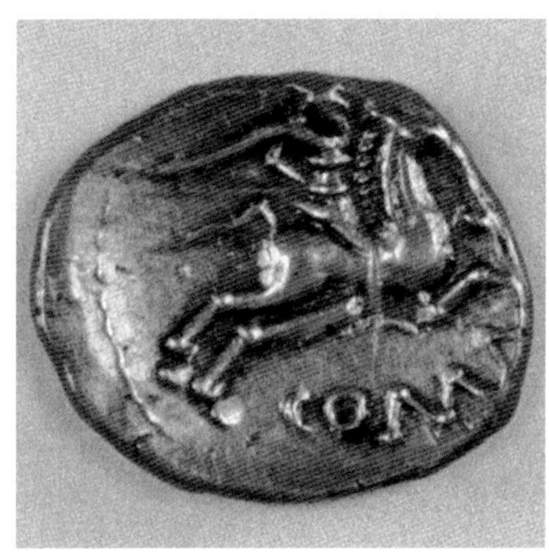

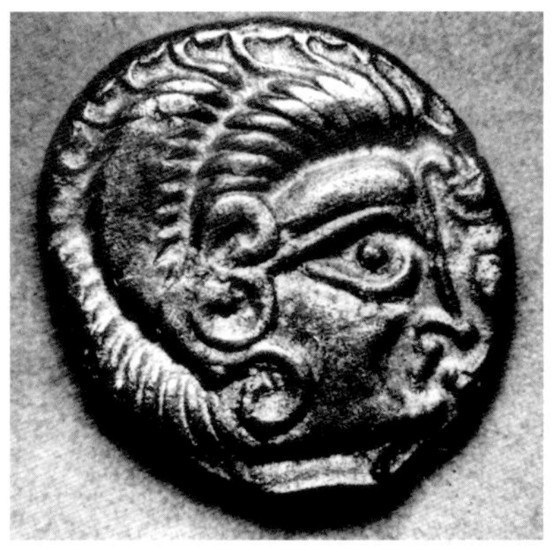

56.
Billon (silver alloy) stater, 19.1 mm, 6.26 g
Mint: Coriosolitae (Gaul), second-first century B.C.
Obverse: stylized male head, to right, diademed
Reverse: stylized horse, to right, above, a pearled cord, below, wild boar, to right
Ref. BN 6598; Blanchet p. 315, fig. 217; Forrer I, p. 261, 464
Gift of Mr. and Mrs. Arthur J. Frank, 1980.21, ex col. Changarnier, ex Treasure of Island of Jersey (English Channel)

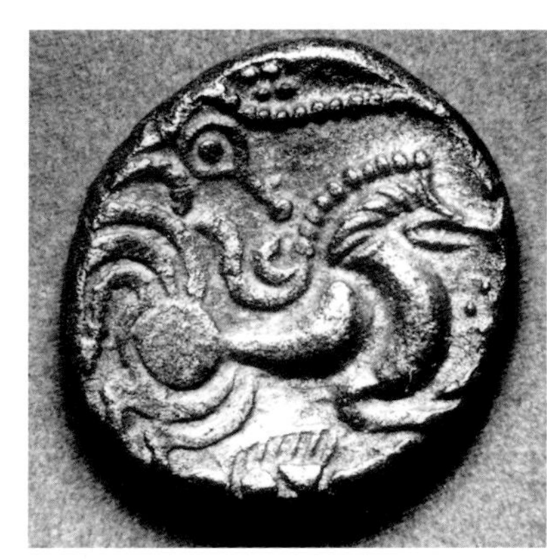

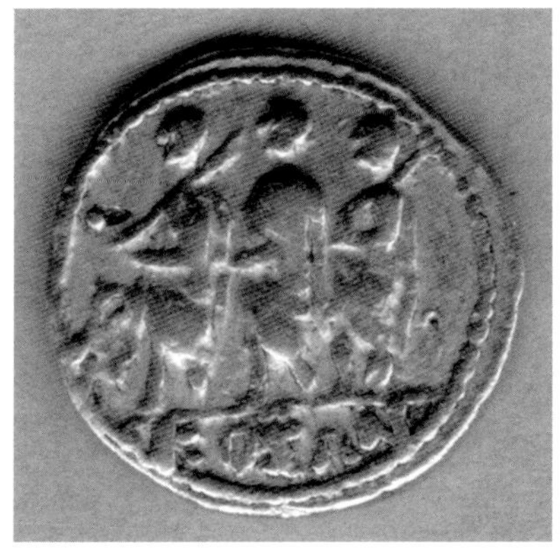

57.
AU stater, aureus, 19.1 mm
Mint: Thrace or Lower Moesia (Bulgaria), 42 B.C., Sythian workmanship
Probably Coson, king of the Sythians
Obverse: the consul L. Brutus walking left between two lictors; in exergue, ΚΟΣΩΝ (of Cosi)
Reverse: eagle with wings spread
Ref. BM Thrace 201.1, on Coson, see Numismatic Fine Arts Catalogue, spring 1975, 109
Lent anonymously, 1.1991.2

This coin was probably struck by M. Brutus just before his defeat at Philippi.

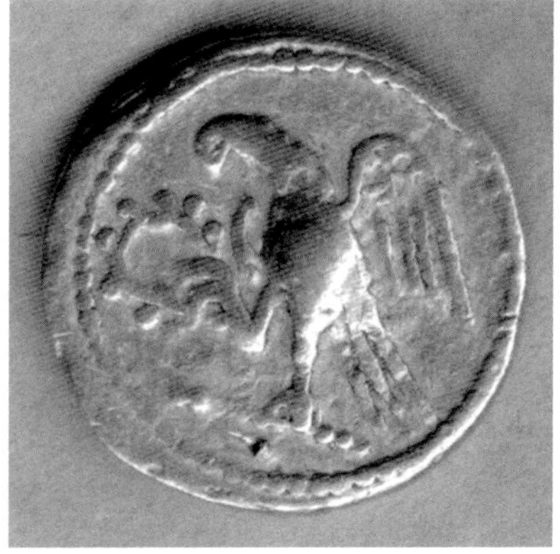

HELLENISTIC COINAGE

In 338 B.C. Philip II of Macedon ended the independence of the Greek cities, and from then on the eastern Mediterranean world was subject to rule by monarchs. Philip was succeeded by his son, Alexander, who at his death in 323 B.C. ruled from the Ionian Sea and Egypt east to the Indus River. With his death his empire fell into the hands of his generals and their descendants: the **Antigonids** in Macedon, the **Seleucids** in Syria and the East, and the **Ptolemies** in Egypt. The Seleucids lost Asia Minor to the **Attalids** of Pergamum in the third century B.C., Parthia (modern Iran) to the Arsacids, and Judaea to the Maccabean rulers in the second. The last of the **Diaduchi** (successors) to fall was the dynasty of the Ptolemies: Cleopatra VII committed suicide in 30 B.C.

In this period the primacy of the ruler was all-important. If subject cities were allowed to coin gold and silver at all, it was on a far smaller scale. The dynasts made use of talented artists to carve magnificent portraits of themselves—not the Olympian gods—on their coins, and the legends that are seen glorify the rulers. When the Olympians do appear, the ruler's name is usually not far off and may be associated with a well-known statue: for example, Alexander with the Olympian Zeus of Phidias, or Demetrius Poliorcetes with Poseidon and with the Victory of Samothrace.

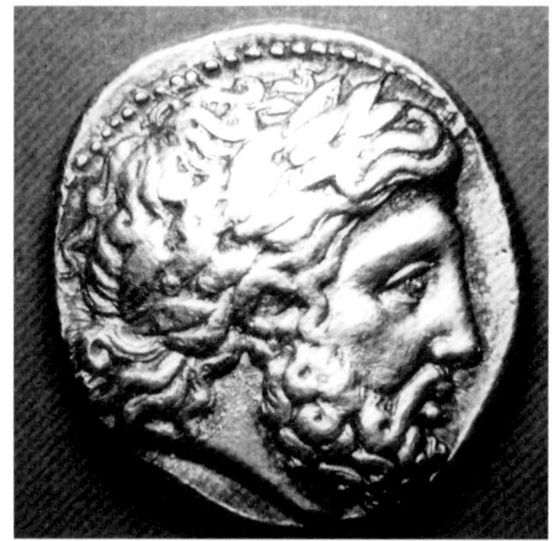

58.
AR tetradrachm, 23.8 mm, 14.40 g
Mint: Pella (Macedon)
Philip II, 359–336 B.C.
Obverse: Zeus, to right
Reverse: little naked jockey on horse, facing right; ΦΙΛΙΠΠΟΥ (of Philip)
Gift of Mr. and Mrs. Arthur J. Frank, 1977.232

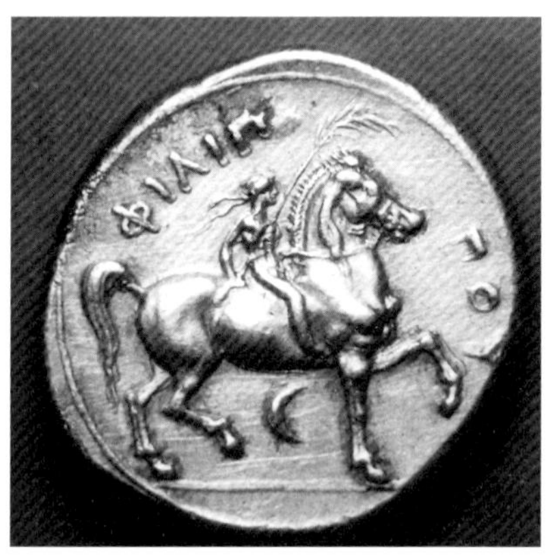

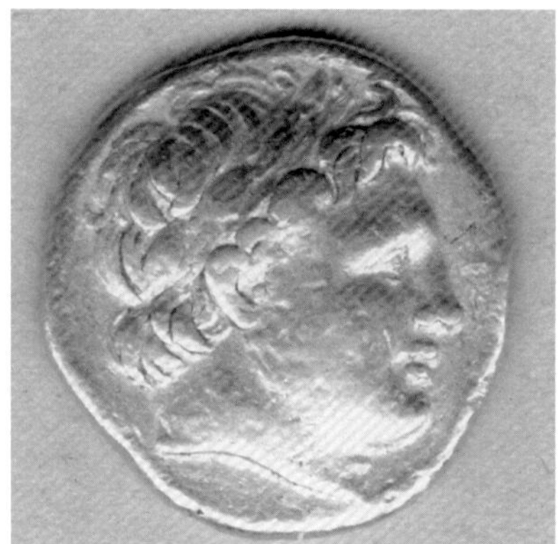

59.
AU stater, 19.1 mm, 133.0 g
Mint: Macedon
Philip II, 359–336 B.C.
Obverse: head of Apollo, to right
Reverse: biga to right; in exergue, ΦΙΛΙΠΠΟΥ (of Philip)
Ref. Mac. I 287.Iff; Head 223
Lent by the Reverends Charles and Evelyn Payson, 3.1991

These coins were struck when Philip captured the gold mines of Thrace from Athens in 356 B.C. Philip is said to have used them for lavish bribery of the leaders of the Greek cities and to have remarked that no city wall was impregnable if the gates were wide enough to admit a mule-load of gold.

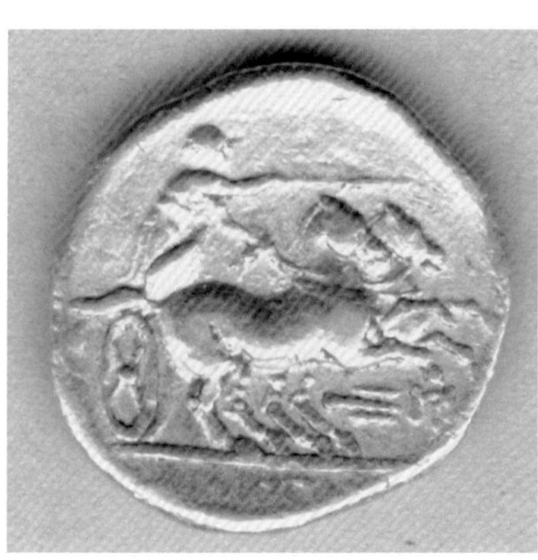

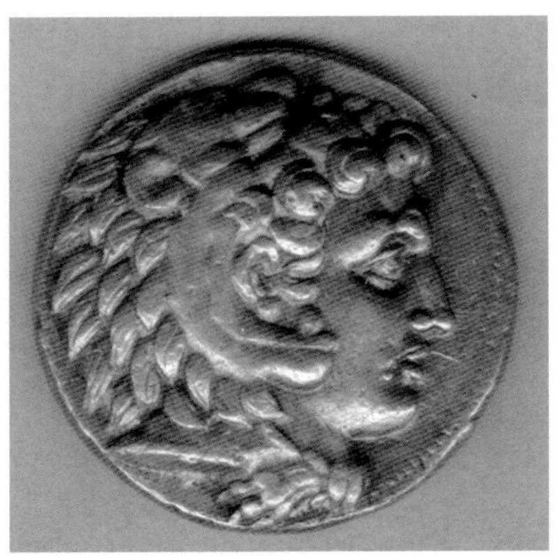

60.
AR tetradrachm, 25 mm
Mint: Side (Asia Minor)
Macedon, Alexander the Great, 336–323 B.C.
Obverse: head of Heracles, to right, wearing skin of Nemean Lion
Reverse: Zeus, seated left, holding eagle; in front, wreath; under seat ΔΙ; ΒΑΣΙΛΕΩΣ ΑΛΕΞΑΝΔΡΟΥ (of King Alexander).
Gift of Mr. and Mrs. Arthur J. Frank, 1977.236

Alexander claimed descent from Heracles through his mother.

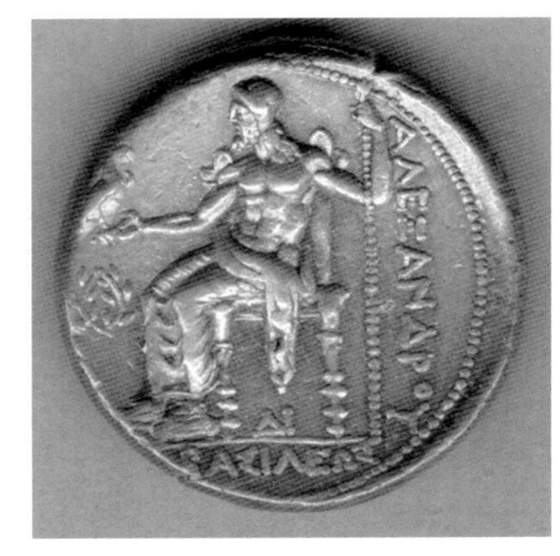

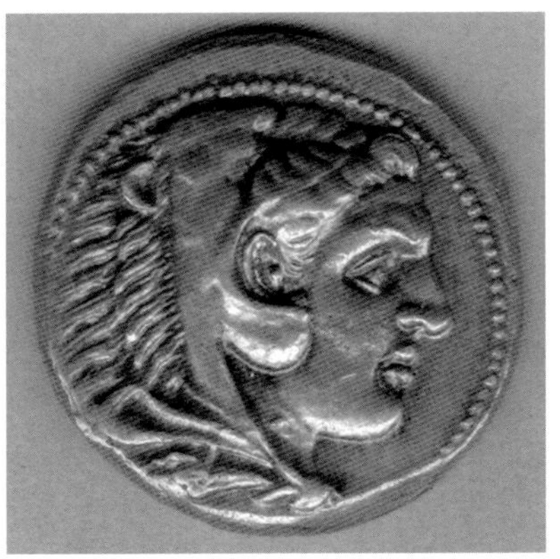

61.
AR tetradrachm, 25 mm
Mint: Damascus, Syria
Macedon, Alexander the Great, 336–323 B.C.
Obverse: head of Heracles, to right, wearing skin of Nemean Lion
Reverse: Zeus, seated left, holding eagle; in front, forepart of ram; under seat: Δ Α; ΑΛΕΞΑΝΔΡΟΥ
Gift of Mr. and Mrs. Arthur J. Frank, 1977.235

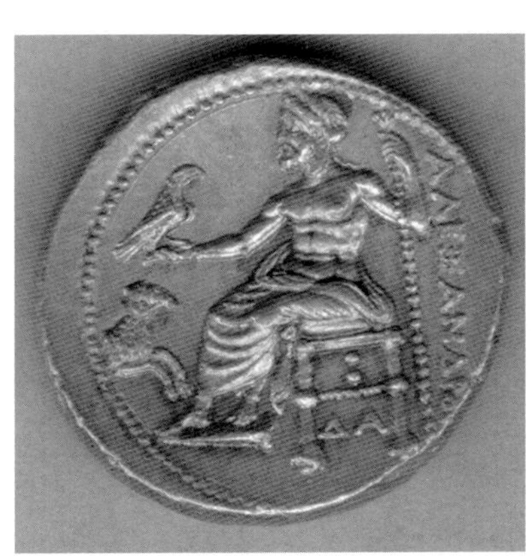

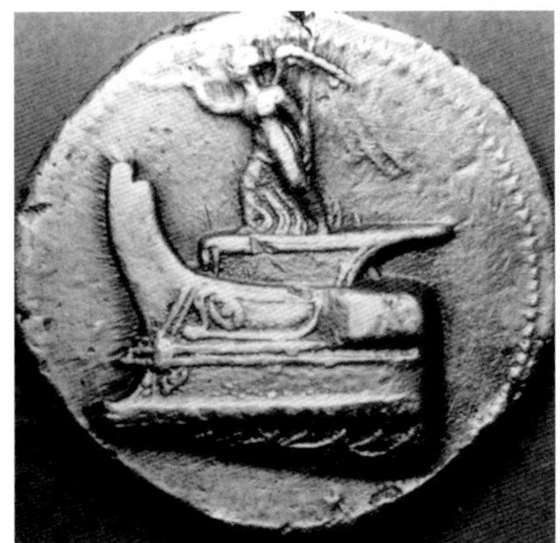

62.
AR tetradrachm, 28.7 mm, 17.04 g
Mint: Salamis, Cyprus
Macedon, Demetrius Poliorcetes, 306–283 B.C.
Obverse: Nike, to left, with trumpet and naval standard on prow of ship
Reverse: Poseidon, naked, striding to left, hurling trident, with chlamys over other arm; ΒΑΣΙΛΕΩΣ ΔΗΜΗΤΡΙΟΥ (of King Demetrius)
Ref. Head 230; Newell (1927) 23
Gift of Mr. and Mrs. Arthur J. Frank, 1979.215

Note that the images of the two deities represented here are very like the great sculptural figures of Victory of Samothrace, now in the Louvre, and Poseidon of Artemisium, now in the National Archaeological Museum, Athens.

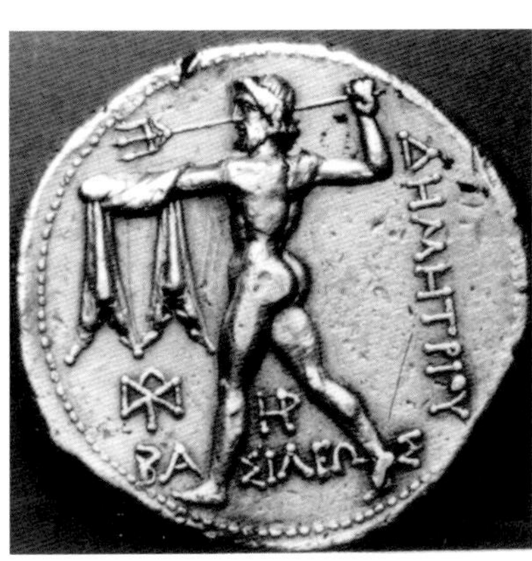

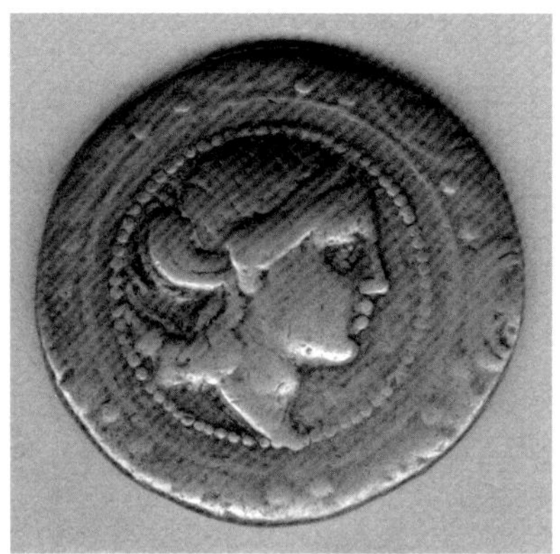

63.
AR tetradrachm, 45 mm
Macedon (Roman domination), 158–148 B.C.
Obverse: Macedonian shield with bust of Artemis in center
Reverse: within oak wreath, a club; ΜΑΚΕΔΟΝΩΝ ΠΡΩΤΗΣ (of the first [district] of the Macedonians), ΔΑ
Ref. BM Mace. 8.8, Head, 238: 151
Gift of Herbert M. Howe, 1980.120

The Romans conquered the last Antigonid in 167 B.C., but took no effective steps to rule for several years. They then divided Macedonia into four regions and made it a province in 146 B.C.

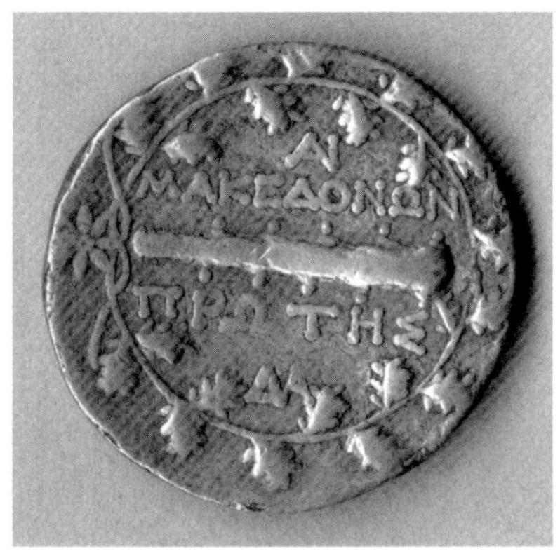

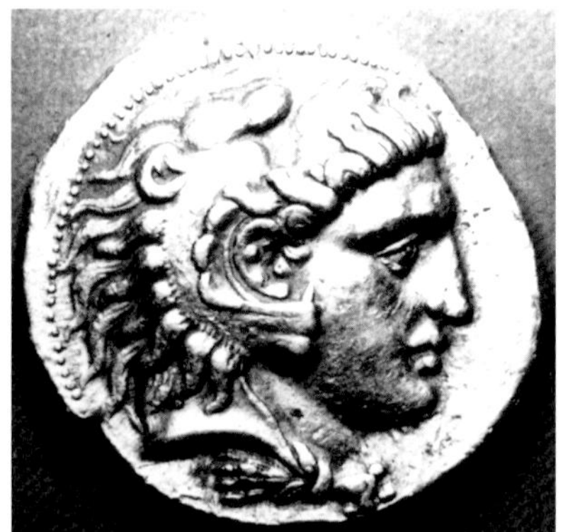

64.
AR tetradrachm, 26 mm, 17.50 g
Mint: Ecbatana
Syria, Seleucus I, 312–280 B.C.
Obverse: head of Heracles, to right, wearing skin of Nemean Lion
Reverse: Zeus seated, to left, with scepter and eagle; feeding horse to left beneath Zeus; in back ΣΕΛΕΥΚΟΥ; in exergue ΒΑΣΙΛΕΩΣ
Gift of Mr. and Mrs. Arthur J. Frank, 1978.317

Compare this coin with cat. nos. 60–61.

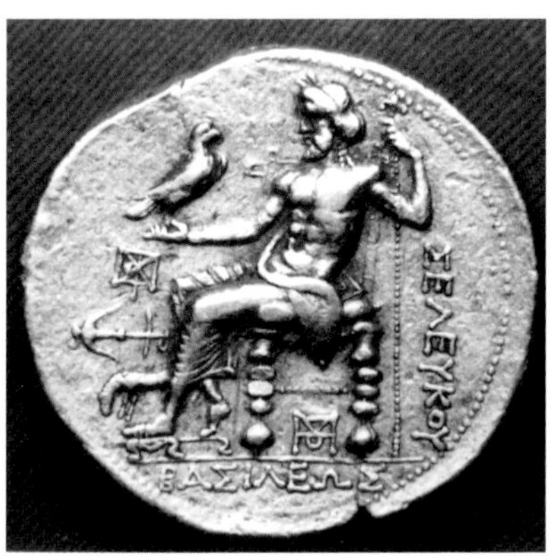

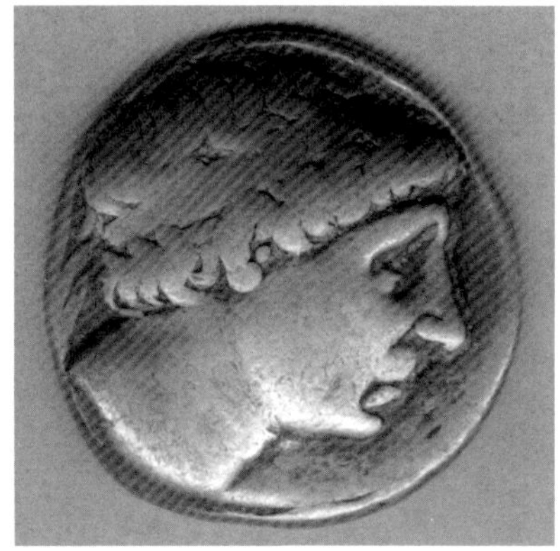

65.
AR tetradrachm, 26 mm, 16.55 g
Syria, Antiochus I, 293–261 B.C.
Obverse: head of middle-aged Antiochus, to right
Reverse: Apollo seated, to left, on omphalos (navel), a stone at Delphi said to be the center of the earth; ΒΑΣΙΛΕΩΣ ΑΝΤΙΟΧΟΥ
Ref. BM Seleucids 9.8
Gift of Herbert M. Howe, 1980.142

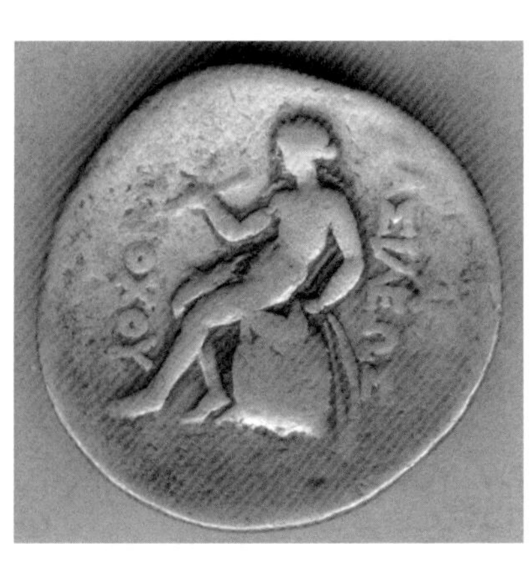

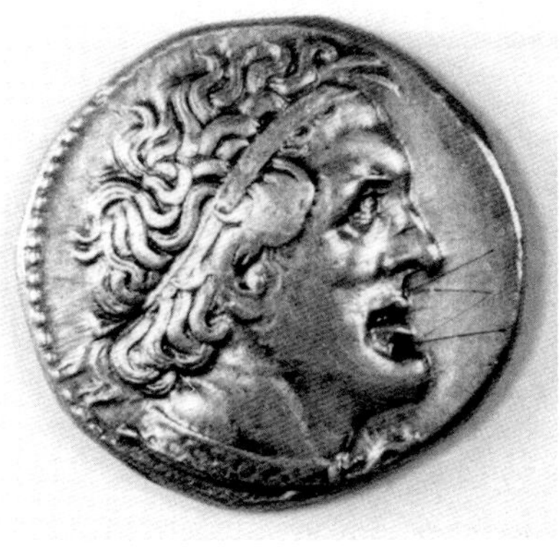

66.
AR tetradrachm, 26 mm
Mint: Egypt
Ptolemy I, 323–283 B.C.
Obverse: head of Ptolemy, to right
Reverse: eagle standing, to left, on thunderbolt;
ΠΤΟΛΕΜΑΙΟΥ ΒΑΣΙΛΕΩΣ (of King Ptolemy)
Ref. Svor. 255, pl. 9.11
Gift of Mr. and Mrs. Arthur J. Frank, 1977.262

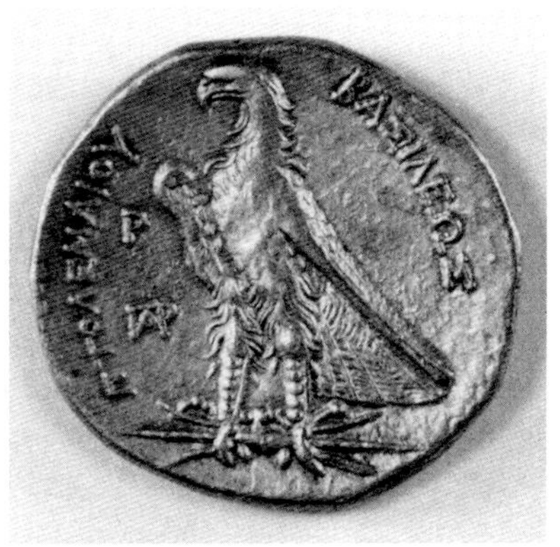

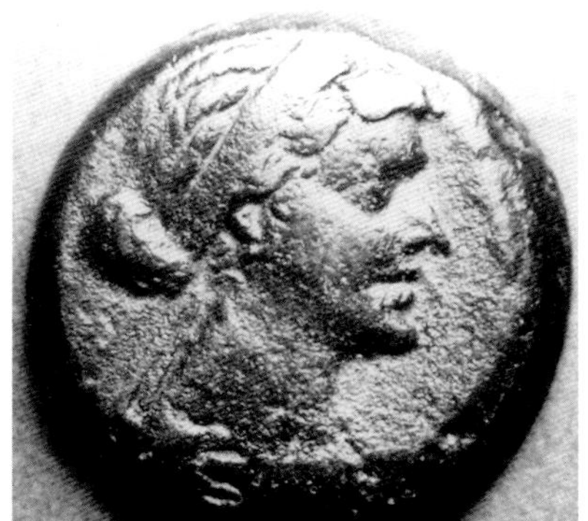

67.
AE (bronze), 27 mm
Mint: Egypt
Cleopatra VII, 51–30 B.C.
Obverse: head of queen, to right, with hair in bun at back with fillet
Reverse: eagle standing, to left, on thunderbolt with cornucopia; ΒΑΣΙΛΙ[ΣΣΗΣ]
Ref. Svor. 1871, pl. 63.3
Gift of Mr. and Mrs. Arthur J. Frank, 1978.324

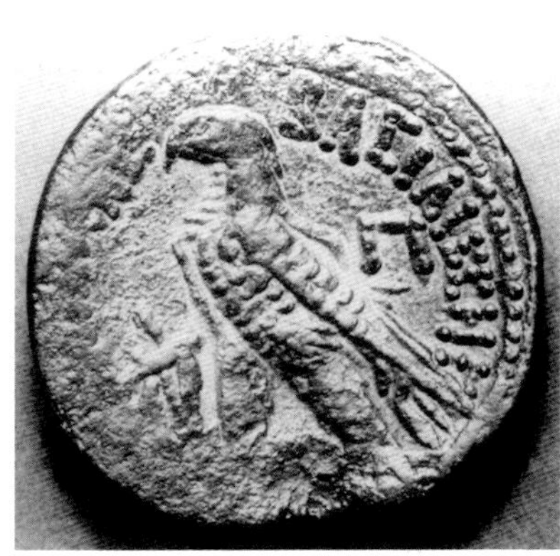

ROMAN REPUBLICAN COINAGE

From the fourth century B.C. onward, Rome, like many other cities of northern Italy, used a bronze coinage whose denominations represented certified weights, multiples of the **uncia**, or ounce. The Roman pound had twelve ounces. The denominations here represented include the **sextans** (one-sixth pound, or two ounces); **quadrans** (one-fourth pound, or three ounces), **triens** (one-third pound, or four ounces), **semis** (one-half pound, or six ounces), **as** (one pound), and the uncommon **bes** (two pounds, or twenty-four ounces). The inconvenience of these enormous coins, aptly called **aes grave**, or "heavy bronze," and the demand for the metal for other uses led to a steady reduction in their size; by the end of the Republic the **as** weighed about half an ounce. From the late third century B.C. the bronze coinage was struck, not cast, but the types remained the same: the **as** had a head of Janus; the **semis**, Saturn; the **triens**, Minerva; the **quadrans**, Hercules; the **sextans**, Mercury; the **uncia**, Roma. All had the prow of a ship and a mark of value on the reverse.

When, in the third century B.C., Rome became supreme in Italy and trade with the Greek world increased, silver became more important, and we find Roman equivalents of the bronze litra and silver didrachm. But from the late third century B.C., the standard Roman silver coin was the **denarius**, worth, as its name suggests, ten asses. Through most of the second century B.C. it had a helmeted head of Roma on the obverse, with an **"X"** as a mark of value. This is the "penny" of the Bible and is the source of the names of many modern coins such as the dinar, dinaro; the English abbreviation d. for penny; and the terms **denier** and **pennyweight** for sizes of thread and nails.

Coins were struck by the members of a committee of three (increased by Julius Caesar to four), who chose their own types. They included punsters like Q. Pomponius Musa, who struck nine types with the Muses, plus two with Apollo and Hercules the Leader of the Muses (cat. nos. 90–100), or L. Valerius Acisculus, who put a little adze (acisculus) on his coins. There were, too, descendants, real or imagined, of ancient worthies. L. Titurius Sabinus, for example, who claimed descent from the Sabine king Titus Tatius, struck coins that illustrated stories in which Tatius played a part (such as the rape of the Sabine women, or the treason of Tarpeia). L. Marcius Philippus also claimed an ancient pedigree and included on his coins a portrait of King Ancus Marcius and an aqueduct, the Aqua Marcia, built by another ancestor. The common denominator of all these is political propaganda—the moneyers were young men with political ambitions, who wanted, in today's terms, "name recognition."

From the death of Caesar in 44 B.C. to the defeat of Antony in 31 B.C., the coins of Octavian (later Augustus, Caesar's great-nephew, adopted by Caesar's will when he was nineteen) and those of Antony give a picture of Antony's attempts to stay on good terms with Octavian, as well as his later attempts to win power in the East with Cleopatra.

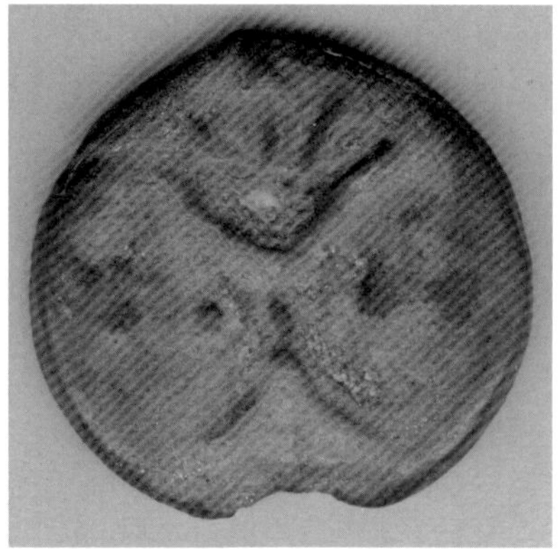

68.
AE triens, cast, 45 mm, 70.80 g
Mint: Rome, 275–270 B.C.
Obverse: thunderbolt; two pellets on each side
Reverse: dolphin; below, four pellets
Ref. Crawford 14/3; CRR 10; BMC Italy 48.8
Gift of Herbert M. Howe, 1980.292

Before the standardization of bronze types in 211 B.C. a variety of types was struck, of which this is one.

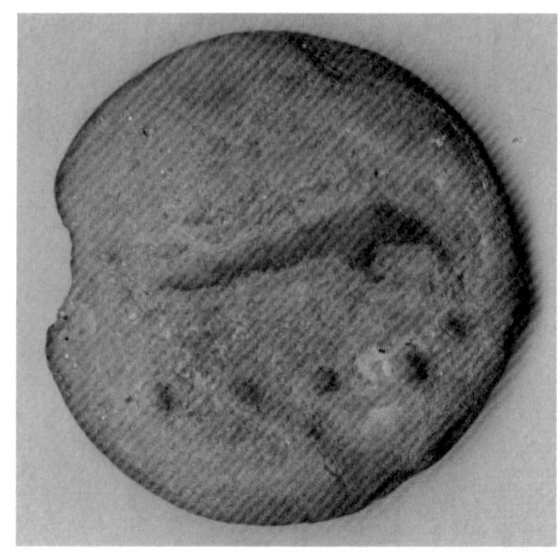

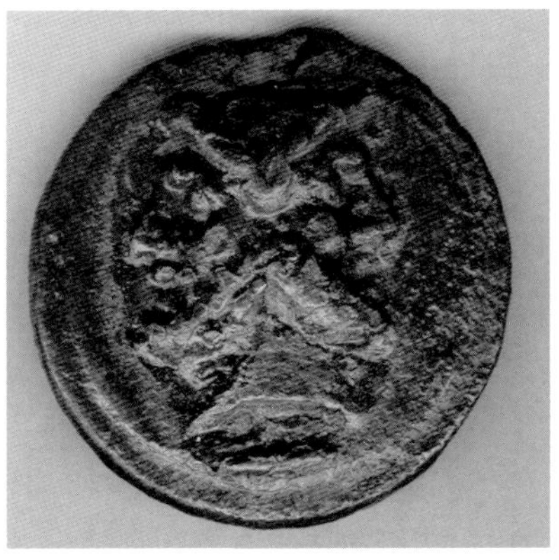

69.
AE as grave, cast, 68 mm, 251.30 g
Mint: Rome, 225–217 B.C.
Obverse: Janus
Reverse: prow. Mark of value: I
Ref. Crawford 35/1; CRR 71
Gift of Mr. and Mrs. Arthur J. Frank, 1977.271

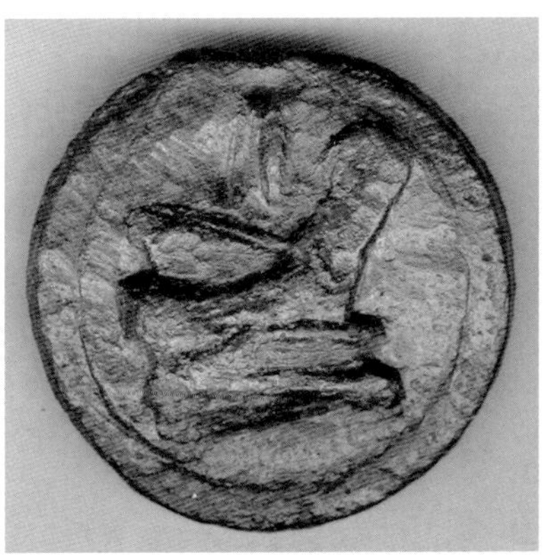

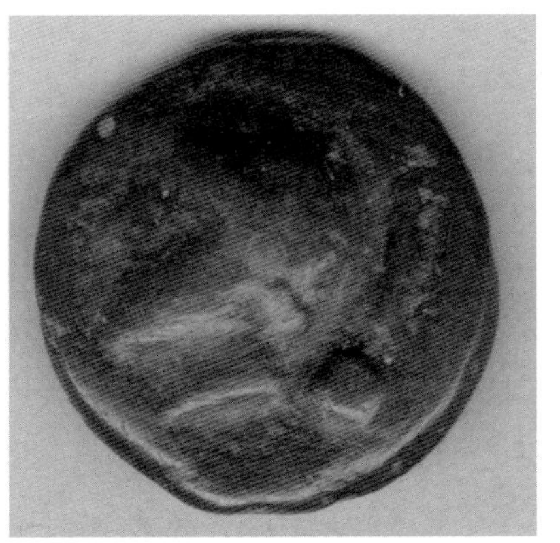

70.
AE uncia, cast, 25 mm, 19.60 g
Mint: Rome, 225–215 B.C.
Obverse: Roma
Reverse: prow. Mark of value: o
Ref. Crawford 38/6; BMCRR Rome 88
Gift of Herbert M. Howe, 1980.156

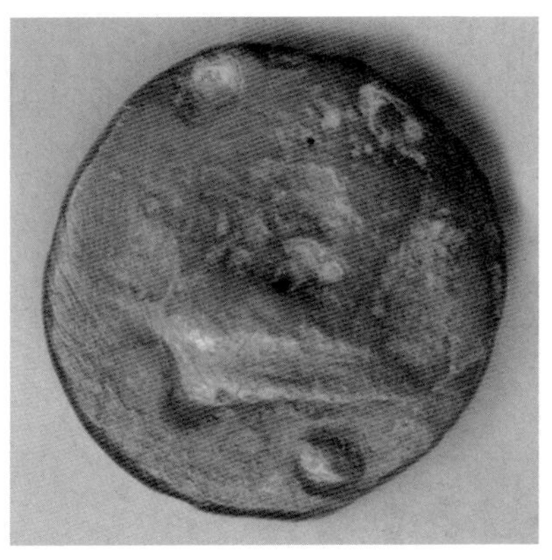

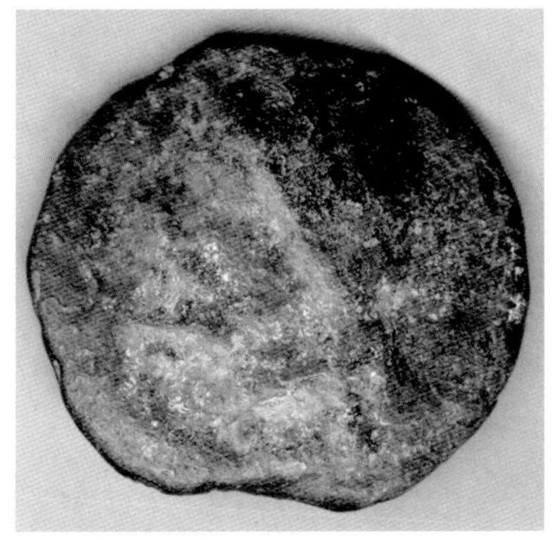

71.
AE semis, cast, 34.9 mm, 115.40 g
Mint: Rome, 225–217 B.C.
Obverse: Saturn
Reverse: prow. Mark of value: S
Ref. Crawford 35/2; CRR 73
Gift of Herbert M. Howe, 1980.482

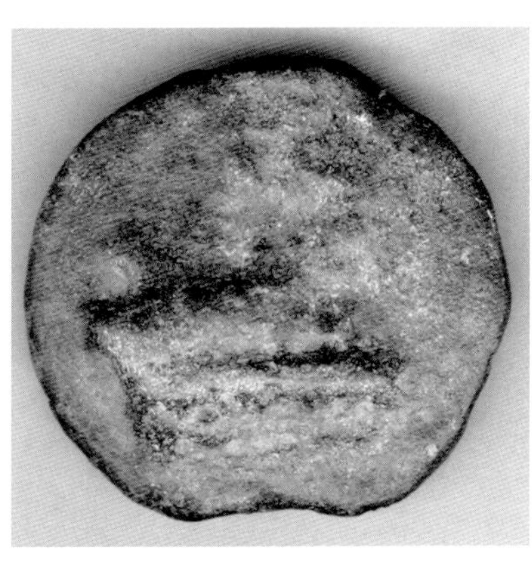

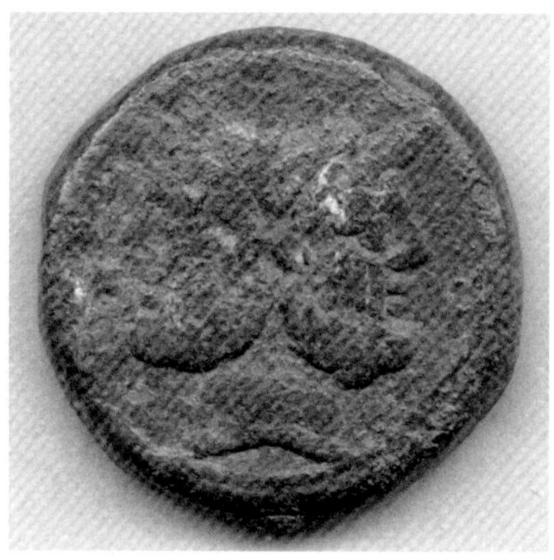

72.
AE as, 32 mm, 40.30 g
Mint: Rome, after 211–208 B.C.
Obverse: Janus
Reverse: prow. Mark of value: I
Ref. Crawford 110/2; CRR 279; BMCRR I 326
Gift of Herbert M. Howe, 1980.459

The earliest denarii (silver coins of ten asses) we have date from 211 B.C. The bronze was standardized at the same time, but gradually fell in weight: compare this coin with cat. no. 77.

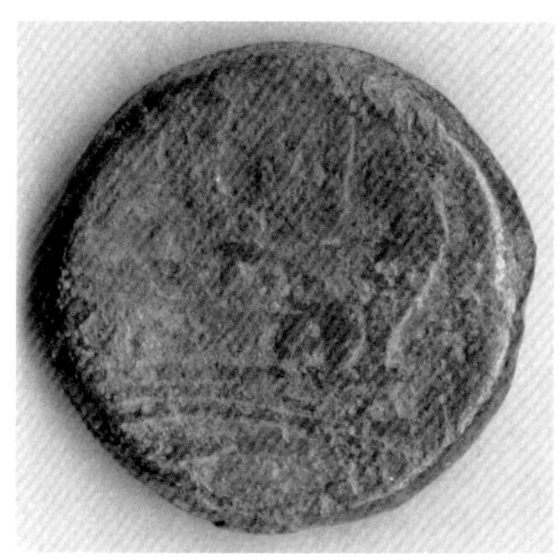

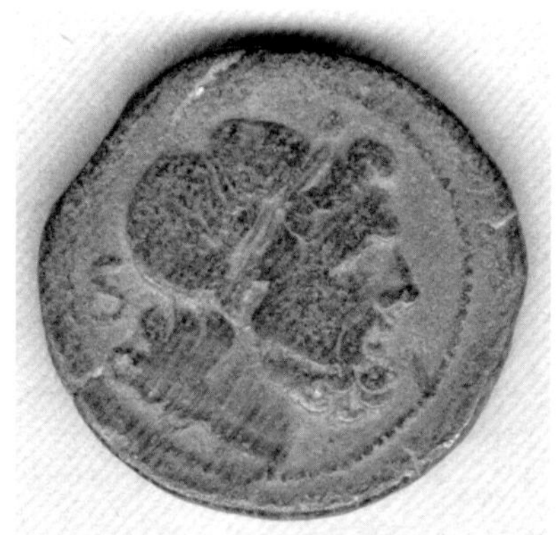

73.
AE semis, 28 mm, 17.30 g
Mint: southeastern Italy, 211–210 B.C.
Obverse: Saturn
Reverse: prow. Mark of value: S
Ref. Crawford 85/3; CRR 175a; BMCRR Italy 206
Gift of Herbert M. Howe, 1980.479

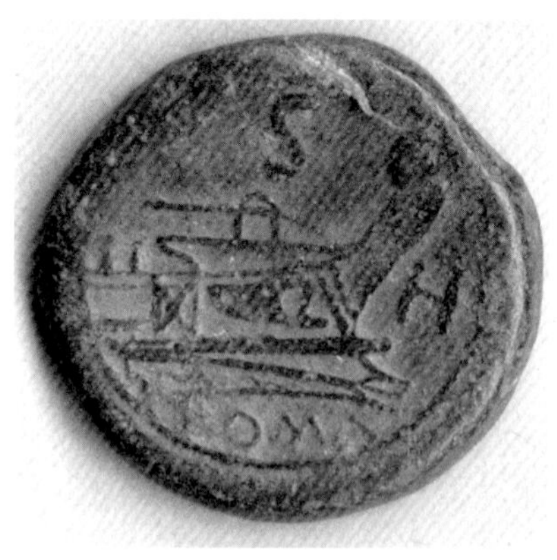

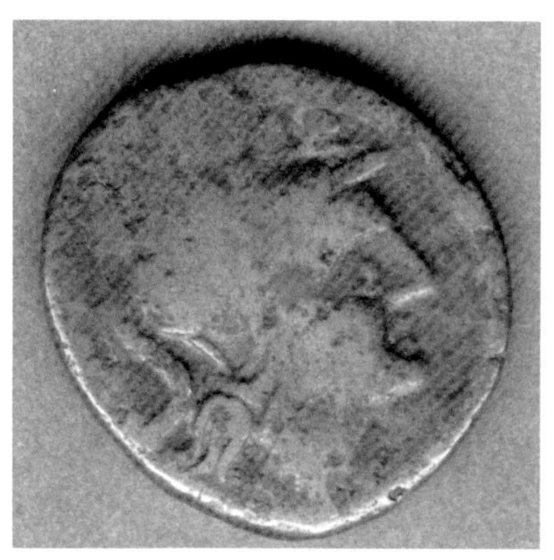

74.
AE triens, 25 mm, 11.40 g
Mint: Rome, 211–210 B.C.
Obverse: Minerva
Reverse: prow. Mark of value: oooo
Ref. Crawford 56/4; CRR 143b; BMCRR Italy 245
Gift of Herbert M. Howe, 1980.104

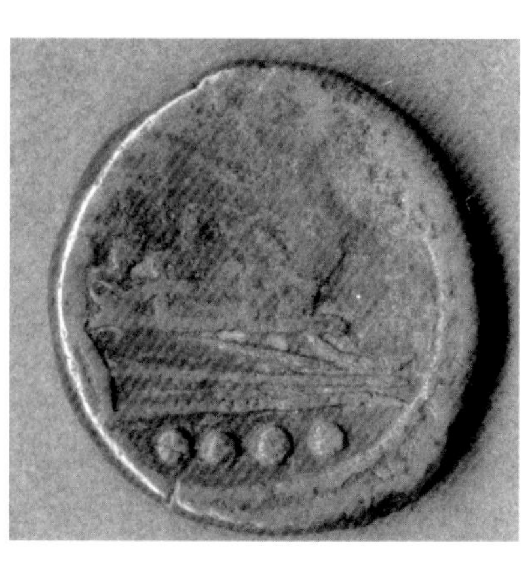

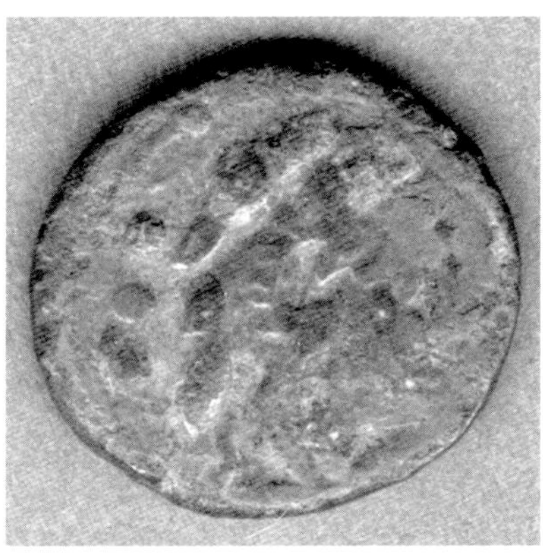

75.
AE quadrans, 20.6 mm, 5.80 g
Mint: central Italy, 211–208 B.C.
Obverse: Hercules
Reverse: prow. Mark of value: ooo
Ref. Crawford 61/5; CRR 148c; BMCR Italy II 344
Gift of Herbert M. Howe, 1980.495

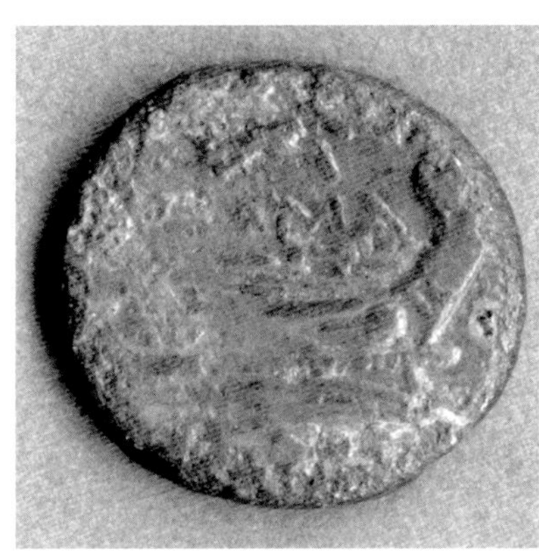

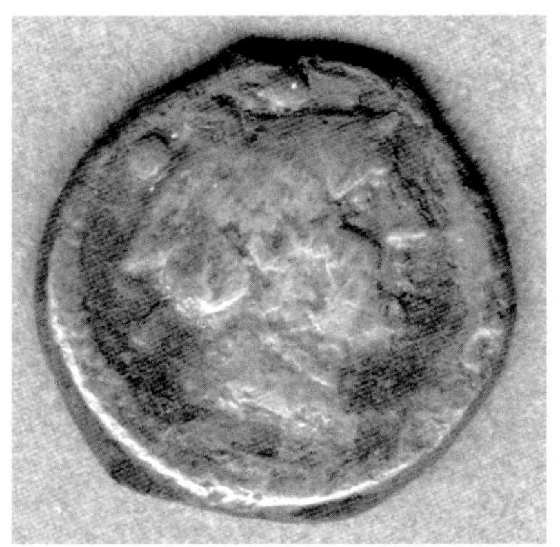

76.
AE sextans, 19.1 mm, 5.10 g
Mint: central Italy, 211 B.C.
Obverse: Mercury
Reverse: prow. Mark of value: oo
Ref. Crawford 63/6; CRR 157d; BMCRR Italy 187
Gift of Herbert M. Howe, 1980.484

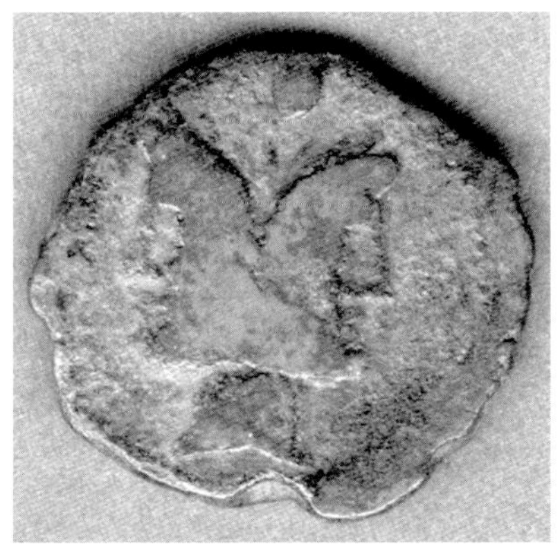

77.
AE as, 25 mm, 10.20 g
Mint: Rome, ca. 91 B.C.
Obverse: Janus
Reverse: prow
Ref. Crawford 339/1; CRR 679; BMCRR 2194
Gift of Herbert M. Howe, 1980.460

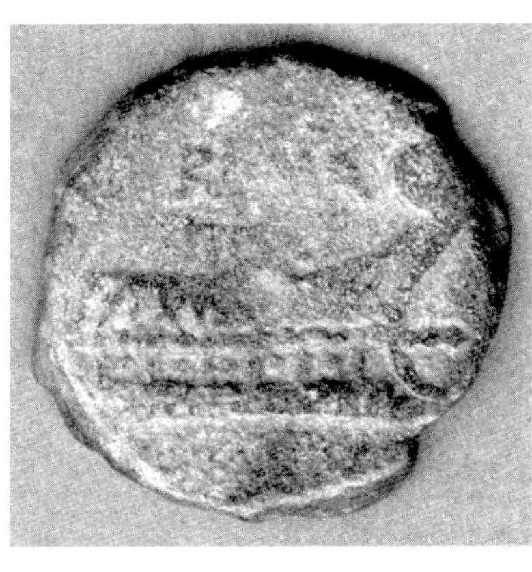

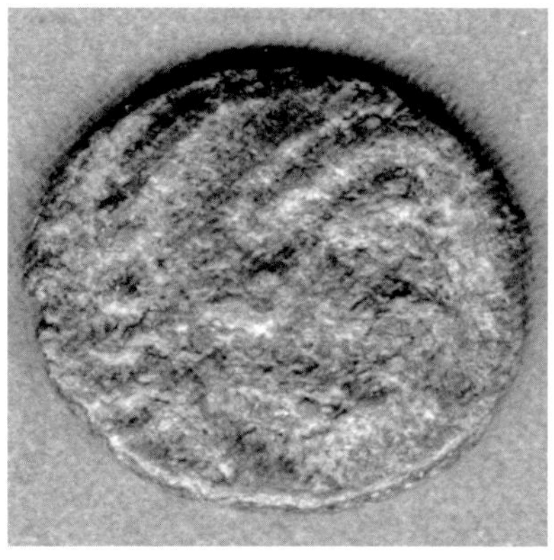

78.
AE uncia, 17.5 mm, 1.20 g
Mint: Rome, ca. 91 B.C.
Obverse: Bellona
Reverse: prow
Ref. CRR 679e
Gift of Herbert M. Howe, 1980.157

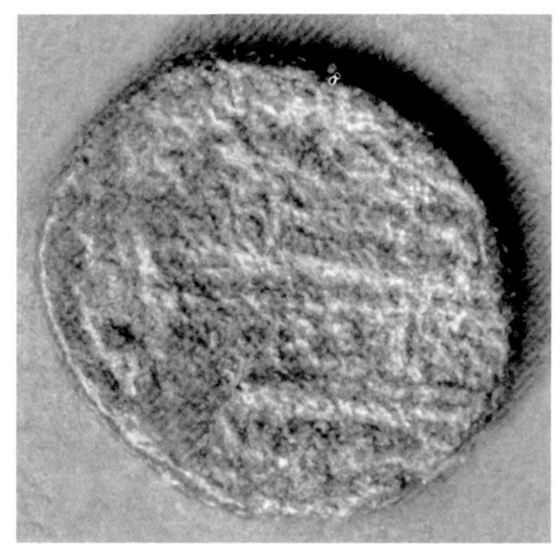

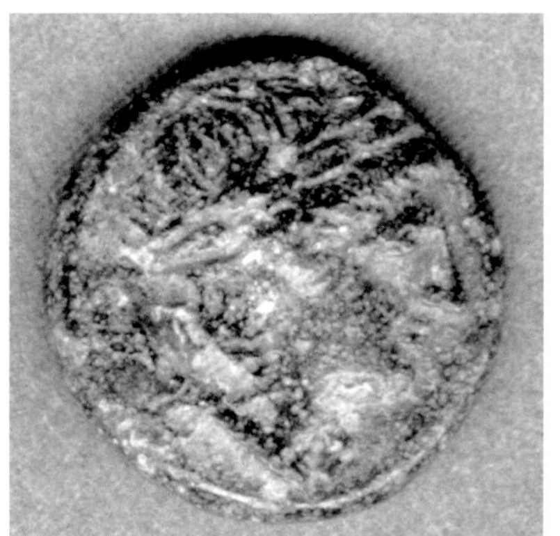

79.
AE litra, 14.3 mm, 2.0 g
Mint: Rome, 234–231 B.C.
Obverse: Apollo
Reverse: galloping horse
Ref. Crawford 26/3; CRR 29; BMCRR 70
Gift of Herbert M. Howe, 1980.470

The litra was a coin made to fit the Greek bronze standard of southern Italy.

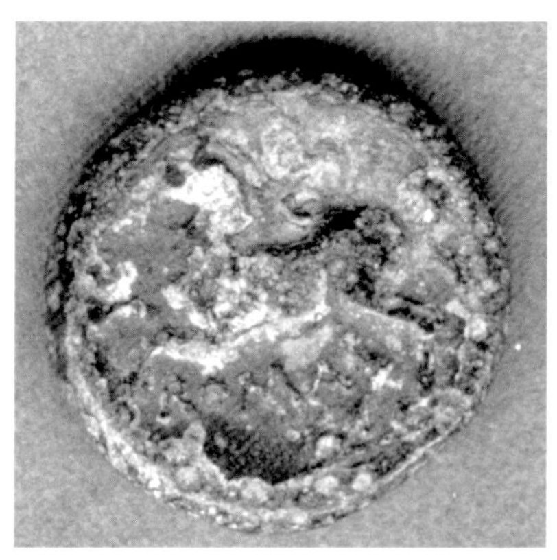

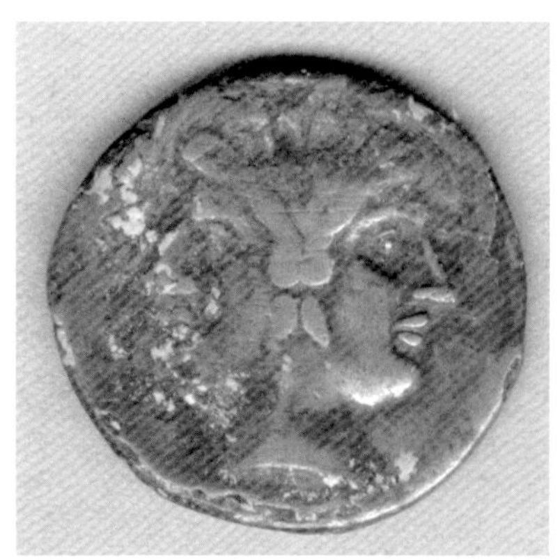

80.
AR didrachm, 22.2 mm, 6.40 g
Mint: Rome, 225–212 B.C.
Obverse: janiform head of Dioscuri
Reverse: Jupiter, with thunderbolt and scepter, and Victory in quadriga (four-horse chariot); beneath, tablet with ROMA, incuse
Ref. Crawford 28/3; CRR 64a
Gift of Herbert M. Howe, 1980.467

This was produced to correspond to the silver coinage of the Greek-speaking cities of South Italy and Sicily.

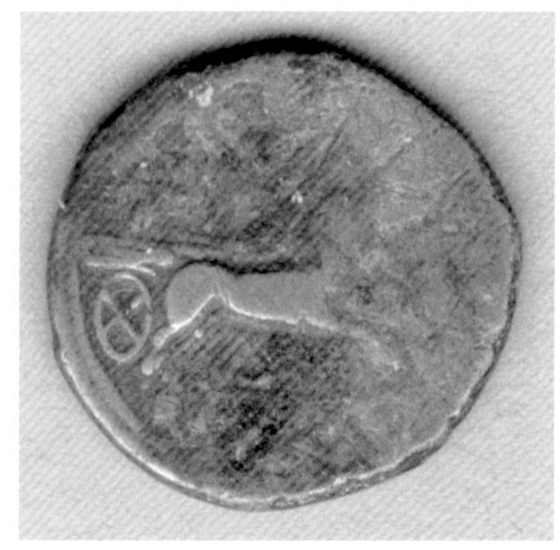

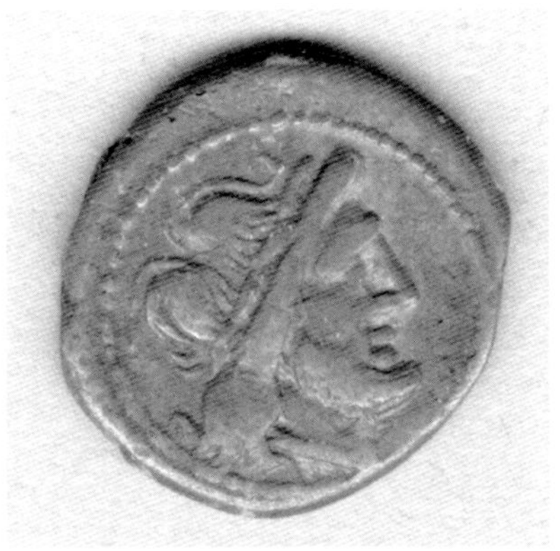

81.
AR victoriate, 15.9 mm, 2.40 g
Mint: Rome, after 211 B.C.
Obverse: head of Jupiter
Reverse: Victory crowning trophy (conquered armor on pole)
Ref. Crawford 53/1; CRR 83; BMCRR 296
Gift of Herbert M. Howe, 1980.130

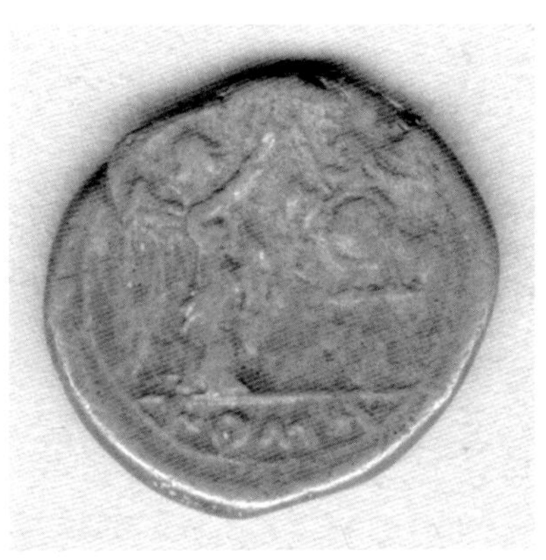

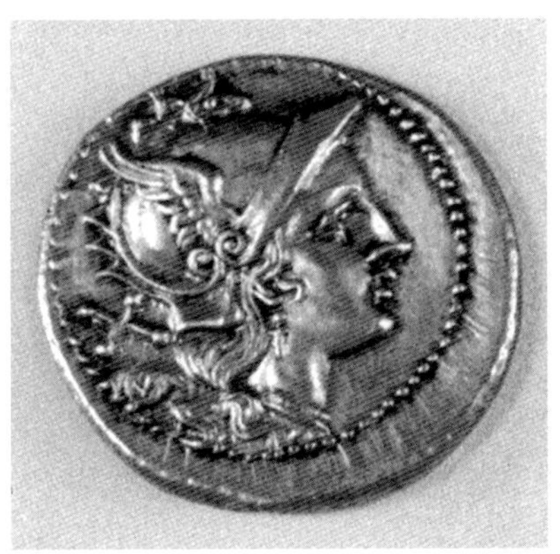

82.
AR denarius, 20.6 mm, 4.50 g
Mint: Rome, ca. 175–168 B.C.
Obverse: helmeted head of Roma to right; behind, X (Roman numeral)
Reverse: Dioscuri to right
Ref. CRR 207
Gift of Mr. and Mrs. Arthur J. Frank, 1977.272

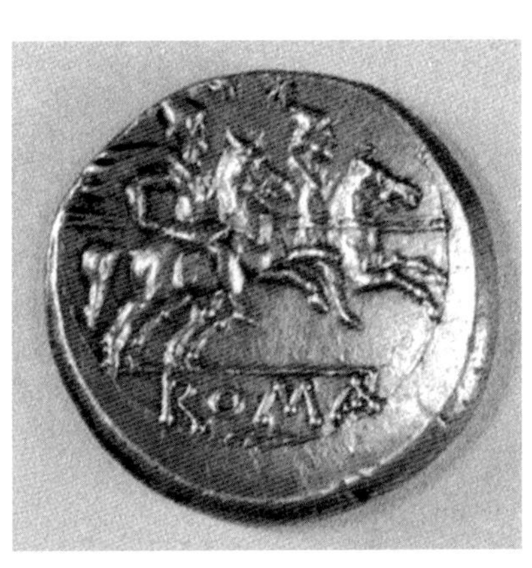

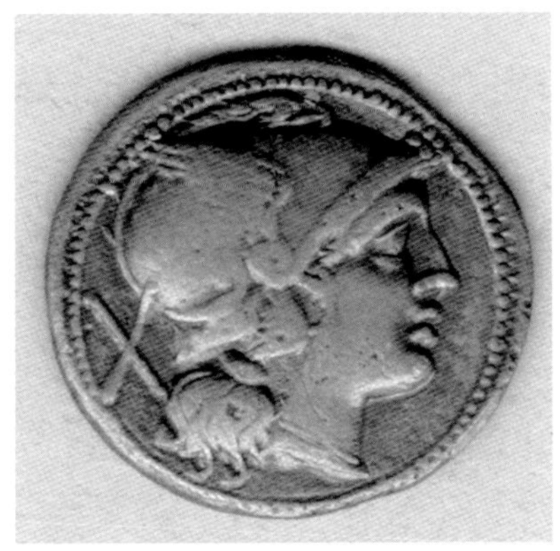

83.
AR denarius, 19.1 mm, 4.50 g
Mint: Rome, after 211 B.C.
Obverse: helmeted head of Roma; behind, X (Roman numeral)
Reverse: Dioscuri galloping right; incuse on tablet, ROMA
Ref. Crawford 44/5; CRR 140; BMCRR Rome 1
Gift of Herbert M. Howe, 1980.461

This coin, with different reverses, was in production for about four-hundred years.

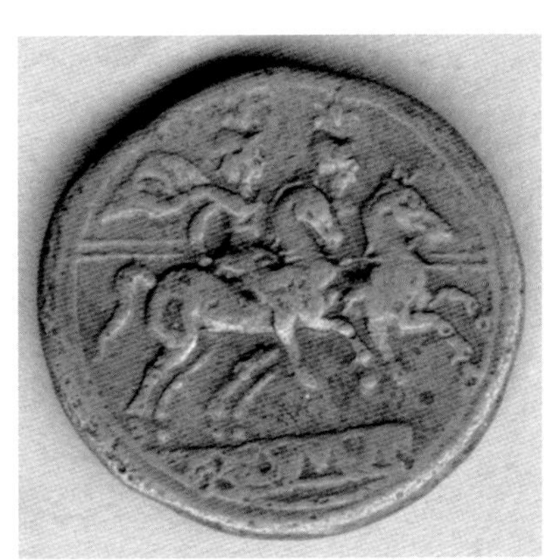

Roman Mythology, History, and Religion

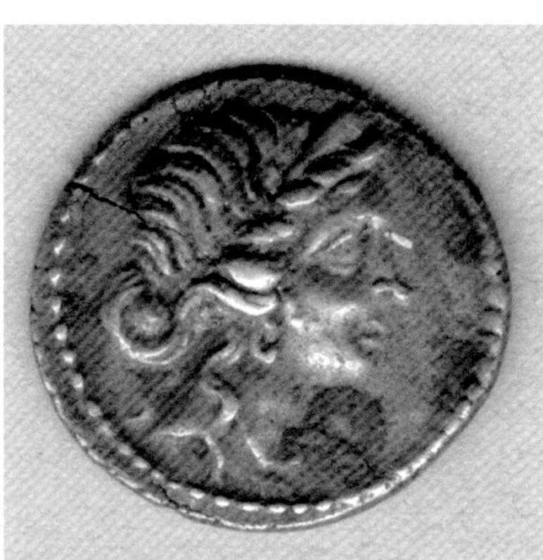

84.
AR denarius, 19.1 mm, 3.80 g
Mint: Africa
Julius Caesar, 47–46 B.C.
Obverse: head of Venus
Reverse: Aeneas walking, to left, carrying Palladium in right hand and his father, Anchises, on his left shoulder; on right, CAESAR
Ref. Crawford 458/1; CRR 1013; BMCRR Ea 31
Gift of Herbert M. Howe, 1980.308

The Julian family claimed descent from Venus and her Trojan lover Anchises, via their son Aeneas and his son Iulus. When Troy fell, Aeneas rescued the Palladium, a statue of Athena which had fallen from heaven (on which the safety of the city depended), lifted his old father onto his shoulders, and fled from the city with his little son Iulus and a band of followers, eventually reaching Italy.

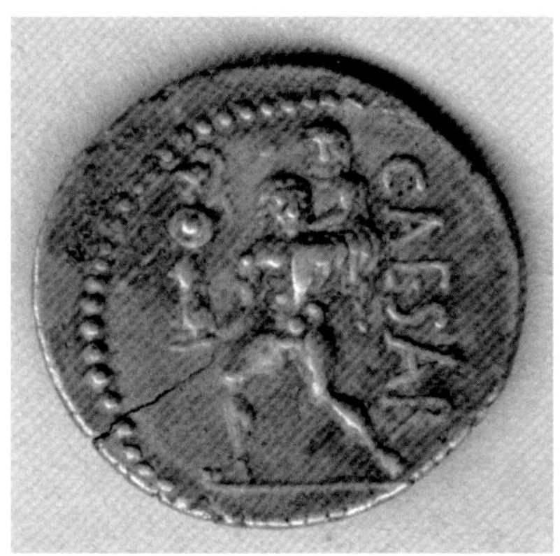

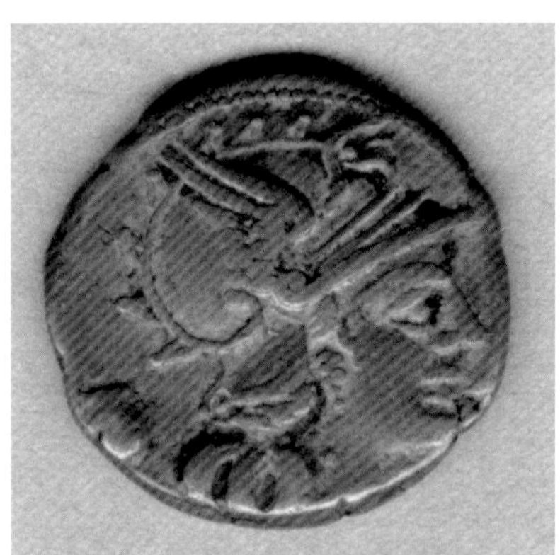

85.
AR denarius, 19.1 mm, 3.84 g
Mint: Rome; Sex. Pompeius Faustulus, 137 B.C.
Obverse: head of Roma
Reverse: wolf and twins; behind, fig tree with one bird (a woodpecker) on trunk and two in branches; to right, the shepherd Faustulus; behind him, FOSTLVS; to right, SEXtus Pompeius
Ref. Crawford 235/1c; CRR 461; BMCRR Italy 926
Gift of Herbert M. Howe, 1980.365

The last legitimate king of Alba Longa had been exiled by his wicked brother and his daughter forced to become a Vestal Virgin. When she became pregnant by Mars, her twin sons, Romulus and Remus, were exposed to die. They were put in a basket and thrown into the Tiber. When the basket washed ashore under a fig tree (sacred to the deity Picus, a woodpecker), the twins were fed by a she-wolf. They were rescued and raised by the shepherd Faustulus.

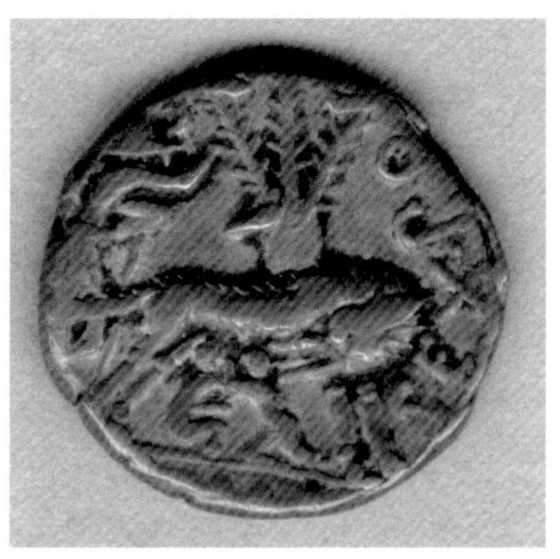

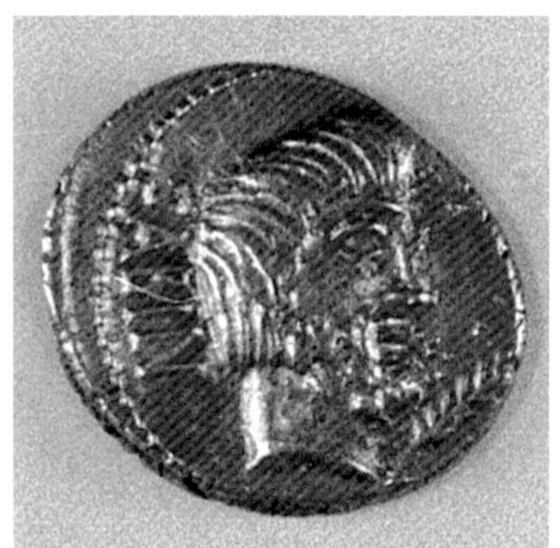

86.
AR denarius, 19.1 mm
Mint: Rome; L. Titurius Sabinus, 89 B.C.
Obverse: bearded head of Titus Tatius; SABINus
Reverse: two Roman soldiers, each bearing a Sabine woman in his arms, below, L. Tituri
Ref. Crawford 344/1b; CRR 698a; BMCRR Italy 2325
Gift of Mr. and Mrs. Arthur J. Frank, 1979.248

When Romulus founded the city, his men had no wives. Romulus therefore ordered a great festival, to which he invited the neighboring Sabines and their families. When he gave the signal, his men pounced on the women and carried them off.

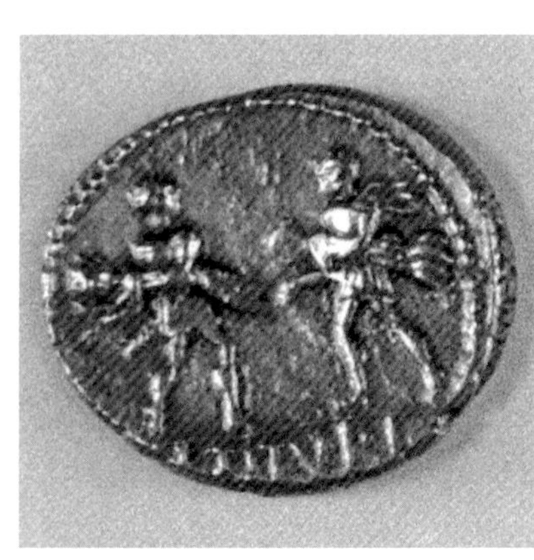

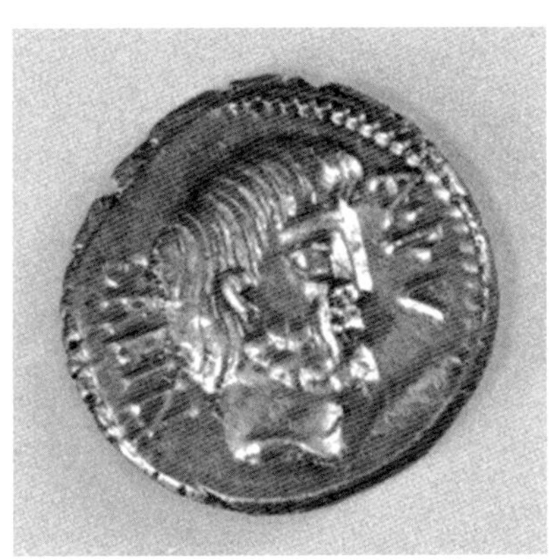

87.
AR denarius, 19.1 mm
Mint: Rome; L. Titurius Sabinus, 89 B.C.
Obverse: bearded head of Titus Tatius to right; behind SABIN; before A.PV, palm branch
Reverse: two soldiers threatening kneeling Tarpeia with their shields, below, L. TITVRI
Ref. CRR 699a; BMCRR Italy 2326
Gift of Mr. and Mrs. Arthur J. Frank, 1979.247

Tarpeia, daughter of the commander of the Romans guarding the Capitoline Hill, offered to open the gates to the Sabines if they would give her "what they had on their left arms"—meaning the gold bracelets they wore. The Sabines agreed. Once inside, they crushed the girl with what they had on their left arms—the weight of their shields.

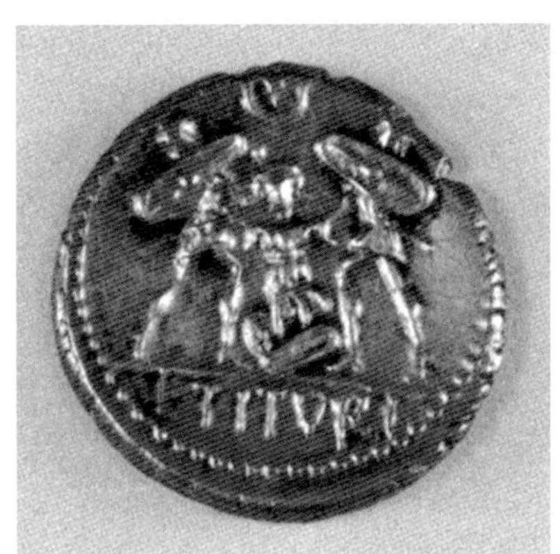

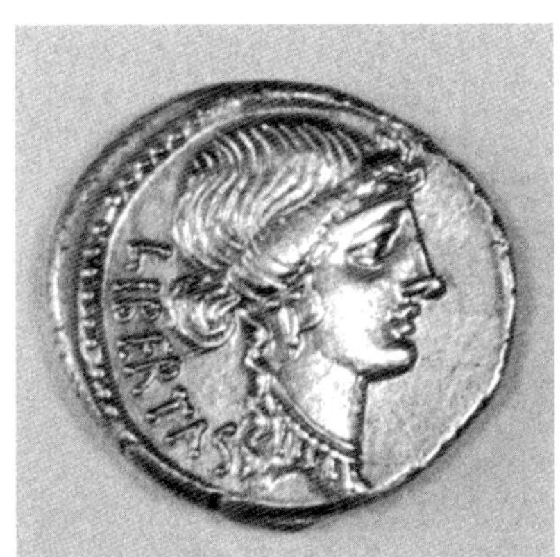

88.
AR denarius, 19.1 mm
Mint: Rome; M. Junius Brutus (adoptive name of Q. Servilius Caepio Brutus), 54 B.C.
Obverse: bust of Liberty, to right; LIBERTAS
Reverse: L. Junius Brutus walking between two lictors (see cat. no. 57) preceded by an accensus; below BRVTVS
Ref. CRR 906; BMCRR 3861
Gift of Mr. and Mrs. Arthur J. Frank, 1977.283

When the last king, Tarquin the Proud, was expelled, the Romans chose two consuls as leaders, of whom L. Junius Brutus was one. His descendant, M. Brutus, struck this coin as well as one showing another ancestor, the tyrannicide C. Servilius Ahala. Brutus himself was to be chief of the assassins of Caesar. But at the time of this coin the chief foe of "liberty" was Pompey, not Caesar.

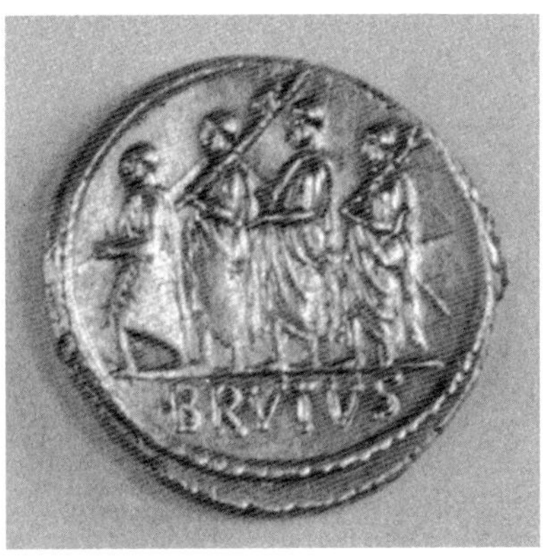

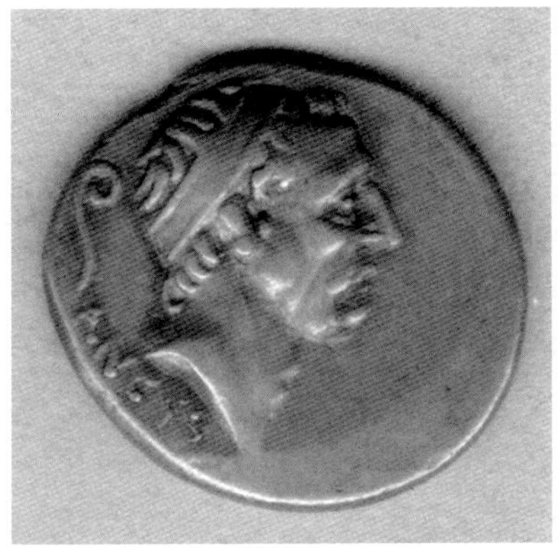

89.
AR denarius, 19.1 mm, 4.00 g
Mint: Rome, L. Marcius Philippus, 56 B.C.
Obverse: head of Ancus Marcius; below, ANCVS
Reverse: equestrian statue on aqueduct of five arches, within which AQVA MR; around, PHILIPPVS
Ref. Crawford 425/1; CRR 919; BMCRR Italy 3890
Gift of Herbert M. Howe, 1980.327

The moneyer is recalling two of his ancestors: the fourth king of Rome and the builder of the Aqua Marcia, upon which was a statue of him on horseback.

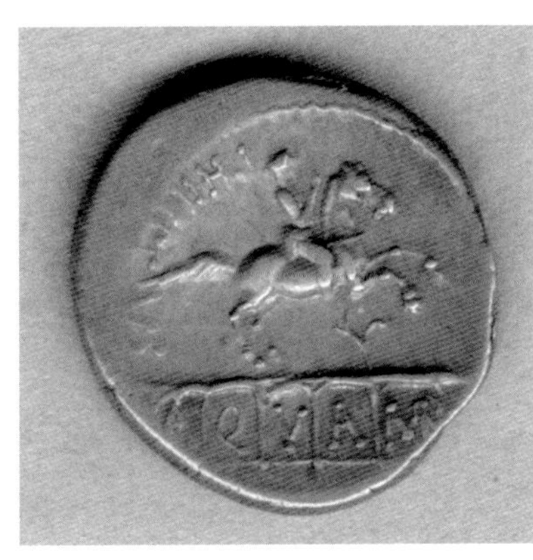

On the following coins, each of the Muses is shown with one of her attributes. However, the functions ascribed to each are late and uncertain. All reverses except cat. no. 100 bear the name Q. POMPONI MVSA (cat. no. 100 has it on the obverse). We know nothing about Pomponius Musa except for these coins—a pun on his cognomen, or third name. This is a remarkably fine set of these uncommon coins.

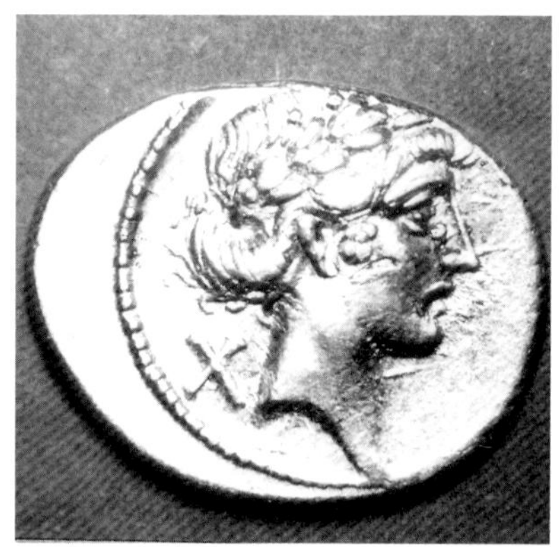

90.
AR denarius, 20.6 mm
Mint: Rome; Q. Pomponius Musa, 66 B.C.
Obverse: laureate head of Apollo, to right; behind two flutes crossed
Reverse: Euterpe, standing to right, holding two flutes in right hand
Ref. Bab. Pomponia 13; CRR 815; BMCRR 3613; Crawford 410/5
Gift of Mr. and Mrs. Arthur J. Frank, 1979.250

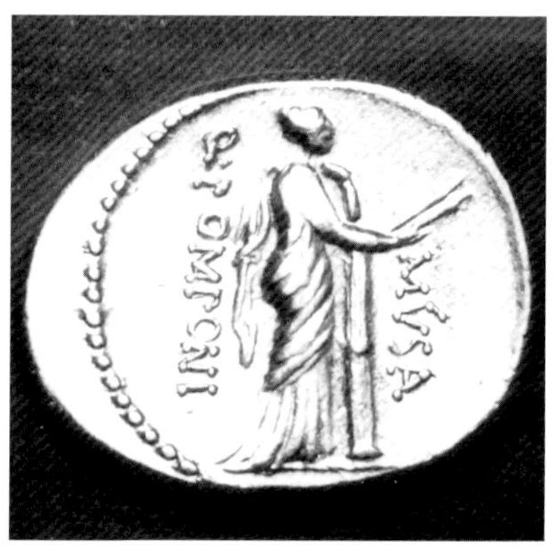

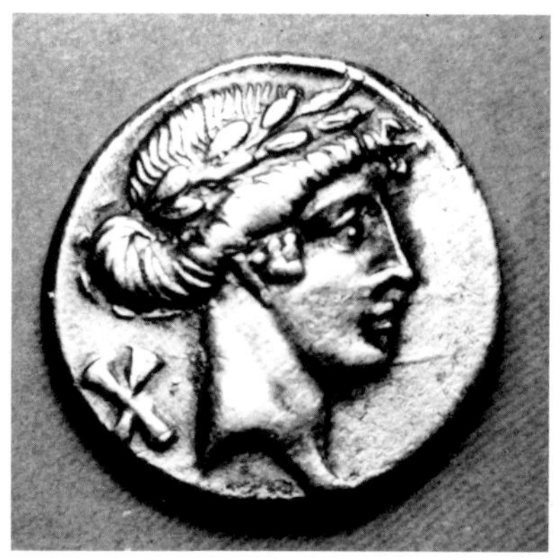

91.
AR denarius, 17.5 mm
Mint: Rome; Q. Pomponius Musa, 66 B.C.
Obverse: laureate head of Apollo, to right, two flutes crossed behind
Reverse: Euterpe, muse of lyric poetry, standing to right, holding two pipes or flutes in right hand
Ref. Bab. Pomponia 13; CRR 815; BMCRR 3613; Crawford 410/5
Gift of Mr. and Mrs. Arthur J. Frank, 1979.251

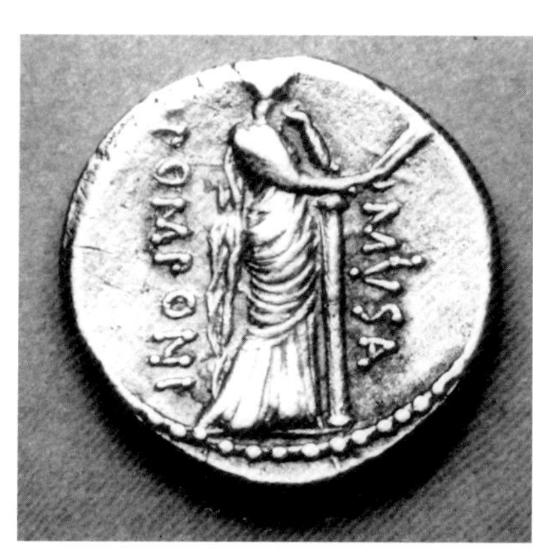

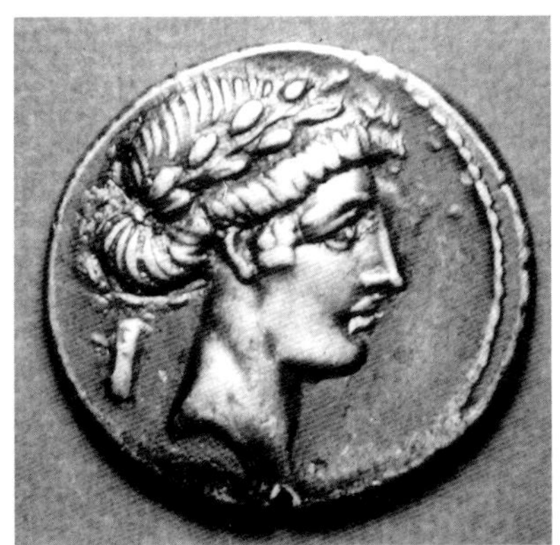

92.
AR denarius, 17.5 mm
Mint: Rome; Q. Pomponius Musa, 66 B.C.
Obverse: laureate head of Apollo, to right, rolled scroll behind
Reverse: Clio, muse of history, standing to left, holding an open scroll between her hands
Ref. Bab. Pomponia 11; CRR 813; BMCRR 3610; Crawford 410/3
Gift of Mr. and Mrs. Arthur J. Frank, 1979.253

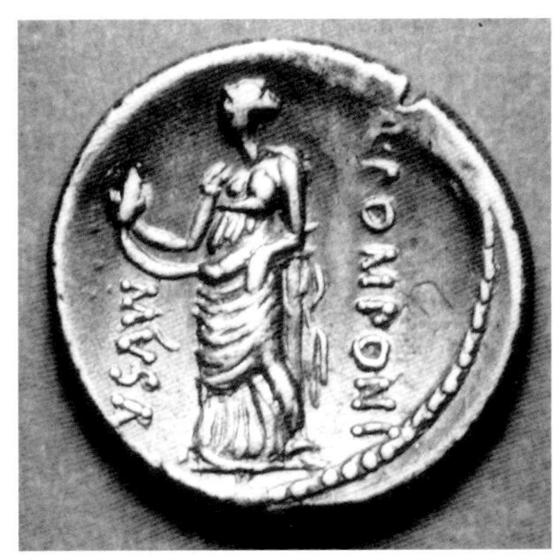

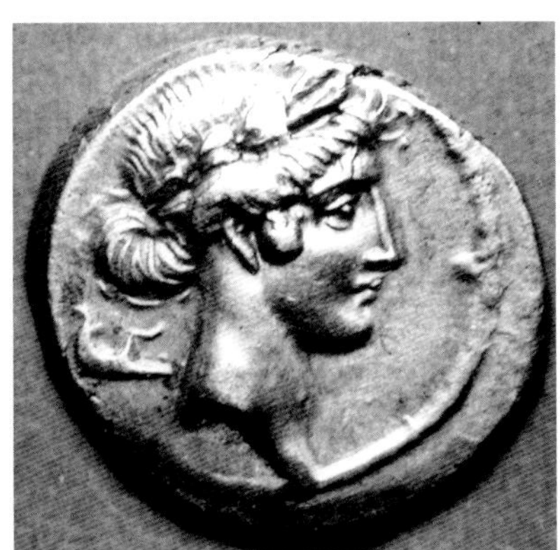

93.
AR denarius, 19.1 mm
Mint: Rome; Q. Pomponius Musa, 66 B.C.
Obverse: laureate head of Apollo, to right, sandal behind
Reverse: Thalia, muse of comedy, standing to left, holding a comic mask in right hand, left elbow resting on pedestal
Ref. Bab. Pomponia 19; CRR 821; BMCRR 3624; Crawford 410/9b
Gift of Mr. and Mrs. Arthur J. Frank, 1979.254

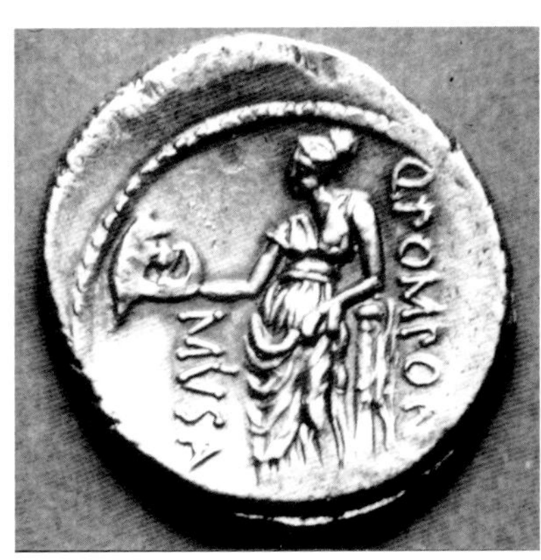

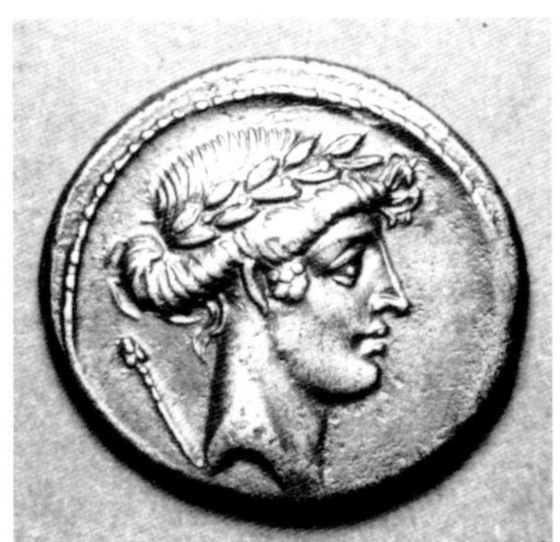

94.
AR denarius, 19 mm, 3.71 g
Mint: Rome; Q. Pomponius Musa, 66 B.C.
Obverse: laureate head of Apollo, to right, scepter behind
Reverse: Melpomene, muse of tragedy, wearing a sword at waist, holding a club and tragic mask
Ref. Bab. Pomponia 14; CRR 816; BMCRR 3615; Crawford 410/4
Gift of Mr. and Mrs. Arthur J. Frank, 1979.252

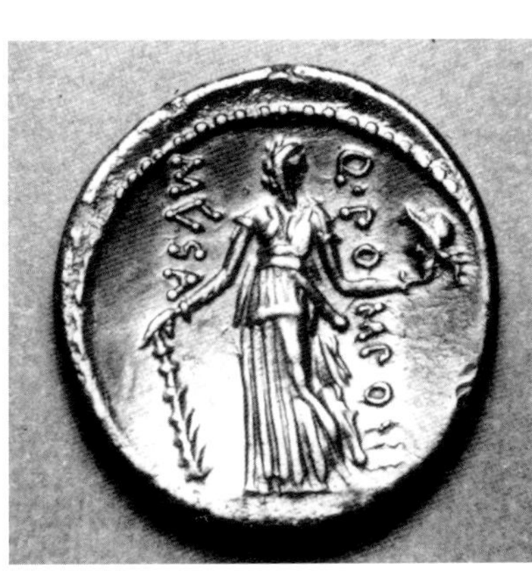

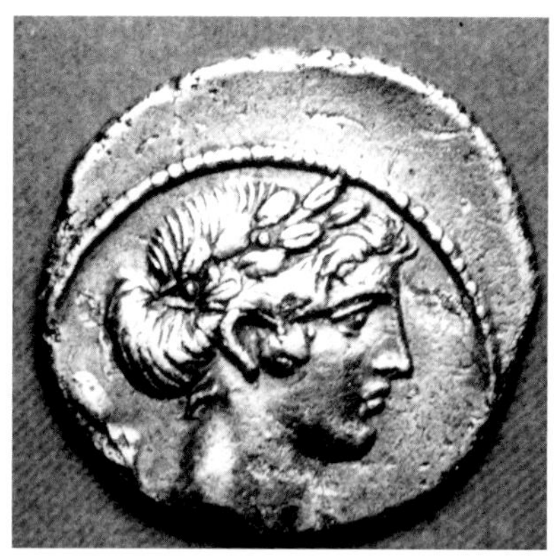

95.
AR denarius, 19.1 mm, 3.52 g
Mint: Rome; Q. Pomponius Musa, 66 B.C.
Obverse: laureate head of Apollo, to right, flower on stem behind
Reverse: Erato, muse of love poetry, standing, playing a lyre, right hand raised to the strings
Ref. Bab. Pomponia 12; CRR 814; BMCRR 3612; Crawford 410/6
Gift of Mr. and Mrs. Arthur J. Frank, 1979.258

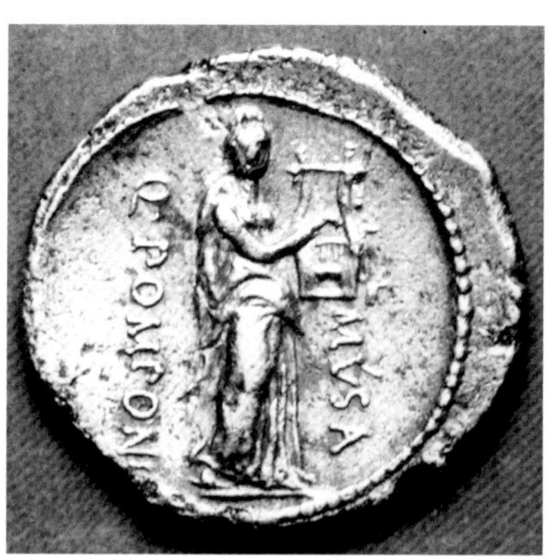

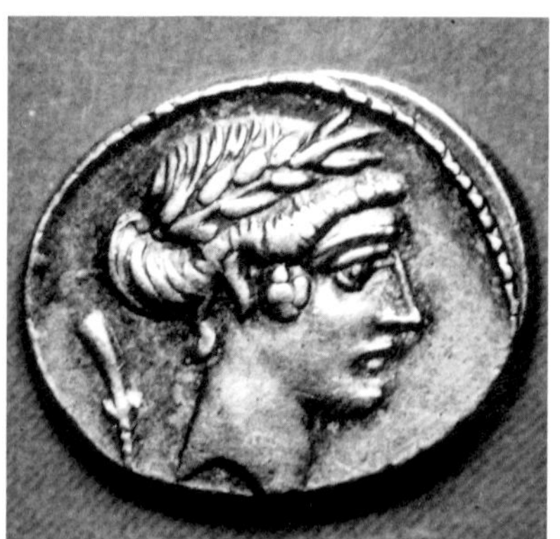

96.
AR denarius, 19.1 mm
Mint: Rome; Q. Pomponius Musa, 66 B.C.
Obverse: laureate head of Apollo, to right, flower on stalk behind
Reverse: Terpsichore, muse of dance, holding lyre in left hand and plectrum in right
Ref. Bab. Pomponia 17a; CRR 820a; BMCRR 3622; Crawford 410/7d
Gift of Mr. and Mrs. Arthur J. Frank, 1979.257

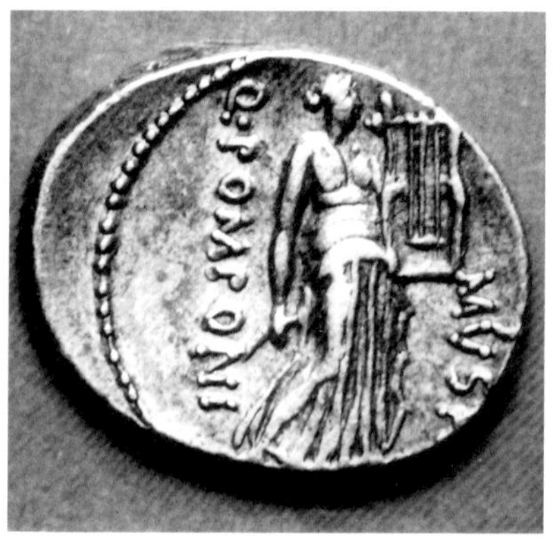

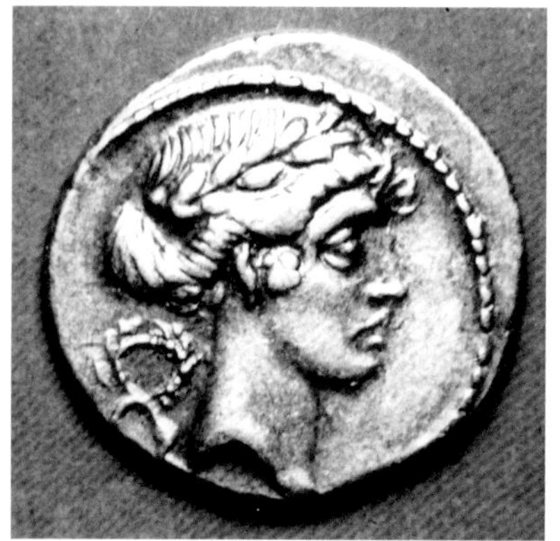

97.
AR denarius, 19.1 mm
Mint: Rome; Q. Pomponius Musa, 66 B.C.
Obverse: laureate head of Apollo, to right, wreath behind
Reverse: Polymnia, muse of sacred song, standing in meditation
Ref. Bab. Pomponia 15; CRR 817; BMCRR 3617; Crawford 410/10a
Gift of Mr. and Mrs. Arthur J. Frank, 1979.256

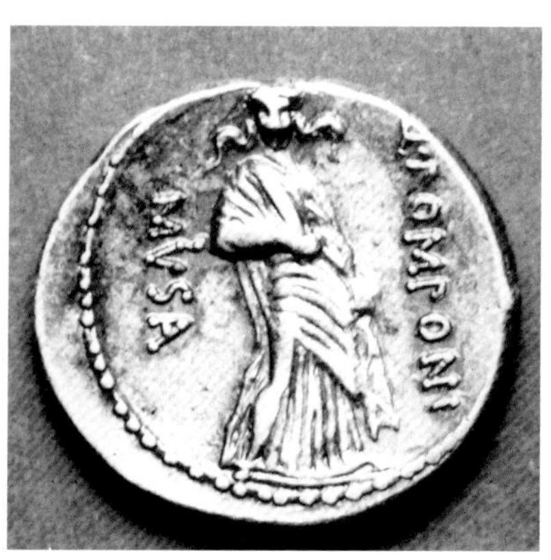

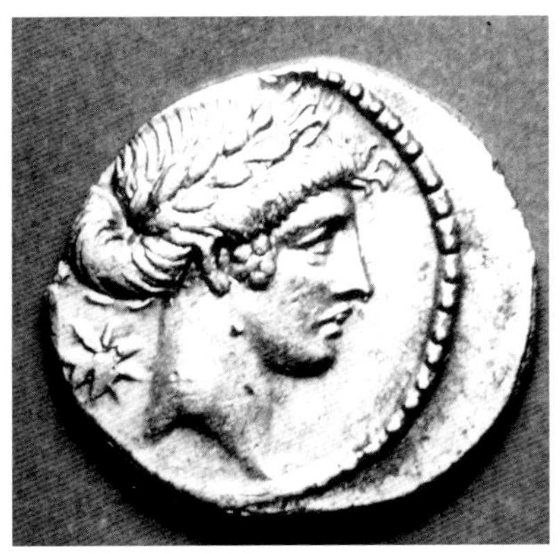

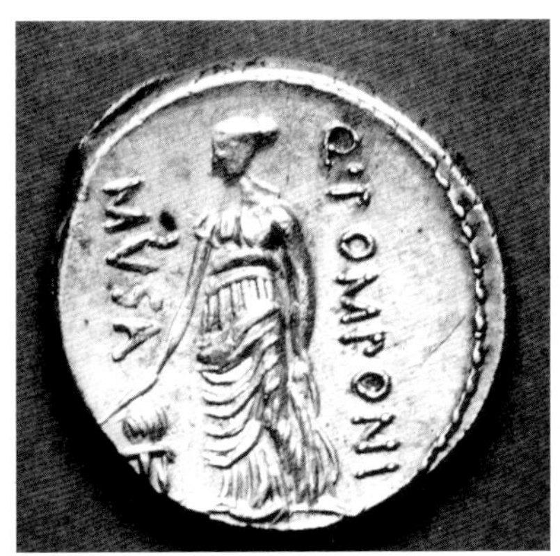

98.
AR denarius, 19.1 mm
Mint: Rome; Q. Pomponius Musa, 66 B.C.
Obverse: laureate head of Apollo, to right, star behind
Reverse: Urania, muse of astrology, holding a rod in right hand and pointing to a globe on a tripod
Ref. Bab. Pomponia 22; CRR 823; BMCRR 3628; Crawford 410/8
Gift of Mr. and Mrs. Arthur J. Frank, 1979.255

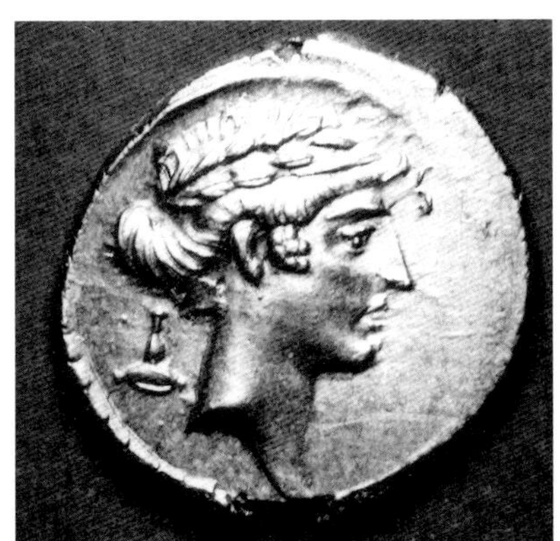

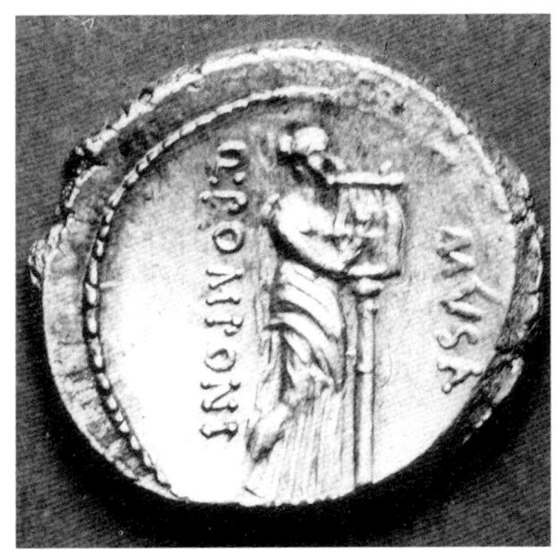

99.
AR denarius, 17.5 mm
Mint: Rome; Q. Pomponius Musa, 66 B.C.
Obverse: laureate head of Apollo, to right, lyre key behind
Reverse: Calliope, muse of epic poetry, playing a lyre on a pedestal
Ref. Bab. Pomponia 10; CRR 812; BMCRR 3608; Crawford 410/2b
Gift of Mr. and Mrs. Arthur J. Frank, 1979.259

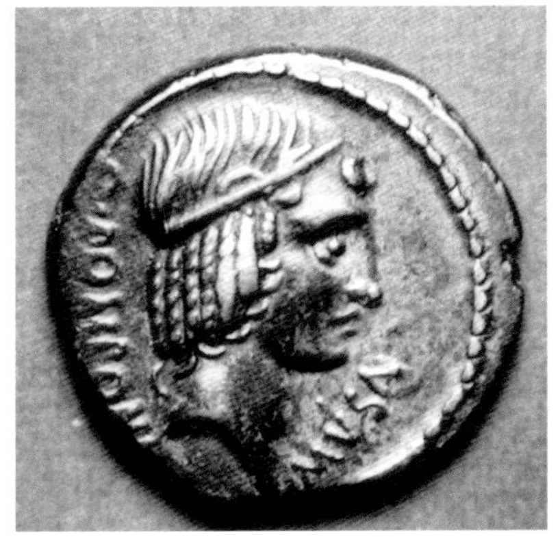

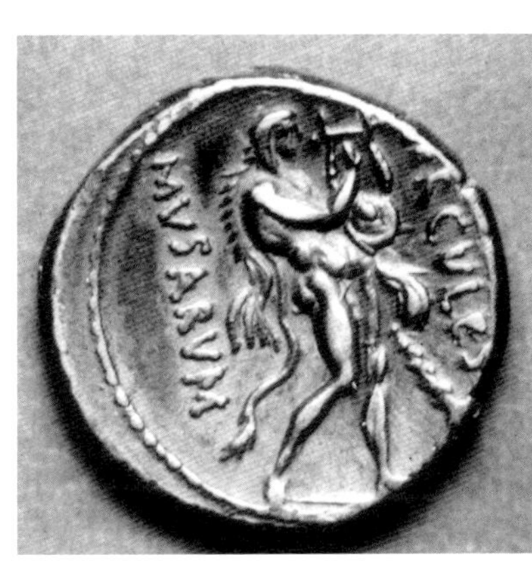

100.
AR denarius, 17.5 mm
Mint: Rome; Q. Pomponius Musa, 66 B.C.
Obverse: laureate head of Apollo, to right
Reverse: Hercules in lion skin, playing lyre; HERCVLES MVSARVM (Hercules, [leader] of the muses)
Ref. Bab Pomponia 8; CRR 810; BMCRR 3602
Gift of Mr. and Mrs. Arthur J. Frank, 1979.260

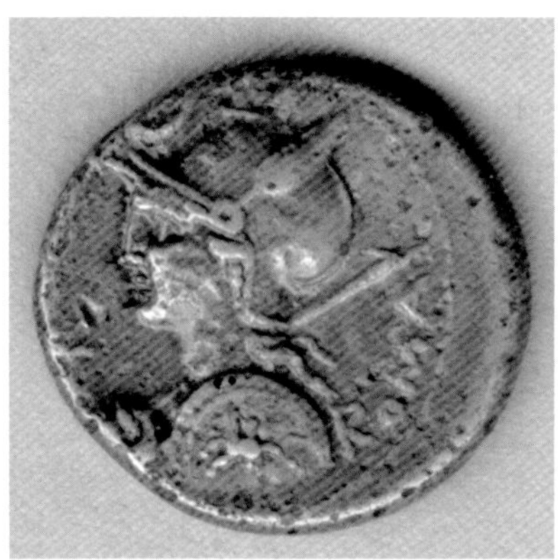

101.
AR denarius, 17.5 mm, 3.85 g
Mint: Rome; P. Licinius Nerva, 113–112 B.C.
Obverse: Roma
Reverse: voting scene: one voter, on the bridge leading to the ballot box, receives his ballot from an attendant; another, on the right, places his ballot in box; P NERVA
Ref. Crawford 292/1; CRR 548; BMCRR II 526
Gift of Herbert M. Howe, 1980.317

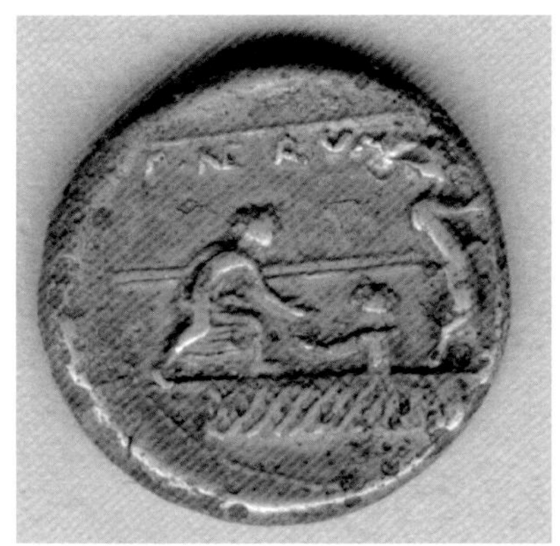

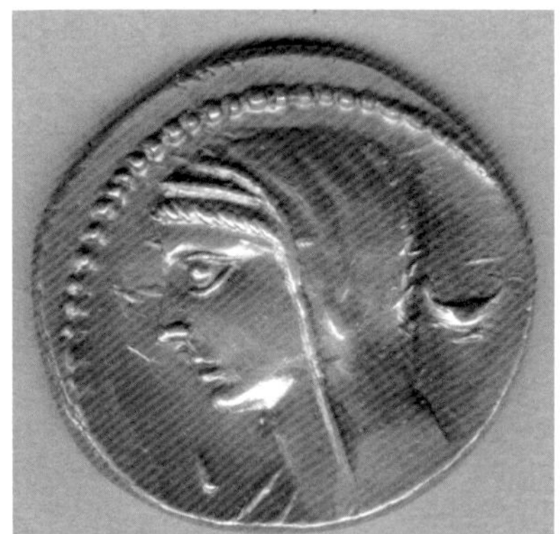

102.
AR denarius, 20.6 mm
Mint: Rome; L. Cassius Longinus, 52–50 B.C.
Obverse: Vesta, to left
Reverse: voter drops ballot marked with his response to a law: Vti ROGAS, (as you propose, aye), on right LONGIN IIIV
Ref. CRR 935; BMCRR 3929–36
Gift of Mr. and Mrs. Arthur J. Frank, 1979.263

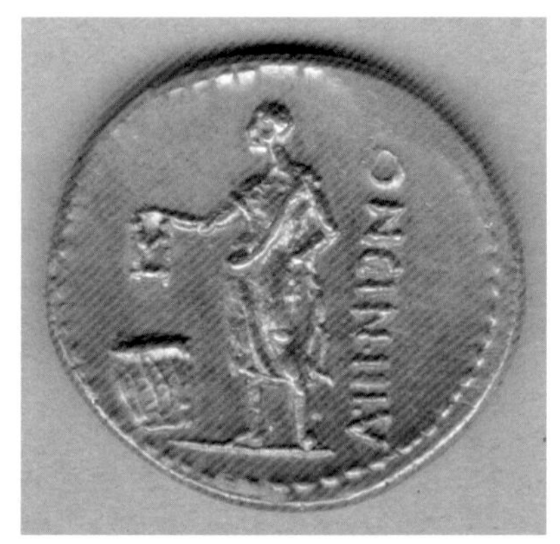

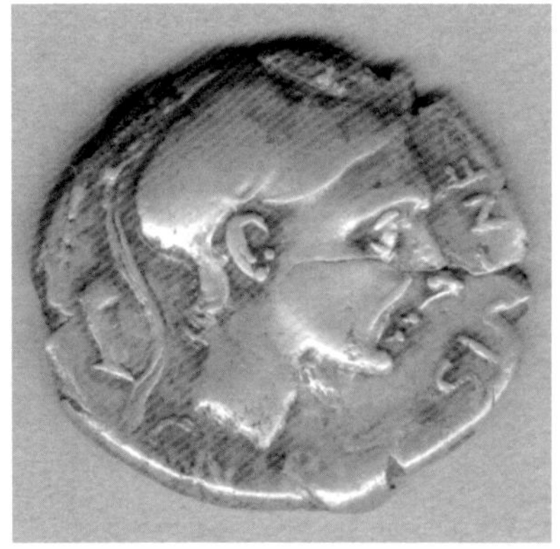

103.
AR denarius, 19.1 mm
Mint: Rome; Cn. Cornelius Blasio, 112–111 B.C.
Obverse: Mars; CN BLASIO CN F (Gnaeus Blasio, son of Gnaeus)
Reverse: Jupiter facing front between Juno to left, and Minerva to right, below ROMA
Ref. Crawford 296/1d; CRR 561b; BMCRR II 626
Gift of Herbert M. Howe, 1980.250

These three deities were the Capitoline Triad, the most important politico-religious cult of Rome.

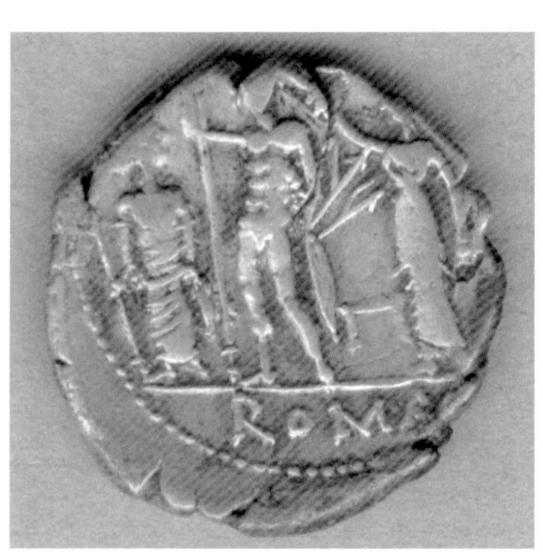

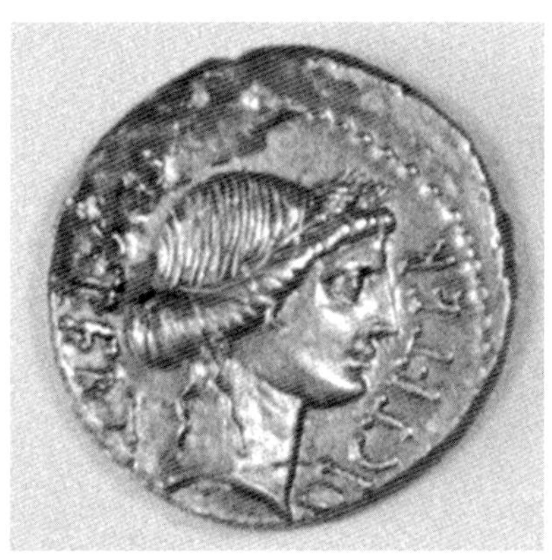

104.
AR denarius, 19.1 mm, 3.25 g
Mint: uncertain; C. Julius Caesar, 46 B.C.
Obverse: Ceres, wearing corn wreath; behind, civil titles of Caesar: COS TERT (consul for the third time); DICT ITER (dictator for the second time)
Reverse: priestly instruments and titles–libation cup, sprinkler, jug, and priestly staff; above, AVGVR; below, PONT MAX
Ref. Crawford 467/1a; CRR 1023; BMCRR Africa 23
Gift of Mr. and Mrs. Arthur J. Frank, 1979.270

Caesar was elected Pontifex Maximus, the head of the Roman state religion, as a young man. The office eventually went to the emperor Augustus and was passed through his successors to Constantine, who relinquished it to the Christian Bishop of Rome.

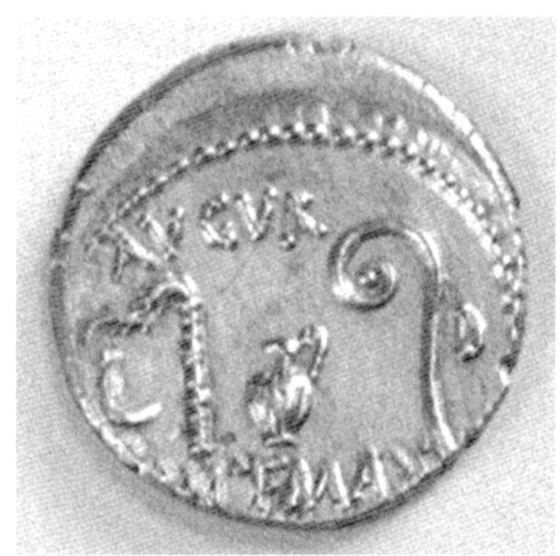

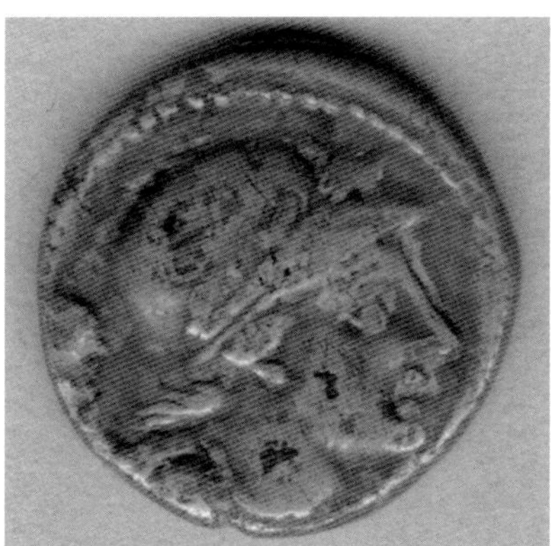

105.
AR denarius, 17.5 mm, 3.76 g
Mint: Rome; M. Volteius, 78 B.C.
Obverse: laureate male bust, to right, possibly Attis, behind mask of Pan
Reverse: Cybele riding, to right, in biga, drawn by lions; she holds patera in right hand; above ΠΑ; (Greek numerals 1–85); in exergue M VOLTEI M F
Ref. Crawford 385/4; CRR 777; BMCRR 3179
Gift of Herbert M. Howe, 1980.455

Volteius struck coins to celebrate the five great games; this one commemorates the Megalensia, in honor of the Great Mother of the Gods, whose wild Asiatic cult was introduced about 210 B.C. and lasted down to the late empire.

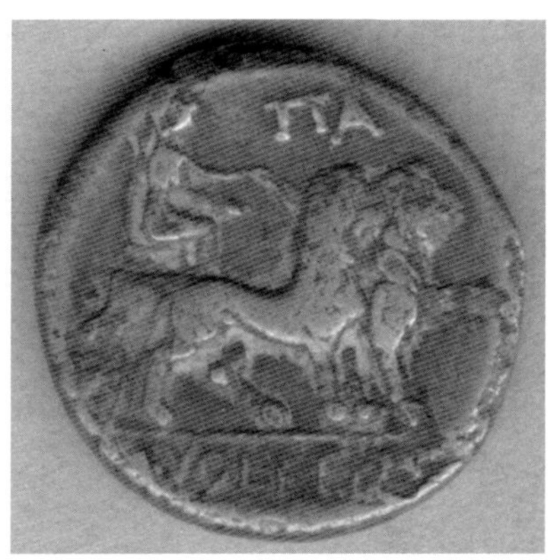

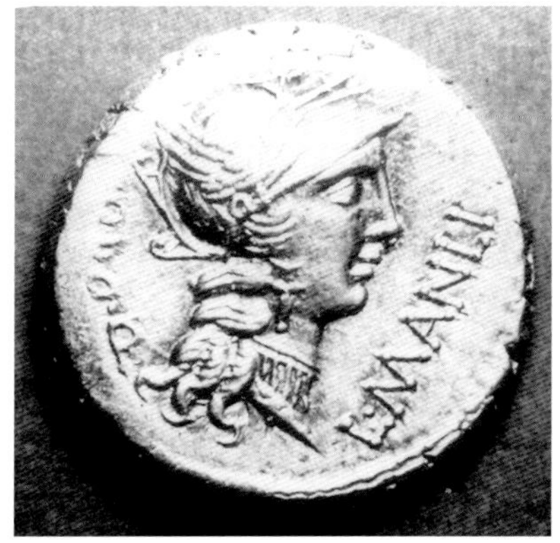

106.
AR denarius, 17.5 mm
Movable mint; L. Manlius Torquatus, 82 B.C.
Obverse: Roma, to right; before, L MANLI
Reverse: triumphal chariot crowned by Victory in quadriga, with reins in left hand and caduceus in right hand; in exergue, L SVLLA IMP
Ref. Crawford 367/5
Gift of Mr. and Mrs. Arthur J. Frank, 1979.249

Sulla, the conservative champion, was the victor in a savage civil war (86–78 B.C.). IMPerator, originally "commander," later came to mean "emperor."

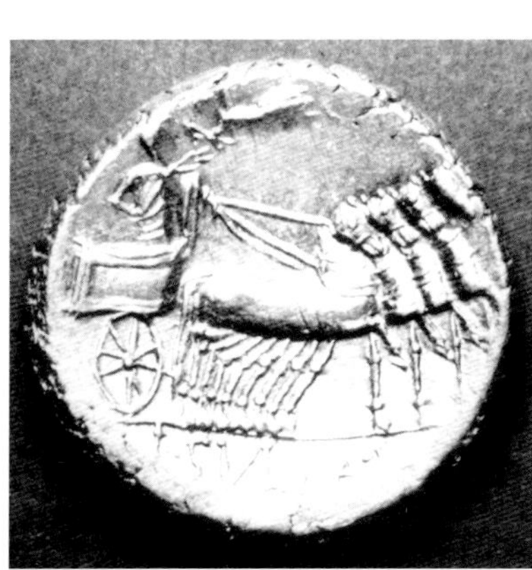

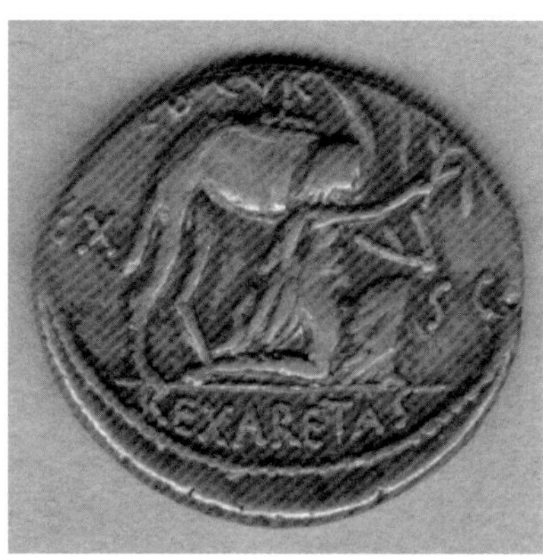

107.
AR denarius, 19.1 mm, 3.70 g
Mint: Rome; M. Aemilius Scaurus, A. Plautius, 58 B.C.
Obverse: Aretas, king of the Nabatean Arabs, kneeling right and holding camel and olive branch; above, M SCAVR; at sides, EX S C (by decree of the Senate); in exergue, REX ARETAS
Reverse: Jupiter in quadriga hurling thunder bolt; below scorpion; above, P HYPSAE; in exergue C HYPSAE COS PREIVE
Ref. Crawford 422/1b; CRR 913
Gift of Herbert M. Howe, 1980.304

Scaurus was sent by Pompey in 64 B.C. to settle the dispute between Hyrcanus and Aristobulus over the rule of Judaea. Two years later he was sent against Aretas, a local sheik, but withdrew, probably heavily bribed.

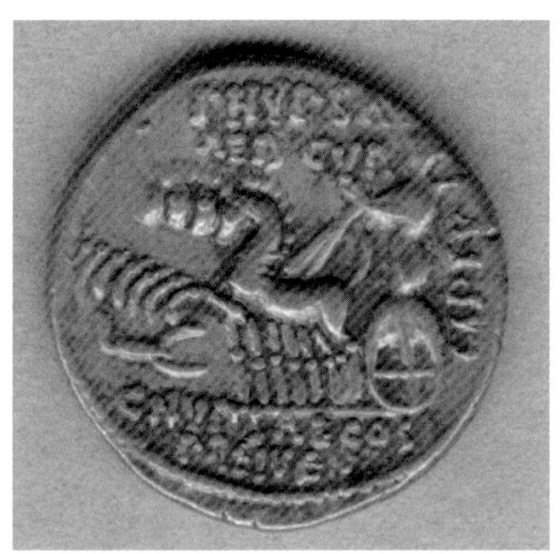

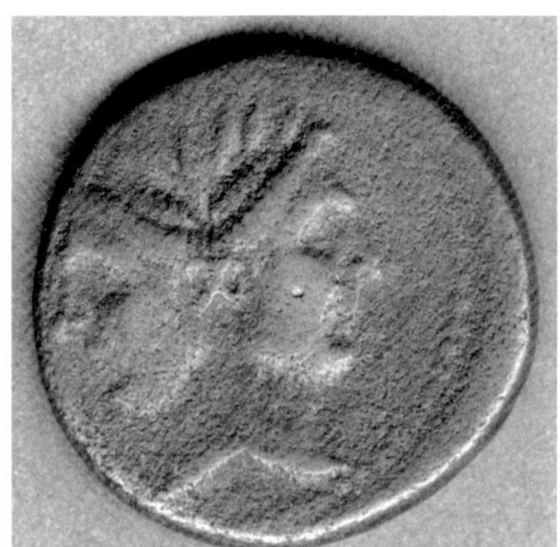

108.
AE as, 28 mm, 17.02 g
Mint: Spain; unknown moneyer, 46–45 B.C.
Obverse: laureate head of Janus with features of Pompey
Reverse: prow, to right; above, CN MAG, (Gnaeus [Pompeius] Magnus); below, PIVS (dutiful to the gods, the state, and one's family)
Ref. Crawford 471/1; CRR 1040; BMCRR Spain 84
Gift of Herbert M. Howe, 1980.363

Defeated by Caesar at Pharsalus in 48 B.C., Pompey fled to Egypt, where he was killed. His sons fought on for a dozen years. One of them may have struck this coin.

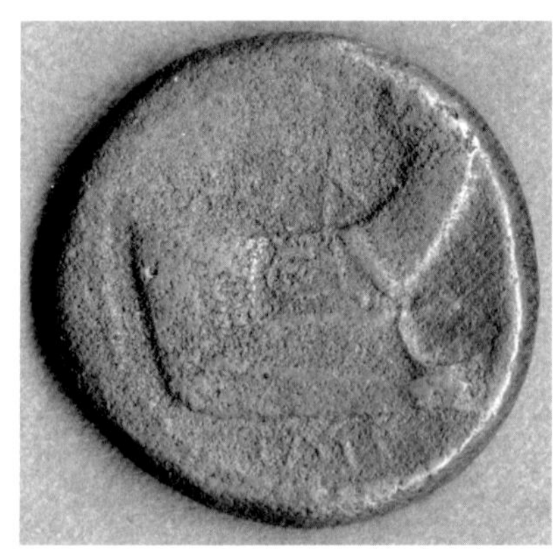

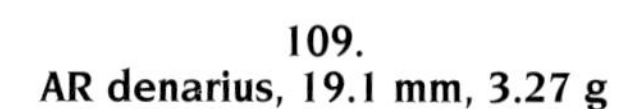

109.
AR denarius, 19.1 mm, 3.27 g
Mint: Sicily; Sex. Pompeius, 42–40 B.C.
Obverse: Pharos (lighthouse) of Messana, with statue of Neptune leaning on trident; before, ship with aquila on tripod at prow and trident, flagstaff, and grappling iron at stern; around, MAG PIVS IMP [ITER] (Magnus, the dutiful [son], general for the second time)
Reverse: Scylla, to left, holding rudder, her body ending in two fishtails and the foreparts of three dogs; around, PRAEFectus CLASsis ET ORAE MARITimae EX S C, (prefect of the fleet and seacoast, by decree of the Senate)
Ref. Crawford 511/4a; CRR 1348; BMCRR Sicily 18
Gift of Herbert M. Howe, 1980.366

Sextus Pompey in Sicily and the Parthians in the East kept Octavian and Antony from settling accounts for a decade.

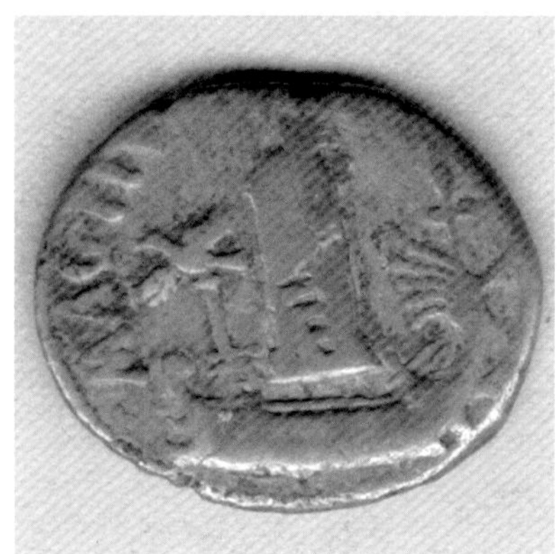

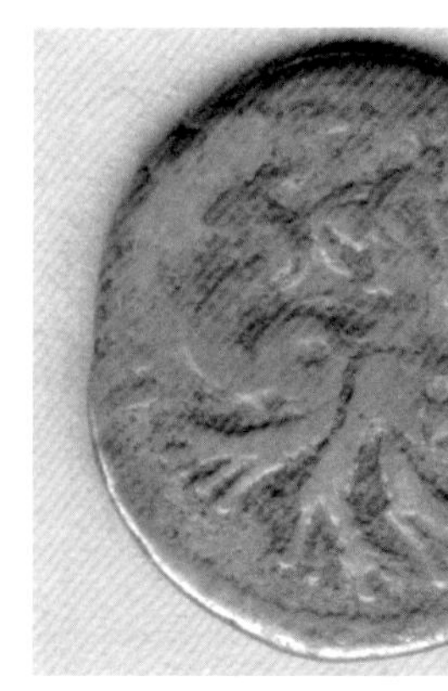

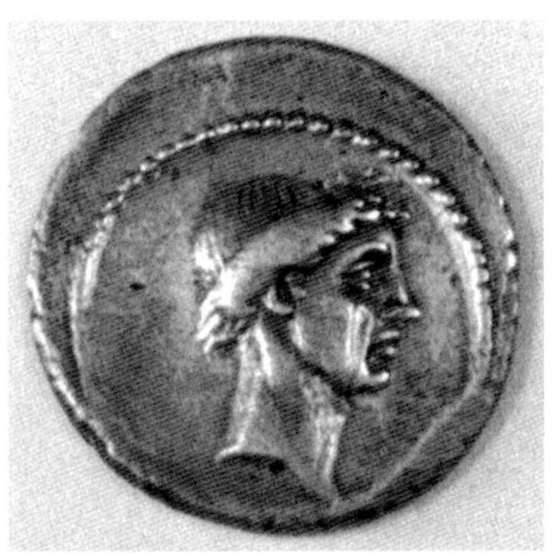

110.
AR denarius, 20.6 mm, 3.80 g
Mint: Rome; L. Flaminius, 42 B.C.
Obverse: laureate head of Julius Caesar, to right
Reverse: Pax (Peace) standing, to left, holding sceptre and caduceus; behind, L FLAMINIVS IIII VIR
Ref. CRR 1089; BMCRR 4201
Gift of Mr. and Mrs. Arthur J. Frank, 1978.328

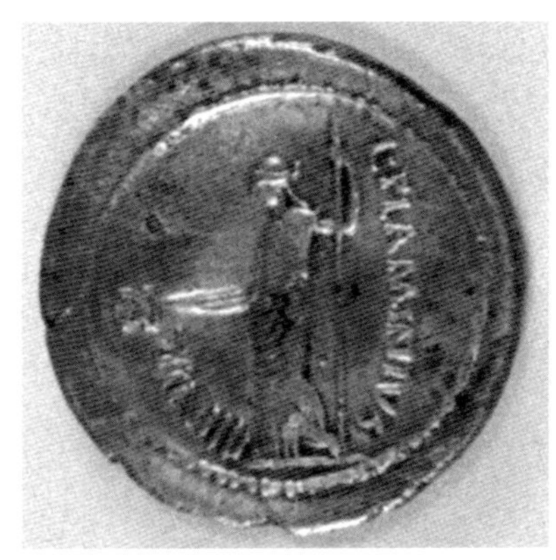

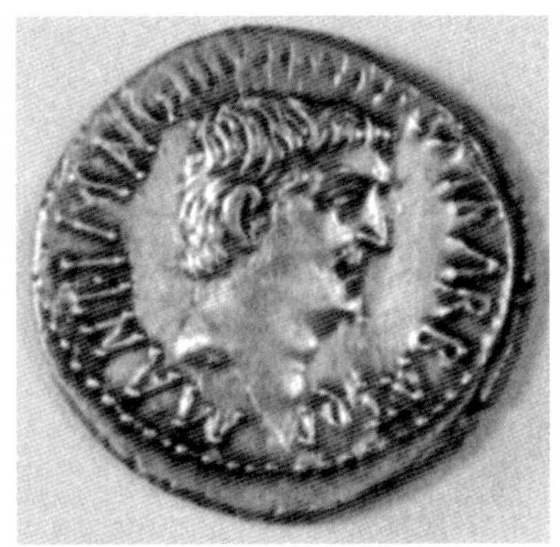

111.
AR denarius, 19.1 mm, 3.95 g
Moving mint, Antony and Octavian, 39 B.C.
Obverse: head of Antony, to right; around, M ANTON IMP III VIR R P C M BARBAT Q P (M. Antonius, general, one of a committee of three for reorganizing the republic; M. Barbatius, quaestor [acting as] praetor)
Reverse: bearded head of Octavian; around, CAESAR IMP PONT III VIR R P C (Triumvir Rei Publicae Constituendae)
Ref. CRR 1181
Gift of Mr. and Mrs. Arthur J. Frank, 1978.329

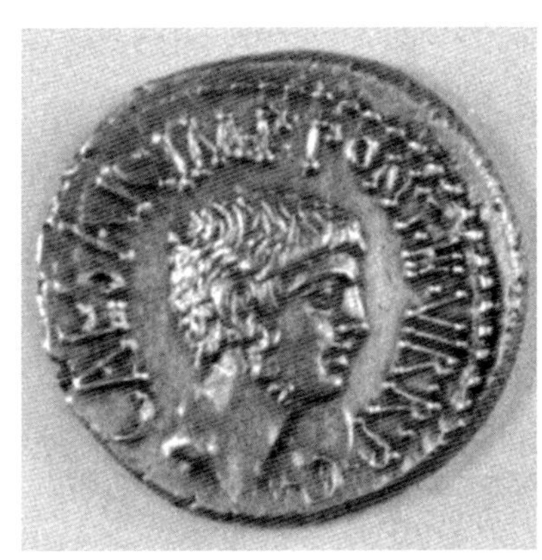

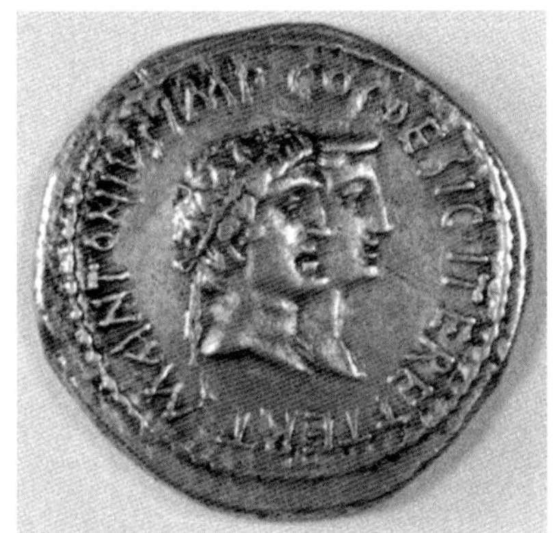

112.
AR cistophorus (chest-bearer), 26.5 mm, 11.65 g
Mint: East; Antony, 39 B.C.
Obverse: conjoined heads of Antony and Octavia, Octavian's sister, whom Antony had married; around, M ANTONIVS IMP COS DESIG ITER ET TERT (M. Antonius, general, consul designate for the second and third times)
Reverse: Bacchus on mystical chest between two serpents
Ref. BMCRR Rep II 135
Gift of Mr. and Mrs. Arthur J. Frank, 1978.330

The **cista mystica** type had originated in Ephesus in about 146 B.C. as a container for sacred objects.

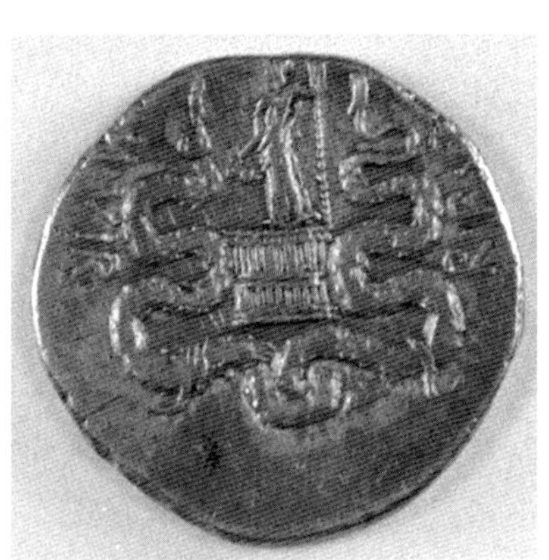

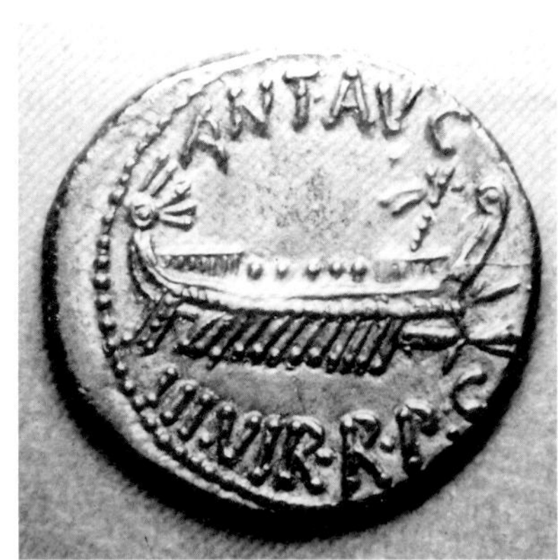

113.

AR denarius, 17.5 mm, 3.60 g

Mint: East, Antony, 32–31 B.C.

Obverse: galley, to right, with rowers; inscription: ANT AVG III VIR R P C. (AVG is for Augur, a high religious office)

Reverse: Legionary eagle between two standards; LEG III

Ref. CRR 1217; Seaby 343 except Leg.III

Gift of Mr. and Mrs. Arthur J. Frank, 1979.271

The combined fleets and armies of Antony and Cleopatra (see cat. no. 54) were gathered in western Greece in 31 B.C. to meet the forces of Octavian. At Actium, on the west coast of Greece, the two navies met, and Antony and Cleopatra, defeated in the battle, fled to Egypt and their deaths. This coin was struck to pay the troops, hence the reverse inscription, different for each legion–here the Third (LEG III).

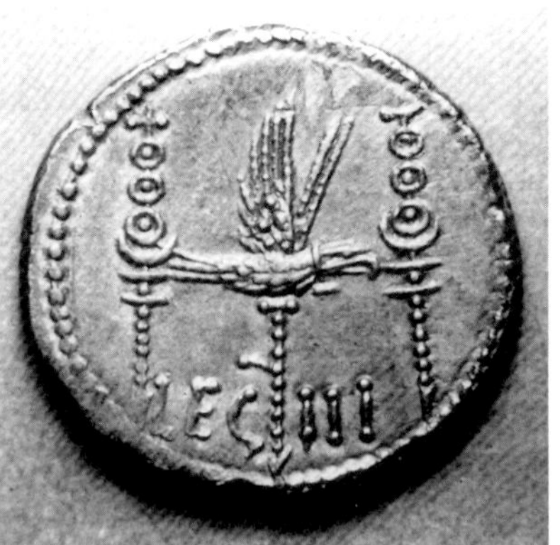

COINAGE OF THE ROMAN EMPIRE

The number of imperial coin types is enormous. The emperor Hadrian averaged over a hundred new ones a year from A.D. 117 to 138. This selection includes only a tiny fraction of the whole coinage, but it can shed light on the political, economic, and artistic currents of the first four centuries of our era.

From the time of Augustus, the coinage is devoted to the emperor's propaganda: his portrait on the obverse, his achievements and virtues or portraits of a few of his family on the reverse. Gold and silver were still struck, but large handsome bronze coins appeared in new denominations: the **sestertius** (two and one-half asses) and **dupondius** (two asses). The Senate decided only what was to appear on bronze, on the reverse of which we often find a large S C, "by decree of the Senate."

Under the empire the Greek cities of the East still struck, but almost entirely in billon (an alloy of silver) or bronze. Such coins have Greek inscriptions. Their reverse types are usually of local deities and legends. For example, cat. no. 175, struck at Antioch, shows the emperor Trebonianus Gallus (A.D. 251–253) on the obverse, but the reverse has the shrine of Tyche (the Good Luck) of the city, containing a statue of Antioch with a turreted crown on her head and the River Orontes under her feet; the inscriptions on both sides are in Greek.

The Roman Empire extended from Scotland to Egypt, from Spain and Morocco to Hungary, Romania, and Armenia. In its eastern provinces Greek was the common language; in the western, Latin. Minor local tongues were everywhere. We are told that at the execution of a certain rebel, a sign was displayed reading "Jesus of Nazareth, King of the Jews" in Hebrew (i.e. Aramaic) and Greek and Latin–the languages of the natives, the Hellenized Jews thronging to the Passover, and the ruling power. A few months earlier, when his fellow Jews had asked, "is it lawful to give tribute to Caesar?," Jesus had called for a penny (denarius; possibly the same sort as cat. no. 118) and asked, "whose are the image and superscription?" They answered, "Caesar's." In the gospels and Acts, very large sums are given in **talents** (a weight, not a coin), some middling sums in "pieces of silver" (probably old Tyrian shekels). The only Jewish coins before the revolt of 66 C.E. were bronze, like the widow's "mite" (the little bronze **prutah**; see cat. no. 48). Only rarely did the Romans allow their subjects to coin gold and silver, though a few regions were permitted billon or potin, alloys of silver. The coins of the Greek-speaking East are misleadingly called "Greek imperial." Some of them, especially from Alexandria and Antioch, are very handsome. Like the Jews, all the subject peoples of the empire were forced to accede to a Roman-controlled exchange, which had little relation to the actual value of the metal. But the Romans had another reason for using copper alloys–prestige. The big, handsome **sestertii** and **dupondii** of the early empire could carry impressive images and, for those who could read, impressive superscriptions. Jesus' question was not an idle one; the right to coin money is the right to express a government's pride and hopes.

But to a ruling people, control of public opinion, especially that of the lower orders, is essential. If a vicious emperor, son of a famous father, succeeds an unpopular one, how can he emphasize his beloved ancestor? Label the coinage "GAIVS SON OF GERMANICVS" and ignore the grim and unpopular Tiberius. Public works, especially spectacular ones, can win acclaim as well. Trajan's bridge over the Danube, Hadrian's travels in Spain, Nero's public meat market—all are subjects for propaganda. Best of all, however, is military victory: a crocodile chained to a palm tree reminds people, even in southern Gaul where it was struck, that Augustus had defeated the Egyptians.

There were other forms of association as well. Names, for instance, made good propaganda. The family name of Vespasian was Flavius, but it does not appear on his coins; he called himself Caesar. Just so the successors of the Antonines (when the line of M. Aurelius died out in A.D. 192) adopted his name, thus establishing a dubious claim to continuity. What is more, an emperor could claim almost any virtue, rightly or not, hoping that those who read the inscription would assume that he would not claim it if he did not possess it.

THE JULIO-CLAUDIAN EMPERORS, 27 B.C.–A.D.68

Republican Rome was ruled for centuries by a land-holding oligarchy, which slowly gave way in the second century B.C. to a few families, whose wealth came from exploiting the new provinces. These great families, especially those whose members had held the consulate, monopolized the control of the state through a network of alliances, economic and marital, euphemistically called *amicitia* (friendship). Portraits on these coins are limited to the emperor himself and a few of his immediate family. Coin portraits, common among the Hellenistic kings, did not appear in Rome until the middle of the first century B.C.; one, possibly of M. Brutus in 43 B.C., may be the first.

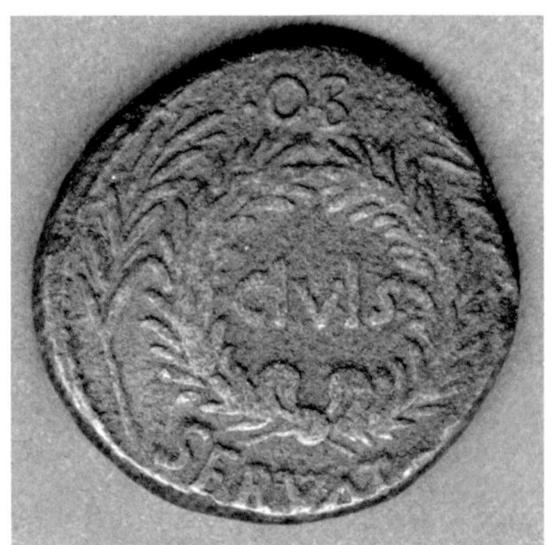

114.
AE sestertius, 20.6 mm, 26.80 g
Mint: Rome, Augustus, 21 B.C.
Obverse: Oak wreath between two laurel branches; OB CIVES SERVATOS (for having saved citizens)
Reverse: C MARCI L F CENSORIN AVG III VIR Auro Argento Aere Feriundo Flando (C. Marcius Censorinus, an augur, one of the Committee of Three for striking and casting gold, silver, and bronze); in center, S C
Ref. RIC Aug. 178
Gift of Herbert M. Howe, 1980.197

The civic crown was given to Augustus in 27 B.C., on the analogy of the decoration, under the Republic, for saving the life of a comrade in battle. It was later voted to other emperors.

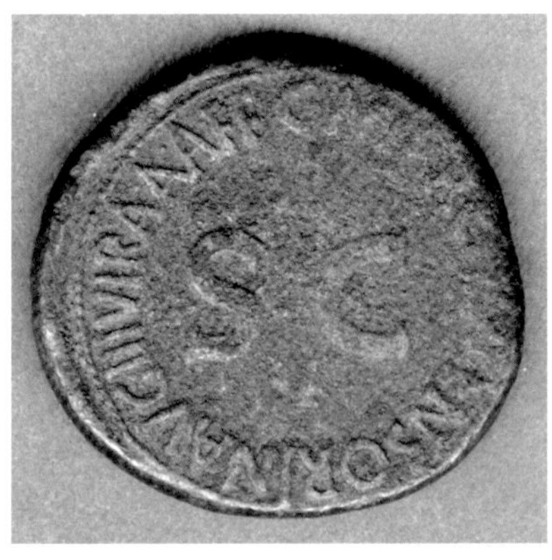

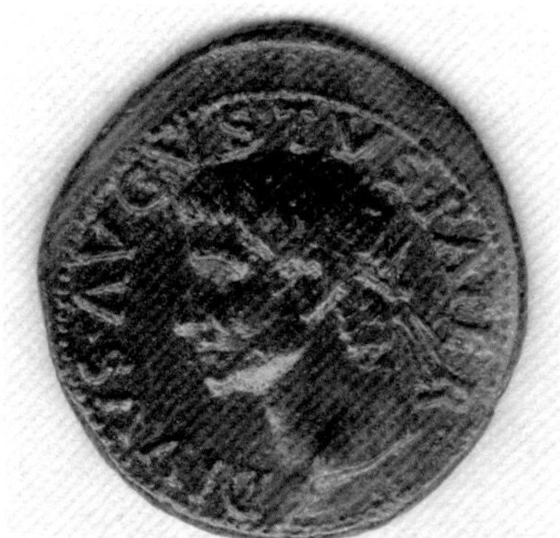

115.
AE as, 19.1 mm
Tiberius, after A.D. 22.
Obverse: bust of Augustus, radiate (wearing a crown with rays), to left; DIVVS AVGVSTVS PATER (Augustus, my deified father)
Reverse: altar; at sides, S C; around, PROVIDENTia (foresight)
Ref. Seaby 424
Gift of Mr. and Mrs. Arthur J. Frank, 1978.331

Augustus had reluctantly adopted his stepson Tiberius in A.D.4. *Divus* (officially listed as a god) was a title decreed by the Senate to some recently dead emperors.

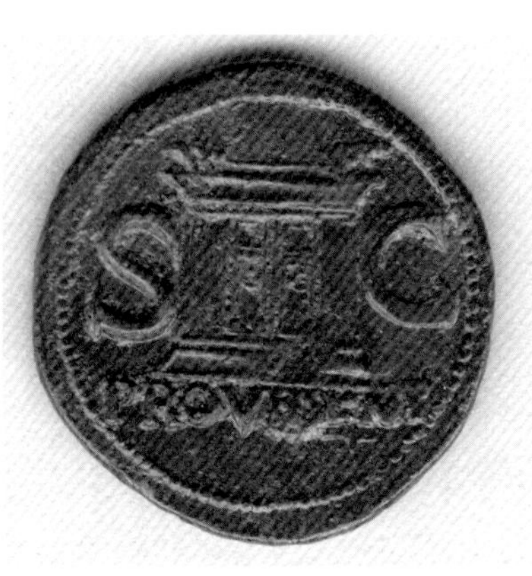

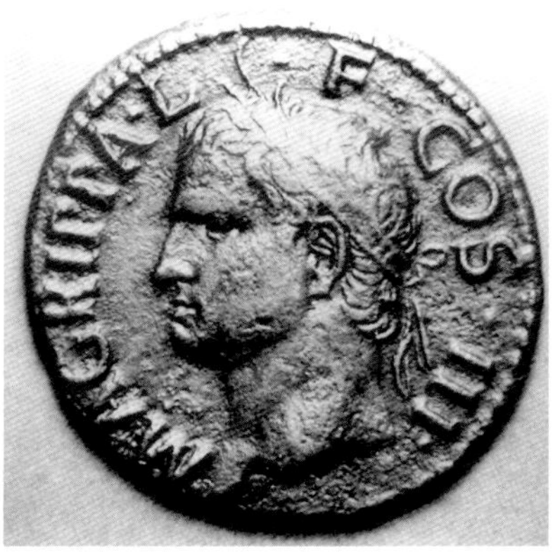

116.
AE as, 28 mm, 10.93 g
Tiberius or Gaius, A.D. 14–37 or 37–41
Obverse: head of Agrippa, to left, wearing rostral crown (one with beaks of ships); M AGRIPPA L F COS III (Marcus Agrippa, son of Lucius, three times consul)
Reverse: Neptune standing, to left, holding dolphin and trident; at sides, S C
Ref. Seaby 456; BMC 161; RIC Tib. 32
Gift of Mr. and Mrs. Arthur J. Frank, 1979.273

Agrippa (d. 12 B.C.) received the naval crown for winning the battle of Actium in 31 B.C. Agrippa was a loyal and expert general and minister of Augustus, and husband of Augustus' daughter, Julia.

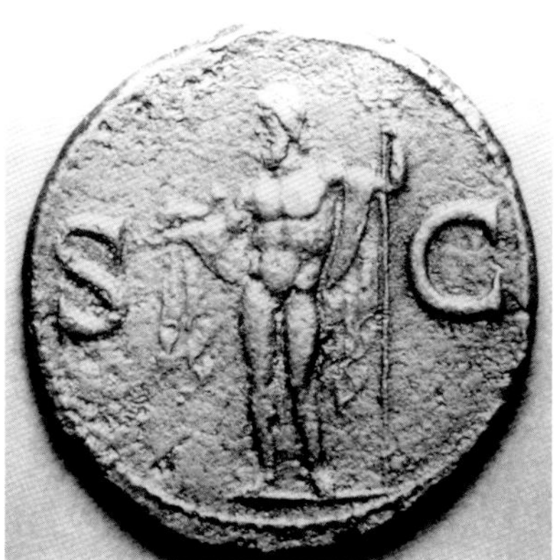

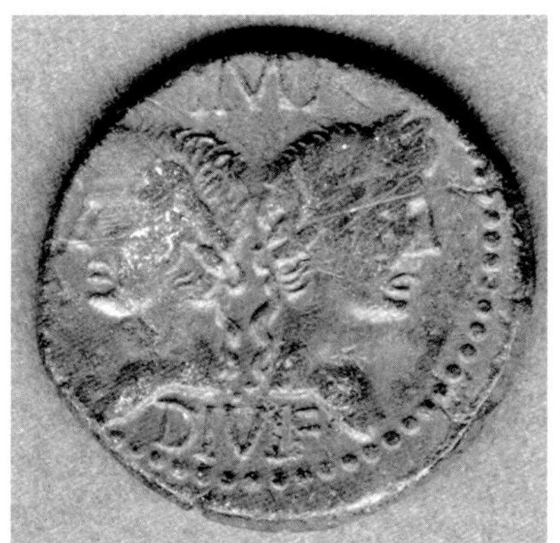

117.
AE dupondius, 26 mm, 12.50 g
Mint: Nemausus (Nîmes), 24–19 B.C.
Obverse: Heads of Augustus, to left, and Agrippa, to right, both laureate; M DIVI F
Reverse: crocodile chained to palm tree; COL NEM (Colonia Nemausiensis)
Ref. Cohen I. 179.7
Gift of Herbert M. Howe, 1980.202

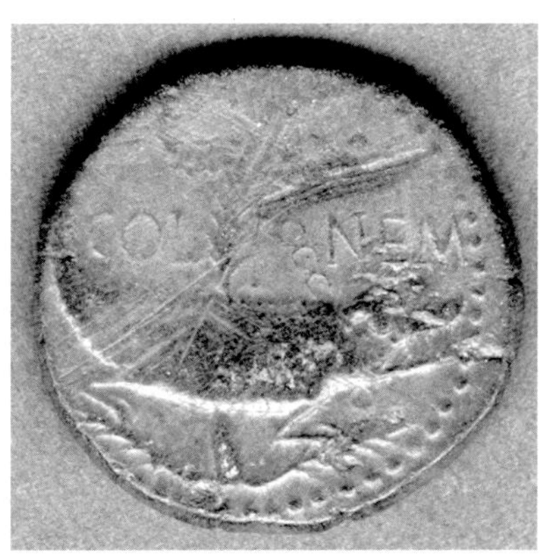

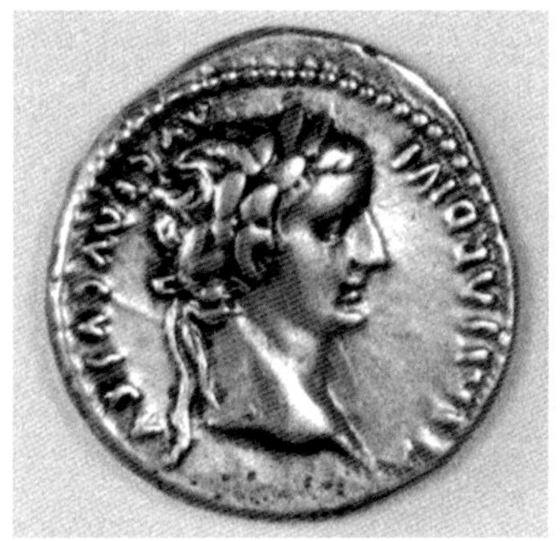

118.
AE denarius, 19.1 mm, 3.70 g
Tiberius, 15–16 B.C.
Obverse: laureate bust of Tiberius, to right; TI CAESAR DIVI AVG F AVGVSTVS (Tiberius Caesar, son of the Deified Augustus, [himself] Augustus
Reverse: Livia, Tiberius' mother, seated, to right; PONTIFex MAXIMus (chief priest).
Ref. Seaby 467
Gift of Mr. and Mrs. Arthur J. Frank, 1977.293

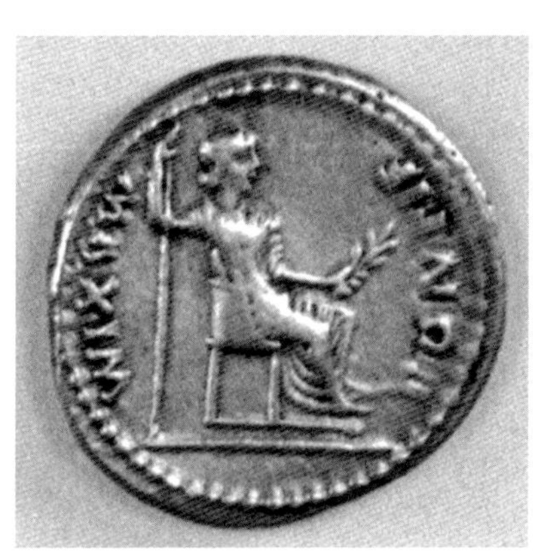

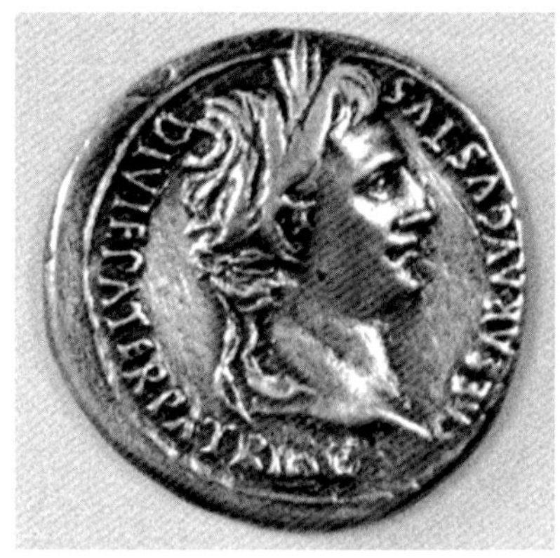

119.
AR denarius, 19.1 mm
Augustus, 27 B.C.– A.D.14
Obverse: bust of Augustus, to right; CAESAR AVGVSTVS DIVI F PATER PATRIAE (Augustus, son of the deified [Julius Caesar], father of the fatherland)
Reverse: Gaius and Lucius Caesar, standing, with shields and spears; above, priestly implements; around, facing out, G L CAESARES AVGVSTI F COS DESIG PRINC IVVENT (Gaius and Lucius Caesar, sons of Augustus, consuls designate, leaders of youth)
Ref. BMC Imp. 519; RIC 350
Gift of Mr. and Mrs. Arthur J. Frank, 1979.272

The two boys were sons of Julia and Agrippa, whom Augustus had adopted in the hope that they would succeed him. Both of them died young.

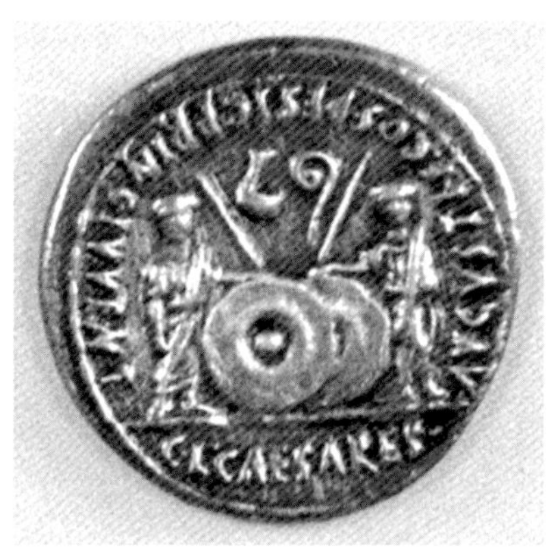

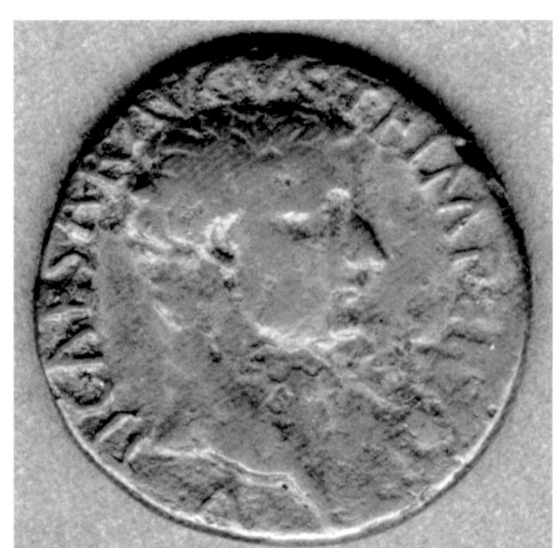

120.
AE as, 28 mm, 10.88 g
Mint: Rome; Augustus, A.D. 10–11
Obverse: bare head of Tiberius, to right; TI CAESAR AVGVST F IMPERATOR V
Reverse: PONTIFEX TRIBVN POTESTATE XII; S C in center
Ref. RIC Aug. 274
Gift of Herbert M. Howe, 1980.203

This coin depicts Tiberius, aged fifty-two.

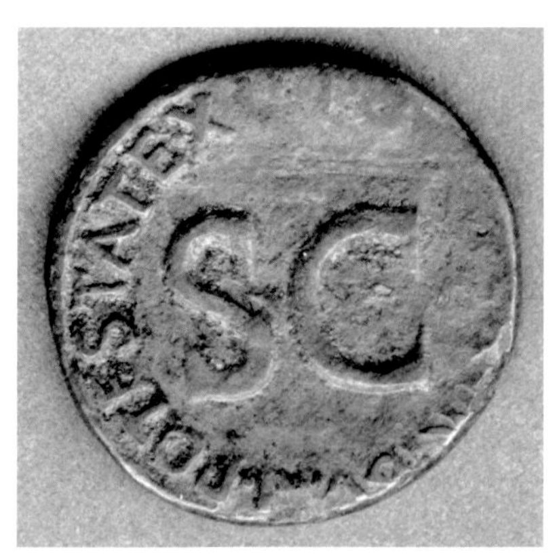

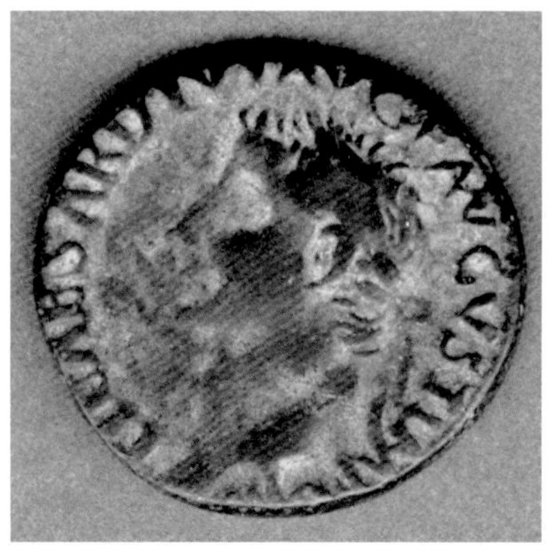

121.
AE as, 26 mm, 11.50 g
Mint: Rome, A.D. 36–37
Obverse: laureate head of Tiberius, to left; TI CAESAR DIVI AVG F AVGVST IMP VIII
Reverse: PONTIF MAX TR POT XXXIIX; at sides, S C
Ref. RIC Tib. 136
Gift of Herbert M, Howe, 1980.415

This example also shows Tiberius, aged seventy-eight.

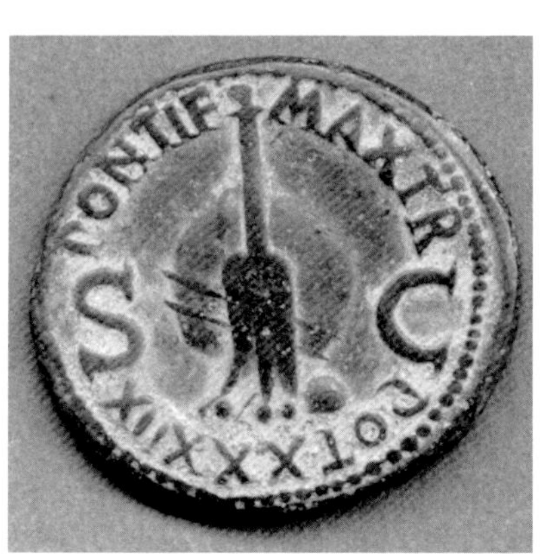

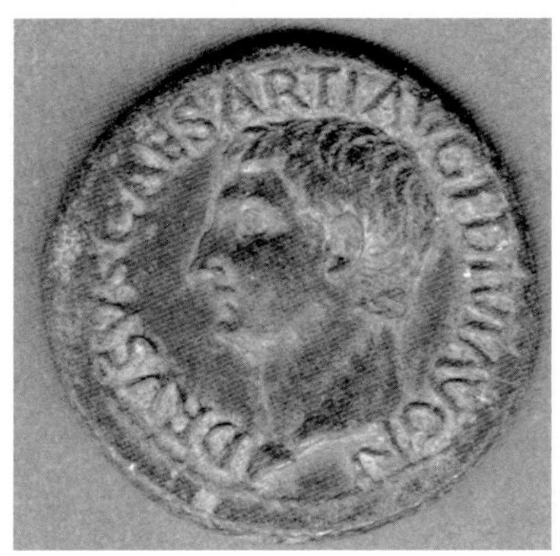

122.
AE as, 28 mm, 11.08 g
Mint: Rome
Tiberius, A.D. 22–23.
Obverse: bare head of Drusus II (son of Tiberius), to left; DRVSVS CAESAR TI AVG F DIVI AVG N (Drusus Caesar, son of Tiberius the emperor, grandson of the deified Augustus)
Reverse: S C; around, PONTIF TRIBVN POTEST ITER ([state] priest, tribunicial power for the second time)
Ref. RIC Tib. 99
Gift of Herbert M. Howe, 1980.414

Drusus II, the only surviving son of Tiberius, married his cousin Livia II. A year or so after this coin, she and the minister Sejanus, her lover, are said to have poisoned Drusus.

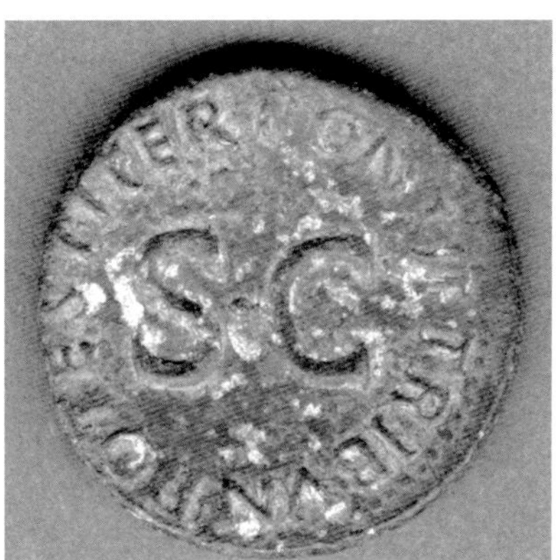

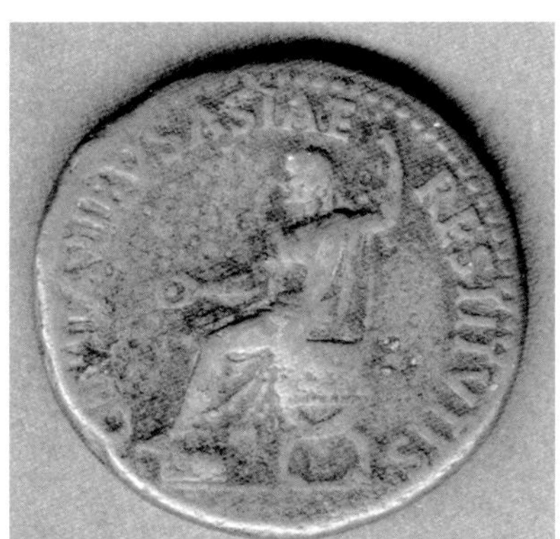

123.
AE sestertius, 22.2 mm, 25.30 g
Mint: Rome
Tiberius, A.D. 22–23
Obverse: Tiberius seated, to left; CIVITATIBVS ASIAE RESTITVTIS, ([commemorating] the rebuilding of the cities of Asia [Minor])
Reverse: S C; around, TI CAESAR DIVI AVG F AVGVST P M TR POT XXIIII.
Lent by State Historical Society of Wisconsin, 1.1990.4

A severe earthquake devastated many cities of western Asia Minor in A.D.17. The emperor immediately sent aid.

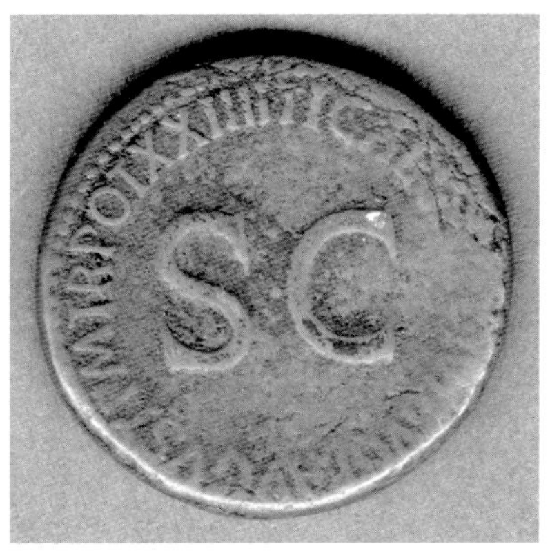

124.
AR denarius, 19.1 mm, 3.78 g
Mint: Rome
Claudius, A.D. 41–54
Obverse: diademed head of Antonia II, to right; ANTONIA AVGVSTA
Reverse: two upright torches joined by ribbon; SACERDOS DIVI AVGVSTI (priestess of the deified Augustus)
Ref. RIC Claud. 114
Gift of Herbert M. Howe, 1980.234

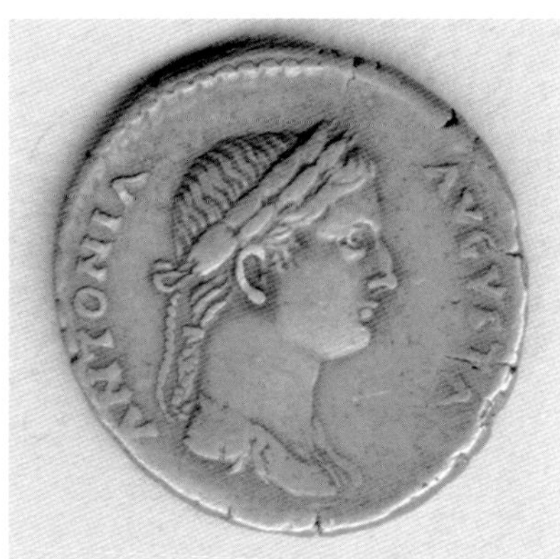

Antonia was the daughter of Octavia I (sister of Augustus) and M. Antonius, the wife of Drusus I (brother of Tiberius), the mother of Germanicus and the emperor Claudius, the grandmother of the emperor Gaius, and the great-grandmother of Nero. Gaius probably gave her the title of "Augusta" (empress), and certainly gave her that of Priestess of Augustus.

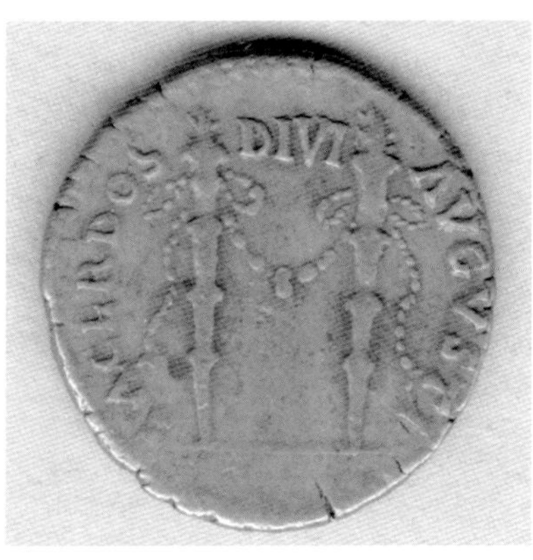

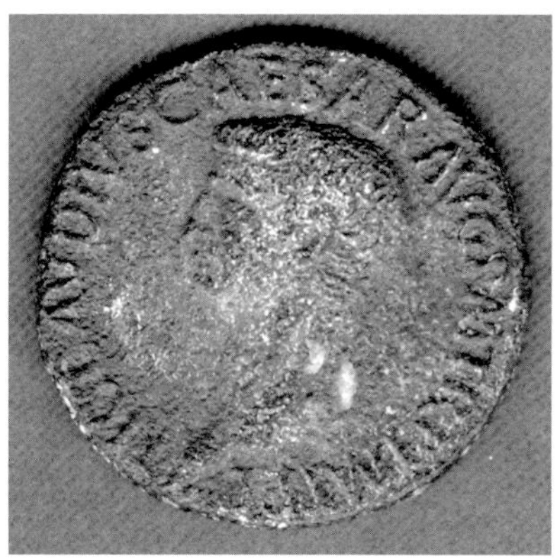

125.
AE as, 28 mm, 10.40 g
Mint: Rome
Claudius, A.D. 41–54
Obverse: bust of Claudius, bare headed, to left; TI CLAVDIVS CAESAR AVG P M TR P IMP Pater Patriae
Reverse: Minerva standing, to left, with spear, shield, and helmet; around CONSTANTIAE AVGVSTI; S C
Ref. RIC Claud. 199
Gift of Herbert M. Howe, 1980.233

Claudius, brother of Germanicus, succeeded his nephew Gaius in A.D.41. He married four times, the last of his wives being his niece Agrippina II, mother (by a previous marriage) of Nero. We are told that he had some deformity of the neck, which appears on many of his coins, carefully minimized.

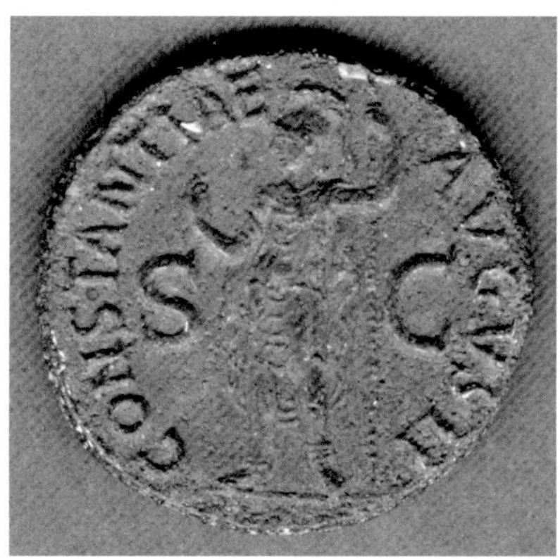

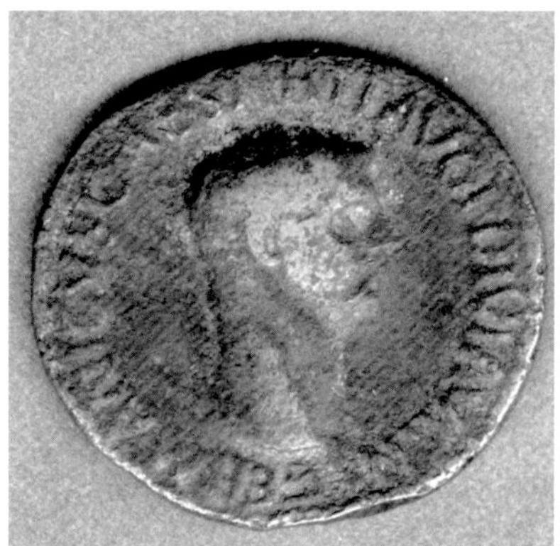

126.
AE as, 28 mm, 10.06 g
Mint: Rome
Claudius, A.D. 41–54
Obverse: head of Germanicus, bare, to right; GERMANICVS CAESAR TI AVG F DIVI AVG Nepos (grandson)
Reverse: S C in center; around, TI CLAVDIVS CAESAR AVG GERM P M TR P IMP P P
Ref. RIC Claud. 215
Gift of Herbert M. Howe, 1980.237

Augustus made Tiberius his successor on condition that Tiberius adopt his nephew, Germanicus, the son of his brother Drusus, as his heir. Germanicus was popular, though hardly competent, but he was the husband of Augustus' granddaughter, Agrippina I, and the father of six children and was favored among the opponents of Tiberius. He died in the East in A.D.19 (possibly by poison), and his family served as a focus for the anti-Tiberian party.

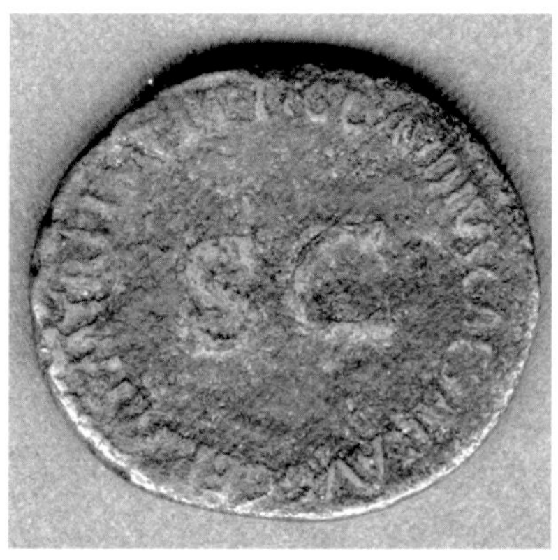

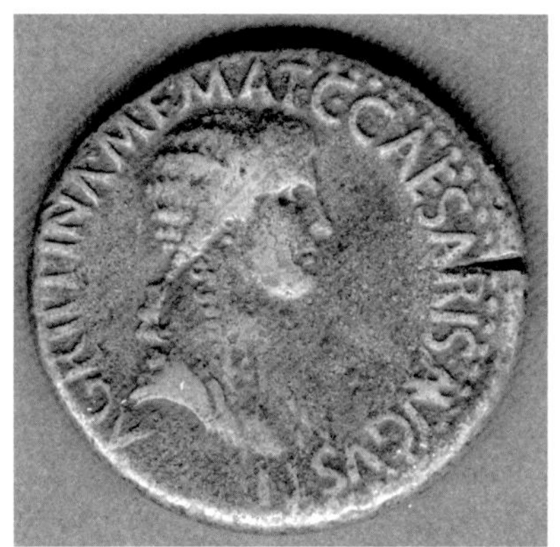

127.
AE sestertius, 35 mm
Mint: Rome
Gaius or Claudius, A.D. 37–41
Obverse: head of Agrippina I, to right; AGRIPPINA M F MATer C CAESARIS AVGVSTI (Agrippina, daughter of Marcus [Agrippa], mother of C. Caesar Augustus)
Reverse: *carpentum* (covered two-wheeled carriage, used especially by ladies of the royal family; Agrippina's appeared at her funeral); Senatus Populus-Que Romanus MEMORIAE AGRIPPINAE (the Senate and the Roman people, to the memory of Agrippina).
Lent by the State Historical Society of Wisconsin, 1.1990.5

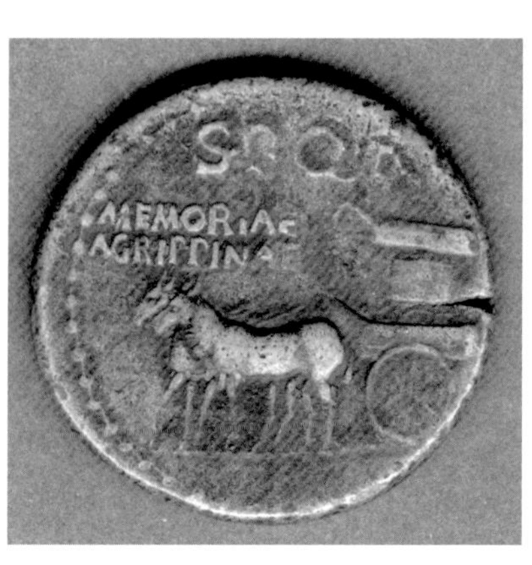

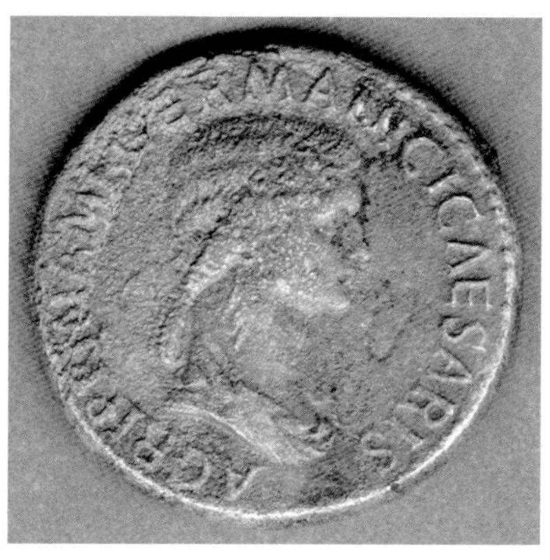

128.
AE sestertius, 35 mm, 25.13 g
Mint: Rome
Claudius, A.D. 41–54
Obverse: bust of Agrippina Major, to right, with hair in braid, AGRIPPINA M F GERMANICI CAESARIS
Reverse: TI CLAVDIVS CAESAR AVG GERM P M TR P IMP P P; S C in center
Ref. RIC Claud. 219
Gift of Herbert M. Howe, 1980.236

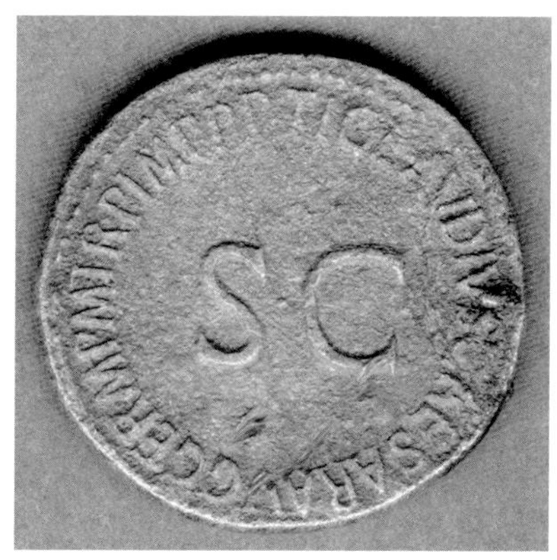

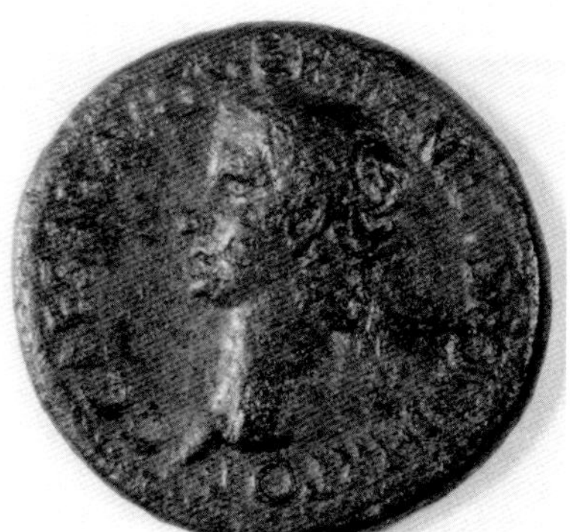

129.
AE sestertius, 45 mm, 26.30 g
Mint: Rome
Gaius, A.D. 37–41
Obverse: laureate bust of Gaius, to left; C CAESAR AVG GERMANICVS PON M TR POT
Reverse: in oak wreath, S P Q R P P OB CIVES SERVATOS.
Gift of Mr. and Mrs. Arthur J. Frank, 1977.294

Gaius, son of Germanicus, was born in an army camp and received the nickname of Caligula ("Bootsy"), by which he is often known. He inherited his father's popularity for a year or so, until his arrogant behavior and his attempt to increase the power of the emperor lost him popular support. He was assassinated in A.D. 41. Later writers accused him of madness and cruelty. Gaius is said to have made his horse, Incitatus, his colleague as consul.

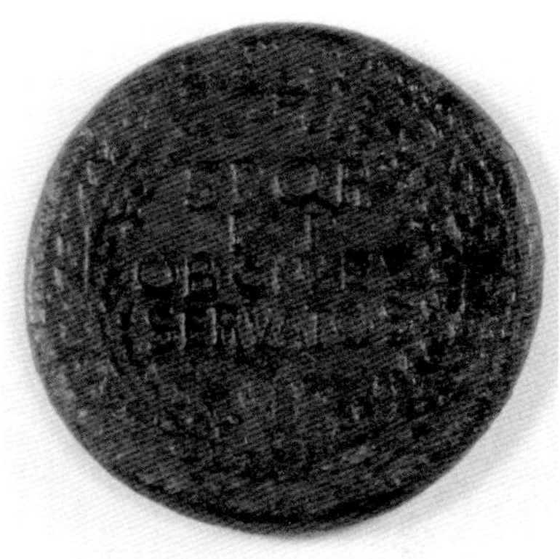

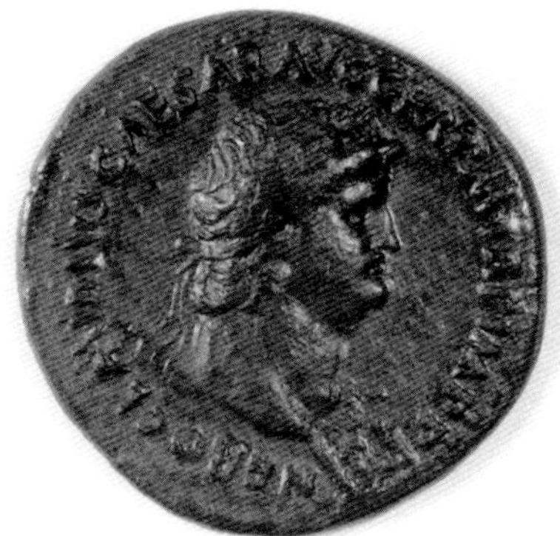

130.
AE sestertius, 37 mm, 27.24 g
Mint: Rome
Nero, A.D. 54–68
Obverse: laureate bust of Nero, to right; NERO CLAVDIVS CAESAR AVG GER P M TR P IMP P P
Reverse: Roma seated, on cuirass to left, with Victory; ROMA S C
Ref. Cohen 264
Gift of Mr. and Mrs. Arthur J. Frank, 1977.295

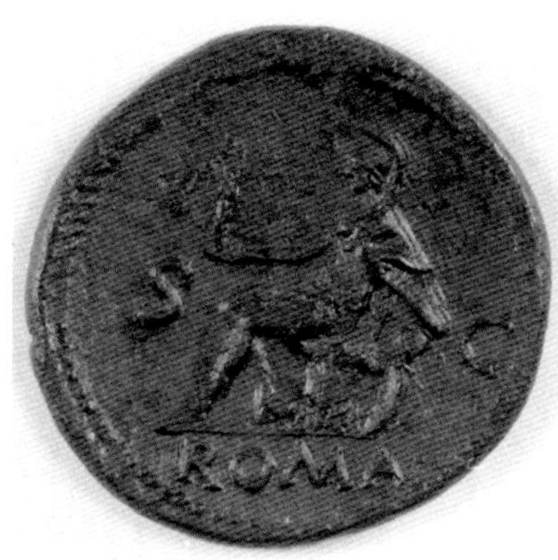

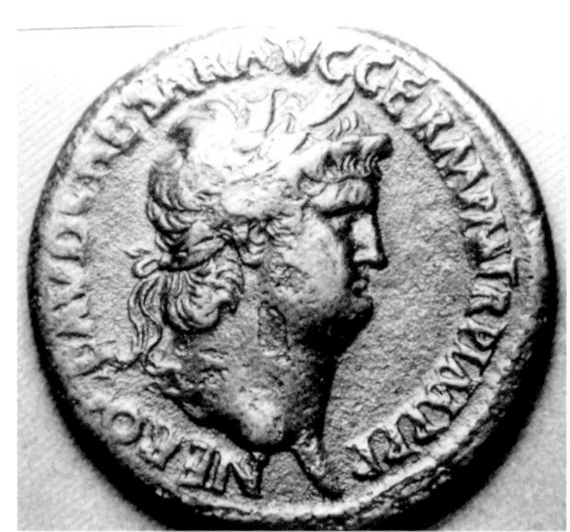

131.
AE sestertius, 42 mm
Mint: Rome, A.D. 64
Nero, A.D. 54–68
Obverse: laureate bust of Nero, to right; NERO CLAVD CAESAR AVG GERM P M TR P IMP P P. (Germanicus, Victor over the Germans)
Reverse: Closed temple of Janus; PACE [P R TERRA] MARIQVE PARTA IANVM CLVSIT (Since peace had been produced [on land and sea], he closed the Temple of Janus).
Gift of Mr. and Mrs. Arthur J. Frank, 1977.296

Augustus had done the same, but before him only two others.

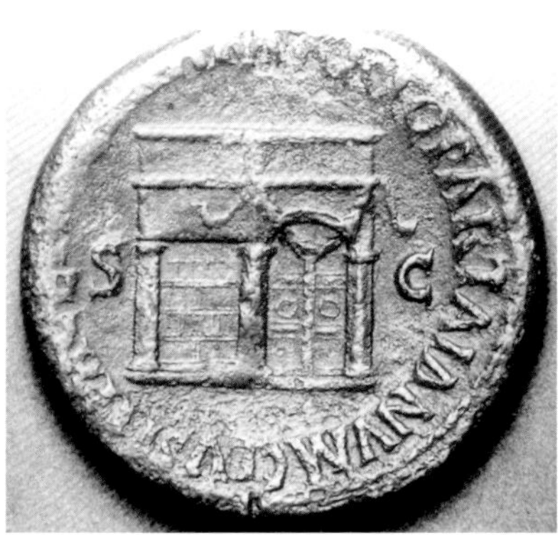

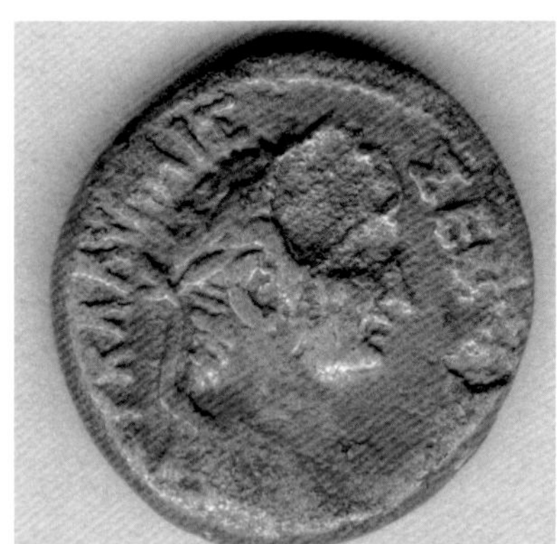

132.
Billon tetradrachm, 22.2 mm, 11.35 g
Mint: Alexandria, A.D. 56–57
Nero, A.D. 54–68
Obverse: laureate head of Nero, to right; ΝΕΡ ΚΛΑΥ ΚΑΙΣ ΣΕΒ ΓΕΡ ΑΥ (Nero Claudius Caesar Augustus Germanicus Imperator)
Reverse: bust of Agrippina II, to right, her hair in pigtail; ΑΓΡΙΠΠΙΝΑ ΣΕΒΑΣΘ (Agrippina Augusta); in front, Lg (year 3)
Ref. BMC Alex. 16.116
Gift of Herbert M. Howe, 1980.348

Agrippina II was the daughter of Agrippina I (and so great-granddaughter of Augustus) and Germanicus (and so great-granddaughter of M. Antonius); great-niece of Tiberius; sister of Gaius; wife of her cousin, Claudius (whom she murdered); mother of Nero (who murdered her); and murderess of her stepson, Britannicus.

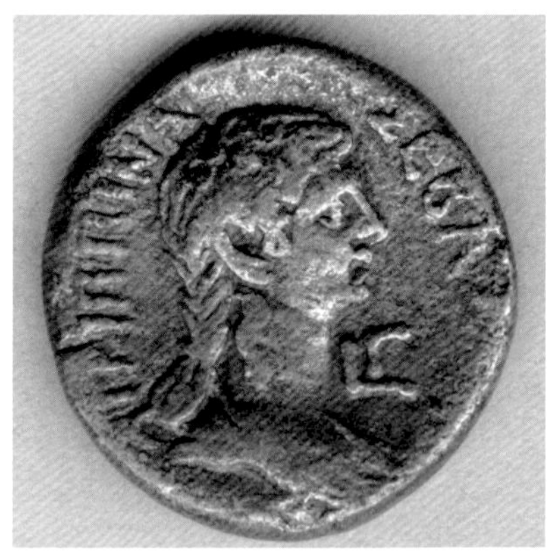

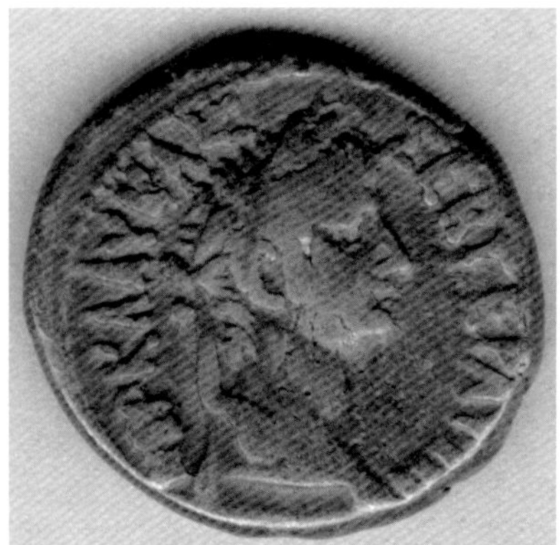

133.
Billon tetradrachm, 26 mm, 13.00 g
Mint: Alexandria, A.D. 56–57
Nero, A.D. 54–68
Obverse: laureate head of Nero, to right; ΝΕΡ ΚΛΑΥ ΚΑΙΣ ΣΕΒ ΓΕΡ ΑΥ
Reverse: bust of Octavia III, to right; in front, Lg (year 3); ΟΚΤΑΟΥΙΑ ΣΕΒΑΣΤΟΥ (Octavia, wife of the emperor)
Ref. BMC Alex. 16.119
Gift of Herbert M. Howe, 1980.349

Octavia was the daughter of Messalina, third wife of Claudius; stepsister and wife of Nero; and great-niece and daughter-in-law of Agrippina. Wishing to marry Poppaea, Nero had Octavia accused of adultery, banished, and murdered.

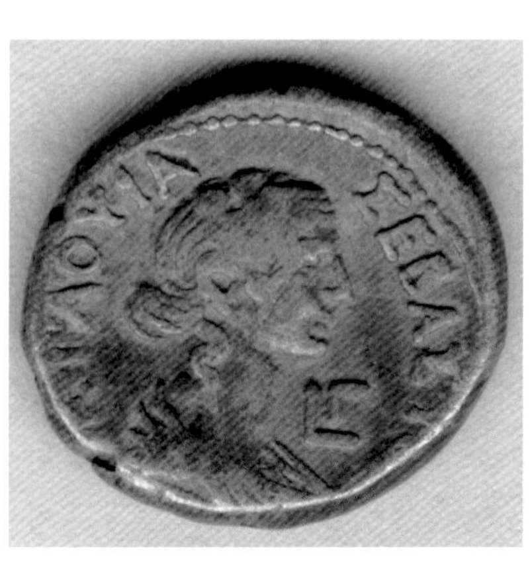

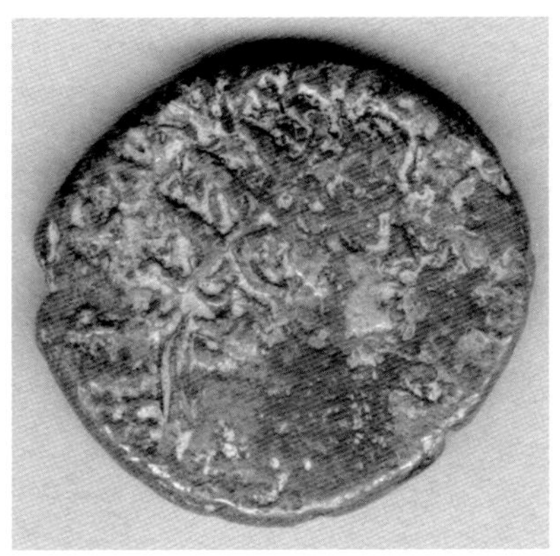

134.
Billon tetradrachm, 26 mm, 11.82 g
Mint: Alexandria, A.D. 63–64
Nero, A.D. 54–68
Obverse: laureate head of Nero, to right; ΝΕΡ ΚΛΑΥ ΚΑΙΣ ΣΕΒ ΓΕΡ ΑΥ
Reverse: bust of Poppaea, to right; in front, Li (year 10); ΠΟΠΠΑΙΑ ΣΕΒΑΣΤΗ (Poppaea the empress)
Ref. BMC Alex. 16.122
Gift of Herbert M. Howe, 1980.350

Poppaea was wife of M. Salvius Otho, who gave her up to Nero in return for a governorship of Portugal, and who was later to be emperor for a few months. Poppaea bore a daughter Claudia, who soon died and was deified as "the Divine Infant." When Poppaea again became pregnant, Nero kicked her in a moment of rage, and she died.

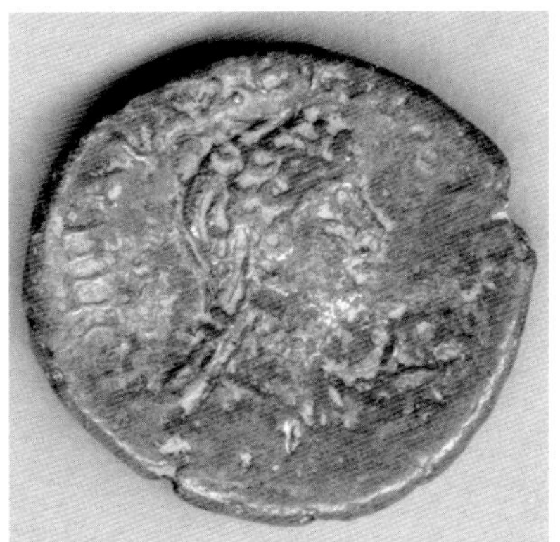

The Flavians And Antonines

The armies in several provinces rose in A.D. 68 against Nero, and he committed suicide, crying, "What a craftsman perishes in me!" Four emperors claimed the throne in A.D. 69—Galba, Otho, Vitellius, and Vespasian. The last of these was not a member of the aristocracy of Rome, but an Italian who had risen to high command in the army and was at the time engaged in the siege of Jerusalem. Leaving the siege to his son Titus, he returned to Italy and secured the throne. Jerusalem fell in A.D. 70 and Masada three years later. Vespasian made no effort to pretend to connections with Augustus, and his coins show him for what he was—a tough army officer with a bull neck. He was succeeded by his son Titus (A.D. 79–81), called "the darling of the human race," in whose reign Mt. Vesuvius erupted and destroyed Pompeii and Herculaneum. Titus was in turn succeeded by his brother Domitian, who was assassinated in A.D. 96. An elderly senator, Nerva, ruled for two years and instituted the policy of succession that saved the empire's internal peace for a century—each emperor named and adopted his successor.

Of the century that followed, the historian Gibbon wrote:

> *If a man were called to fix the period in the history of the world during which the condition of the human race was most happy and prosperous, he would, without hesitation, name that which elapsed from the death of* Domitian *to the accession of* Commodus.

The empire reached its greatest extent. Except for two Jewish revolts, savagely suppressed, it was generally peaceful from A.D. 70 to about 160. Taxation was not yet crushing, and administration was effective. However, the arts and Greek literature stagnated. The coins are competent but imitative. Perhaps the most impressive of the arts were architecture and engineering.

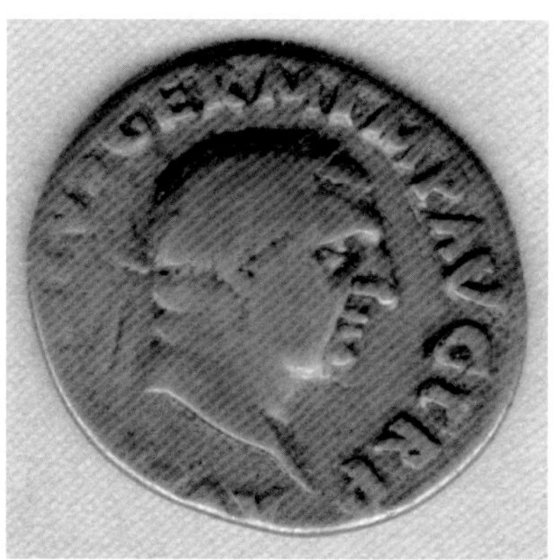

135.
AR denarius, 19.1 mm, 3.02 g
Mint: Rome
Vitellius, A.D. 69
Obverse: laureate head of Vitellius, to right; A VITELLIVS GERM IMP AVG TR P
Reverse: Libertas standing front, looking right; LIBERTAS RESTITVTA
Ref. RIC Vit. 31
Gift of Herbert M. Howe, 1980.453

Vitellius, commander of an army in Germany, was the third emperor in the year A.D. 69. When he was being led to his death, a soldier held a sword, point up, under his chin, to keep him from bowing his head.

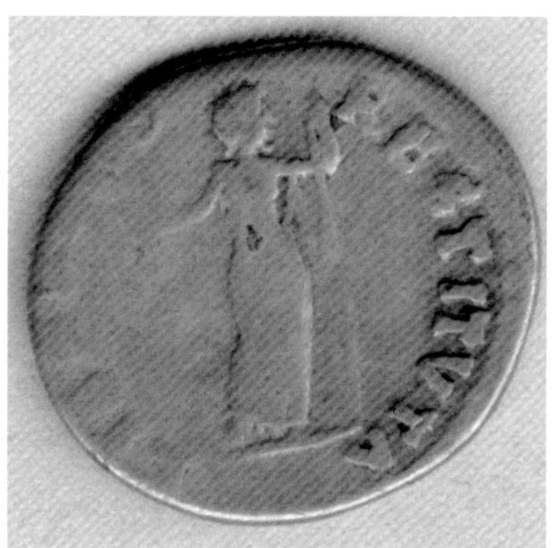

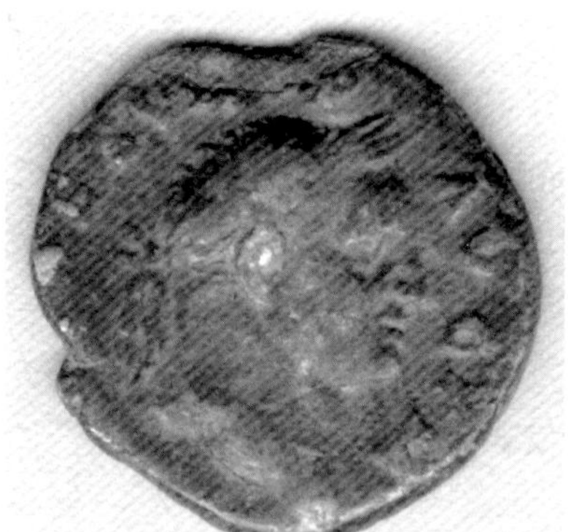

136.
AR denarius, 17.5 mm, 2.92 g
Rome, A.D. 69–70
Vespasian, A.D. 69–79
Obverse: laureate head of Vespasian, to right; IMP CAES VESP AVG P M
Reverse: priestly implements; above, AVGVR; below, TRI POT. Vespasian does not use the name of his own family (Flavius), but keeps the Julio-Claudian titles
Ref. RIC Vesp. 50
Gift of Herbert M. Howe, 1980.444

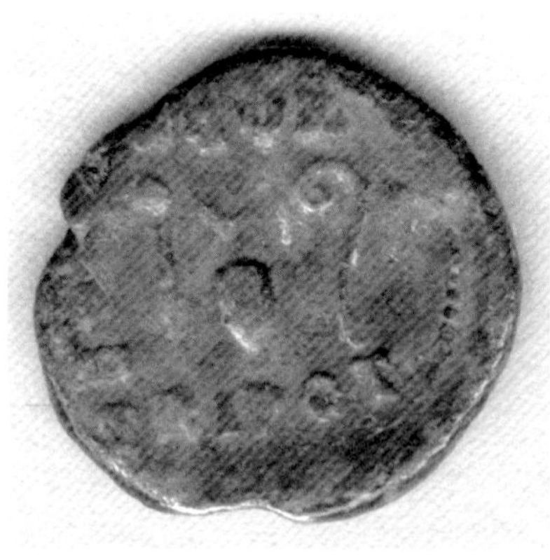

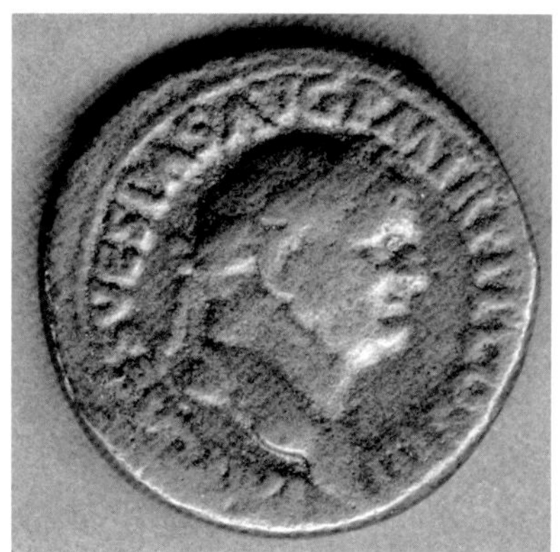

137.
AE sestertius, 71. 33 mm
Mint: Rome, A.D. 69–70
Vespasian, A.D. 69–79
Obverse: laureate head of Vespasian, to right; IMP CAES VESPASIAN AVG P M TR P P P COS III
Reverse: Jewish man standing and woman sitting by palm tree, both bound; IVDAEA CAPTA S C (for the fall of Jerusalem).
Lent by State Historical Society of Wisconsin, 1.1990.6

This coin was struck to commemorate the fall of Jerusalem in A.D. 70.

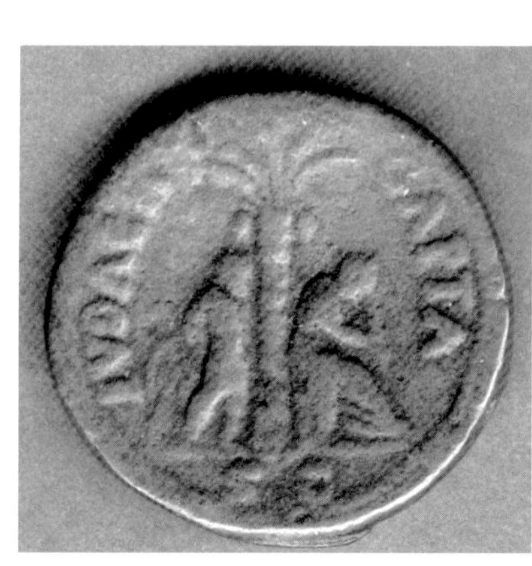

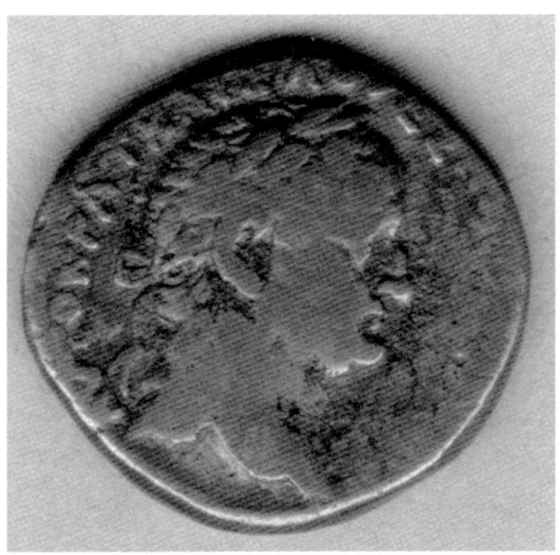

138.
Billon tetradrachm, 23.8 mm, 13.13 g
Mint: Antioch A.D. 70
Vespasian, A.D. 69–79
Obverse: laureate head of Vespasian, to right; ΑΩΤΟΚΡΑΤ ΚΑΙΣ ΟΥΕΣΠΑΣΙΑΝΟΥ
Reverse: laureate head of Titus, to right; Τ ΦΛΑΥΙ ΟΥΕΣΠ ΚΑΙΣ [ΕΤΟΥΣ ΝΕΟΥ ΙΕΡΟΥ] (of the second sacred year of T. Flavius Vespasianus Caesar)
Ref. BMC Galat.179.224
Gift of Herbert M. Howe, 1980.442

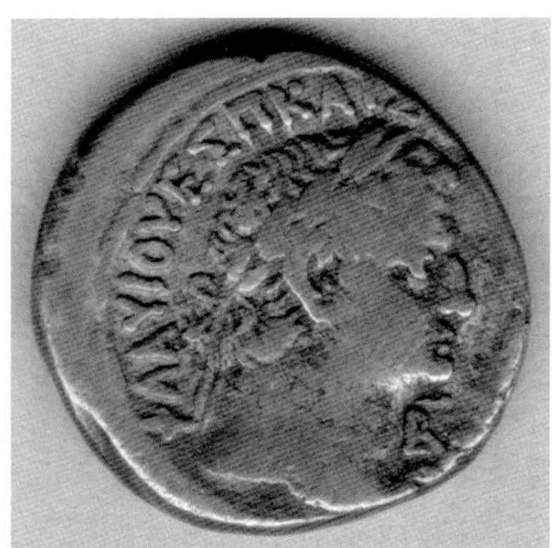

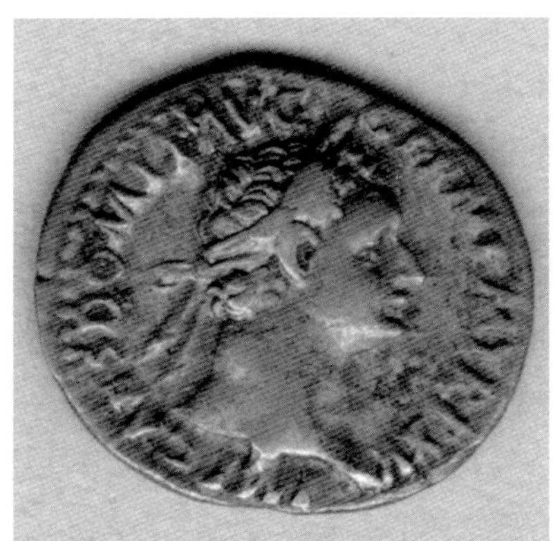

139.
AR denarius, 19.2 mm
Mint: Rome, A.D. 95–96
Domitian, A.D. 81–96
Obverse: laureate head of Domitian, to right; IMP CAES DOMIT AVG GERM P M TR P XV
Reverse: Minerva standing, to left, with spear and thunderbolt; IMP XXII COS XVII CENS P P P (with the power of a censor)
Ref. RIC Dom. 234
Gift of Herbert M. Howe, 1980.265

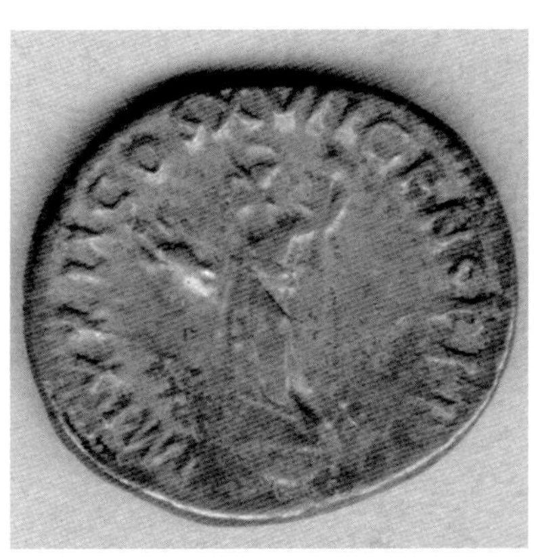

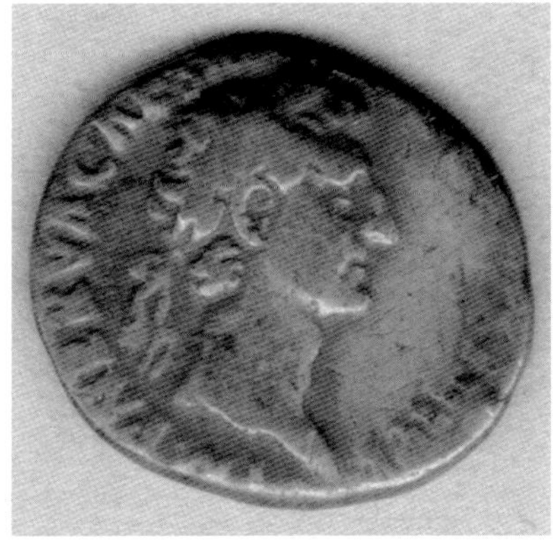

140.
AR denarius, 17.5 mm, 3.30 g
Mint: Rome, A.D. 96
Nerva, A.D. 96–98
Obverse: laureate bust of Nerva, to right; IMP NERVA CAES AVG P M TR P COS II P P
Reverse: Fortuna standing, to left, with rudder and cornucopia; FORTVNA AVGVSTA S C
Ref. RIC Nerva 10
Gift of Herbert M. Howe, 1980.351

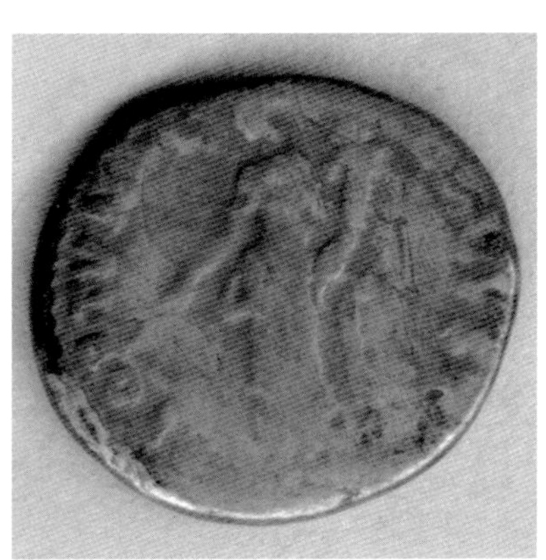

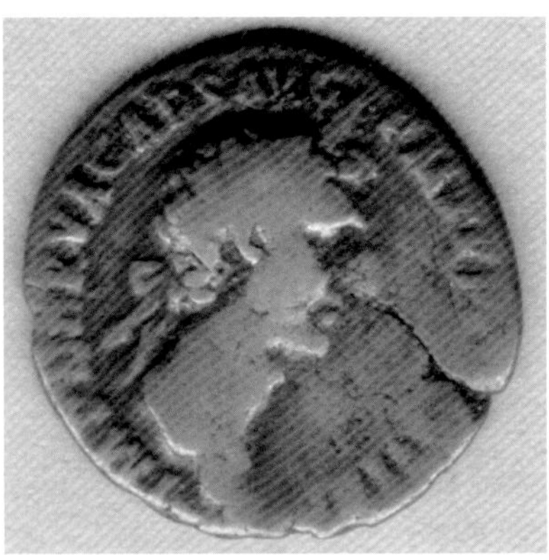

141.
AR denarius, 17.5 mm, 2.60 g
Mint: Rome, A.D. 96
Nerva, A.D. 96–98
Obverse: laureate bust of Nerva, to right; IMP NERVA CAES AVG P M TR P COS II P P
Reverse: clasped hands; CONCORDIA EXERCITVVM (agreement among the armies)
Ref. RIC Nerva 6
Gift of Herbert M. Howe, 1980.352

People still remembered the vicious struggles after the death of Nero. When Domitian was assassinated, power passed smoothly into new hands.

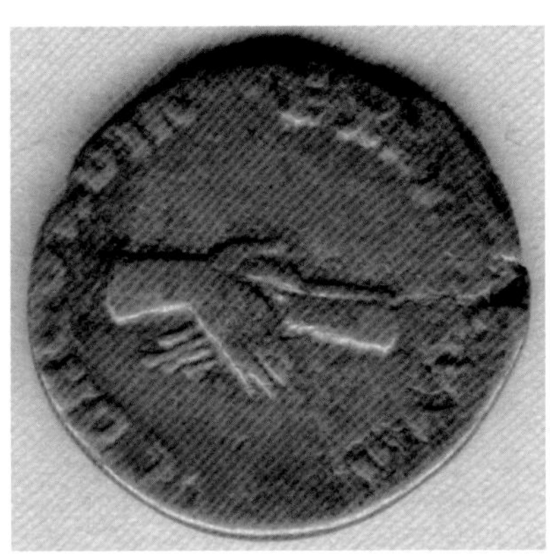

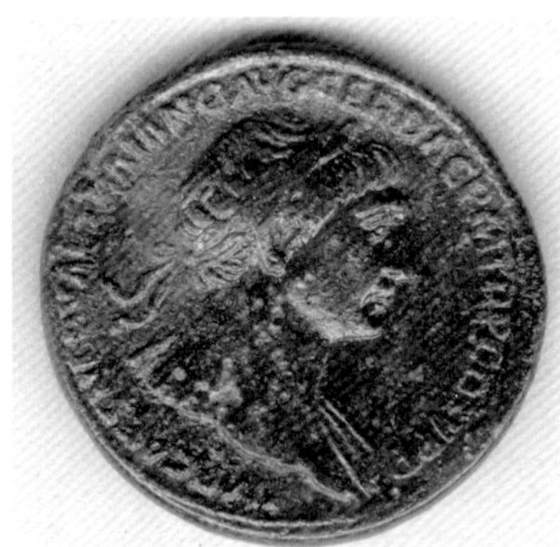

142.
AE sestertius, 33 mm
Mint: Rome, A.D. 103–111
Trajan, A.D. 98–117
Obverse: laureate bust of Trajan, to right; IMP CAES NERVAE TRAIANO AVG GER DACico (victor over the Dacians) P M TR P COS V P P
Reverse: bridge over Danube; S P Q R OPTIMO PRINCIPI (Senate and the Roman people [dedicate this] to the best of rulers) S C
Ref. Cohen 542; Seaby 910
Gift of Mr. and Mrs. Arthur J. Frank, 1977.299, ex Georgi collection

Trajan's Dacian campaign required the building of at least two bridges over the Danube, shown on this coin. Although the Romans remained in Dacia for only about 150 years, the language of the country now known as Romania is still a development of Latin.

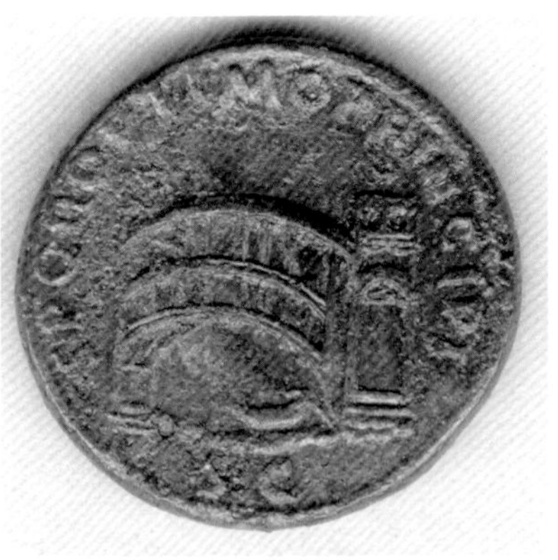

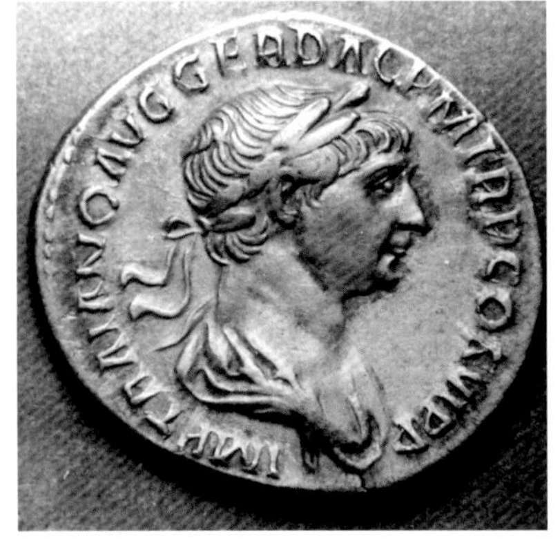

143.
AR denarius, 19.1 mm
Mint: Rome A.D. 112–117
Trajan, A.D. 98–117
Obverse: draped bust of Trajan, to right; IMP TRAIANO AVG GER DAC P M TR P COS VI P P
Reverse: Trajan's Column with two eagles at base; S P Q R OPTIMO PRINCIPI
Ref. RIC 292
Gift of Mr. and Mrs. Arthur J. Frank, 1979.275

In 112 A.D. Trajan dedicated his Forum in Rome, a complex of temples, market, libraries, and palace, including the column, which still stands. Trajan's Column is surrounded by a spiral frieze of scenes from his wars in Dacia, which began in A.D. 101.

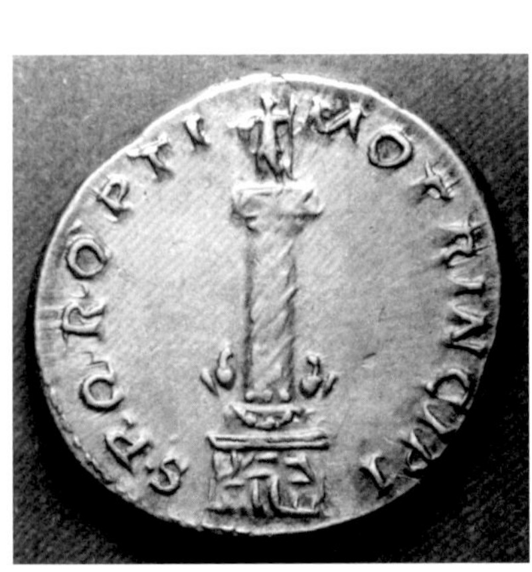

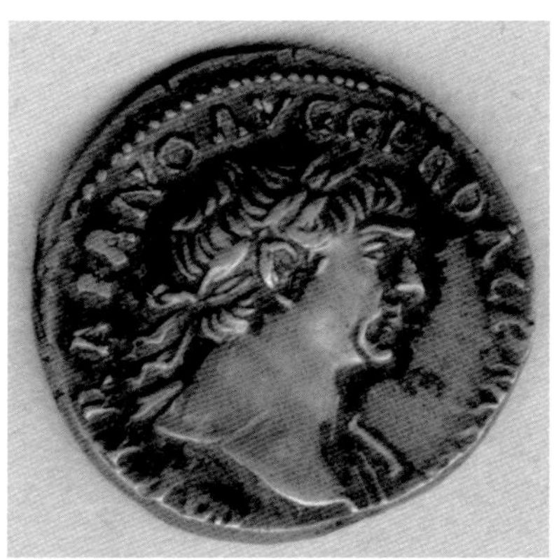

144.
AR denarius, 19.1 mm, 3.30 g
Mint: Rome, A.D. 103–111
Trajan, A.D. 98–117
Obverse: laureate bust of Trajan, to right; IMP TRAIANO AVG GER DAC P M TR P
Reverse: Dacian wearing peaked cap and tunic to knees standing left, hands bound in front; by his side to left oblong shield, two curved swords, and spear; to right round shield. COS V PP S P Q R OPTIMO PRINC; in exergue DAC CAPT
Ref. RIC Traj. 383
Gift of Herbert M. Howe, 1980.427

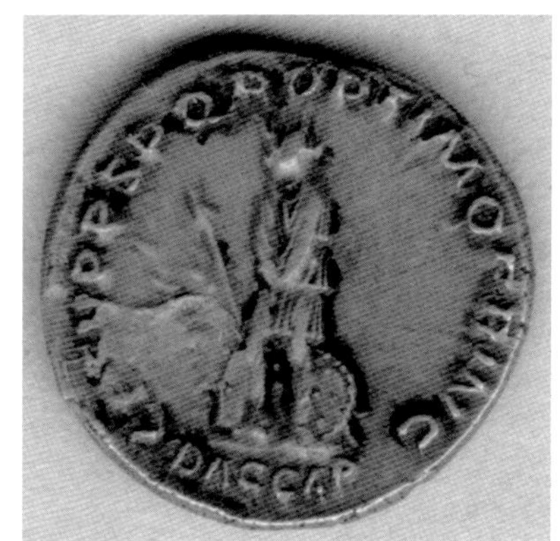

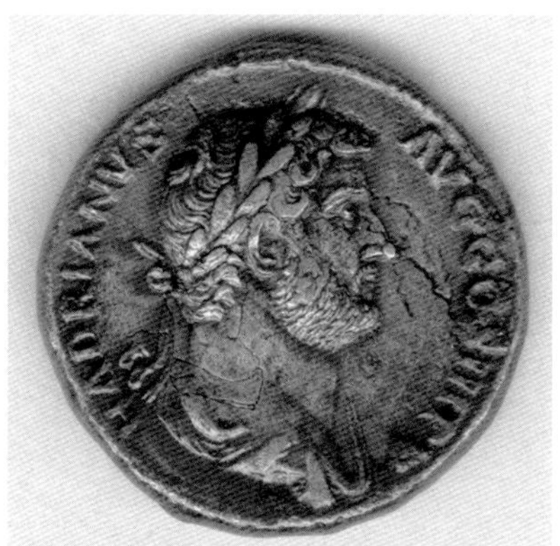

145.
AE sestertius, 32 mm
Mint: Rome, A.D. 134–136
Hadrian, A.D. 117–138
Obverse: laureate, draped bust of Hadrian, to right; HADRIANVS AVG COS III P P
Reverse: Hadrian clasping hands with Fortuna, both standing; FORTVNAE REDVCI (to Good Luck, which has come back again)
Ref. BMC 1519 var
Gift of Mr. and Mrs. Arthur J. Frank, 1979.276, ex Duke of Argyll collection

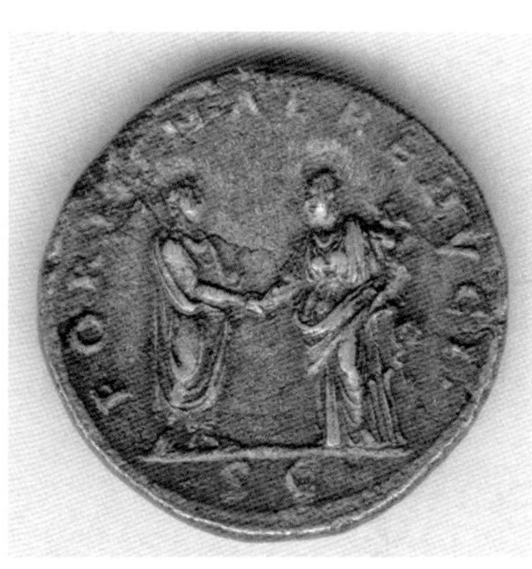

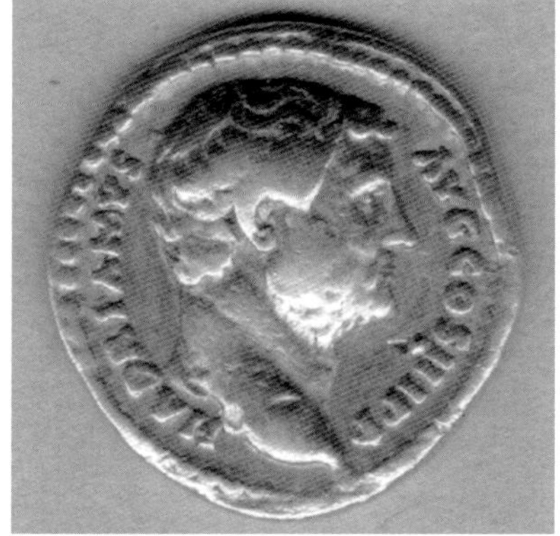

146.
AU aureus, 17.5 mm
Mint: Rome, A.D. 134–138
Hadrian, A.D. 117–138
Obverse: bare head of Hadrian, to left; HADRIANVS COS III P P
Reverse: Victoria, bare to waist, standing front, facing right, with palm and wreath; VICTORIA AVG
Ref. RIC Had. 763
Anonymous loan, 1.1991.1

What victory? The Jews in North Africa and elsewhere in the East had revolted during the last days of Trajan, and in Palestine under Simon Bar Kochba in the early 130s A.D. This revolt, crushed with great difficulty, was the most severe threat to the empire in Hadrian's reign.

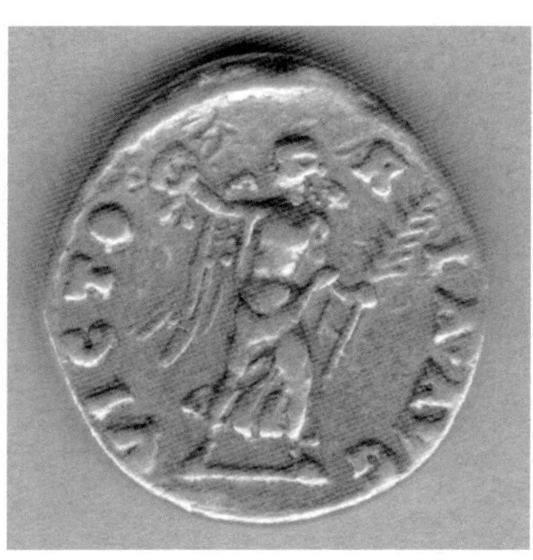

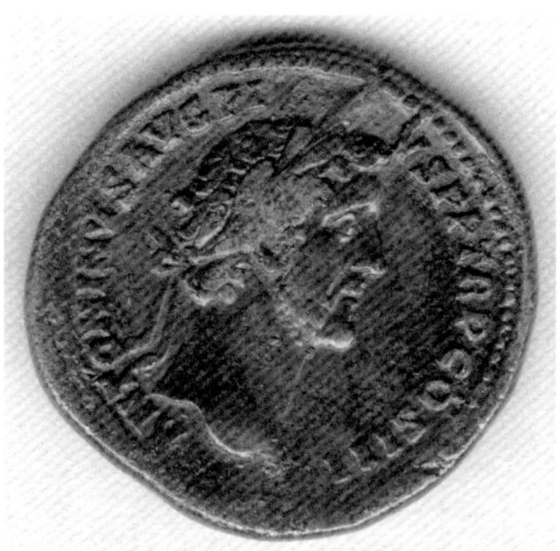

147.
AE sestertius, 33 mm, 27.04 g
Mint: Rome, A.D. 157–161
Antoninus Pius, A.D. 138–161
Obverse: laureate bust of Pius, to right; ANTONINVS AVG PIVS P P TR P COS III
Reverse: Securitas standing, to left; SECVRITAS AVG S C
Gift of Mr. and Mrs. Arthur J. Frank, 1977.303

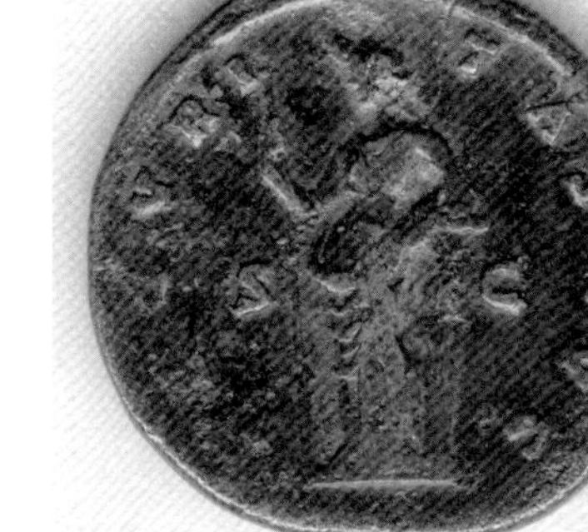

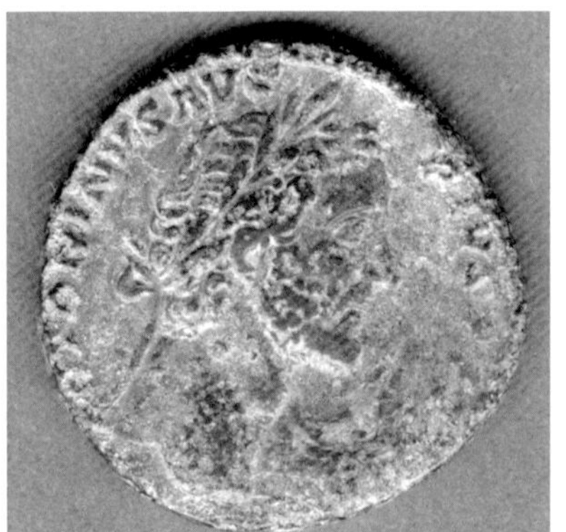

148.
AE sestertius, 30 mm, 16.48 g
Mint: Rome, A.D. 157–158
Antoninus Pius, A.D. 138–161
Obverse: laureate head of Pius, to right; ANTONINVS AVG PIVS P P IMP II
Reverse: she-wolf standing, to right, suckling twins; TR POT XXI COS IIII; in exergue S C
Ref. RIC 2042
Gift of Herbert M. Howe, 1980.182

The patina of a bronze coin, a green, black, or red layer, may be beautiful, but it can make the coin hard to examine.

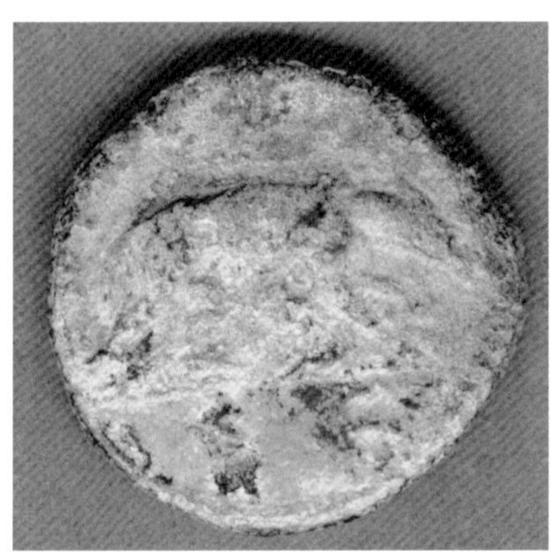

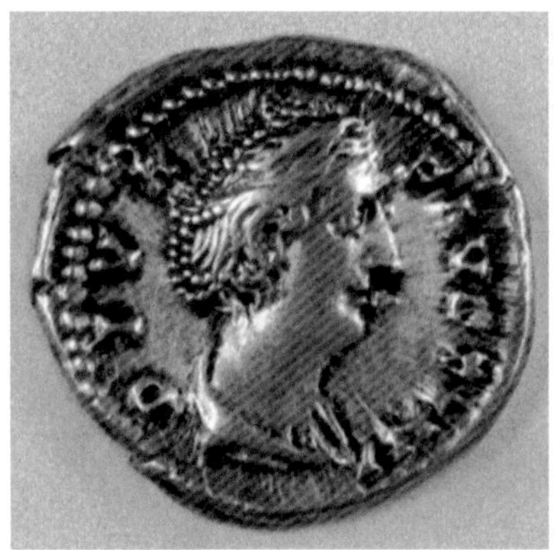

149.
AR denarius, 19.1 mm
Mint: Rome, A.D. 141–143
Antoninus Pius, A.D. 138–161
Obverse: draped bust of Annia Faustina, wife of Pius; DIVA FAVSTINA
Reverse: Ceres standing, to left with scepter and corn ears; AVGVSTA
Gift of Mr. and Mrs. Arthur J. Frank, 1977.304

The later Antonines show many portraits of their women, who were important in cementing political alliances.

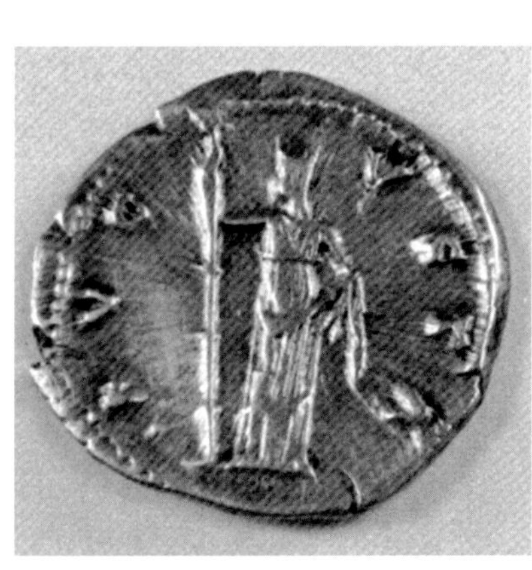

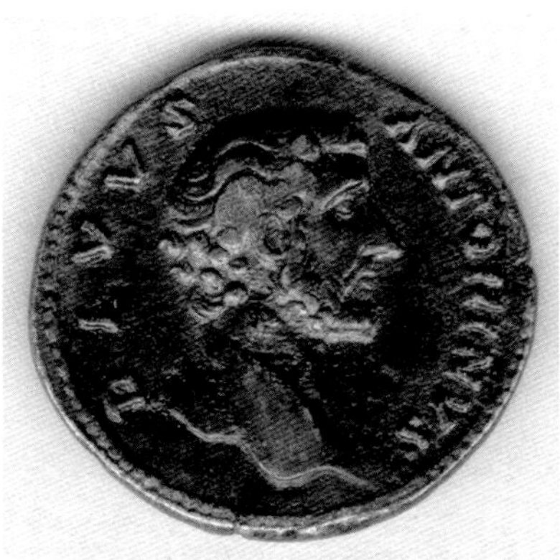

150.
AE sestertius, 32 mm
Mint: Rome, A.D. 161
M. Aurelius, A.D. 161–180
Obverse: bare-headed bust of Pius, to right; DIVVS ANTONINVS
Reverse: funeral pyre surmounted by Pius in quadriga; CONSECRATIO
Ref. RIC 1266; BMC 874; Seaby 1205
Gift of Mr. and Mrs. Arthur J. Frank, 1979.277

This coin commemorates the deification of Pius.

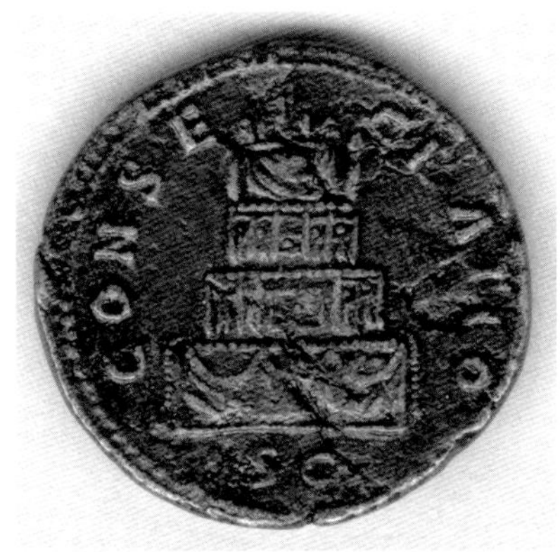

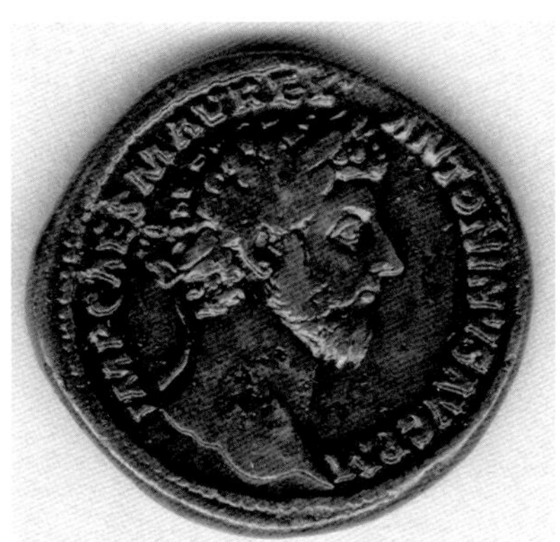

151.
AE sestertius, 33 mm
Mint: Rome, A.D. 161–163
M. Aurelius, A.D. 161–180
Obverse: laureate bust of M. Aurelius, to right; IMP CAES M AVREL ANTONINVS AVG P M
Reverse: M. Aurelius and L. Verus standing, clasping hands; CONCORD AVGVSTOR TR P XVI COS III S C
Gift of Mr. and Mrs. Arthur J. Frank, 1977.305

Pius adopted Marcus Aurelius and L. Verus, with the former as senior emperor. Verus died in A.D. 169.

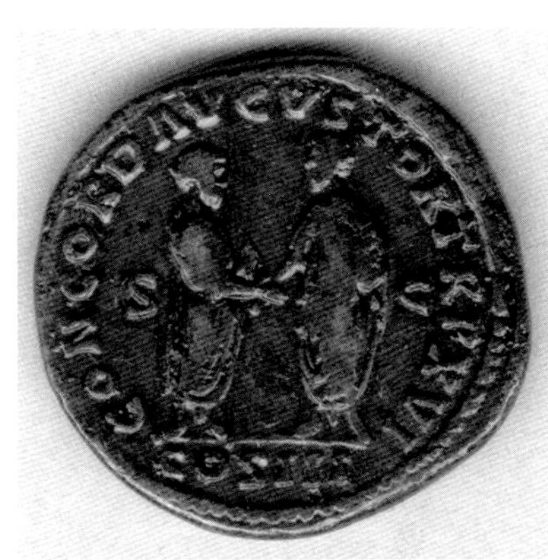

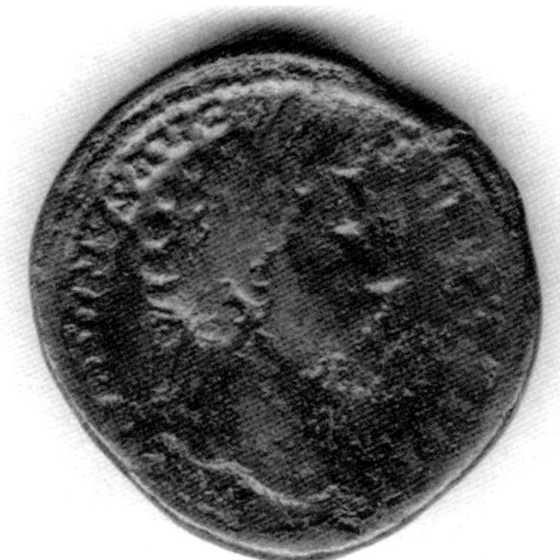

152.
AE sestertius, 32 mm, 28.85 g
Mint: Rome, A.D. 170
M. Aurelius, A.D. 161–180
Obverse: laureate bust of M. Aurelius, to right; M AVRELIVS ANTONINVS AVG TR P XV
Reverse: emperor riding, to right, with four foot soldiers; above, PROFECTIO (setting out to the army); in exergue, AVG
Lent by State Historical Society of Wisconsin, 1.1990.9

Marcus Aurelius spent his last years fighting German invaders with fair success, and, in his spare time, composing his *Meditations*.

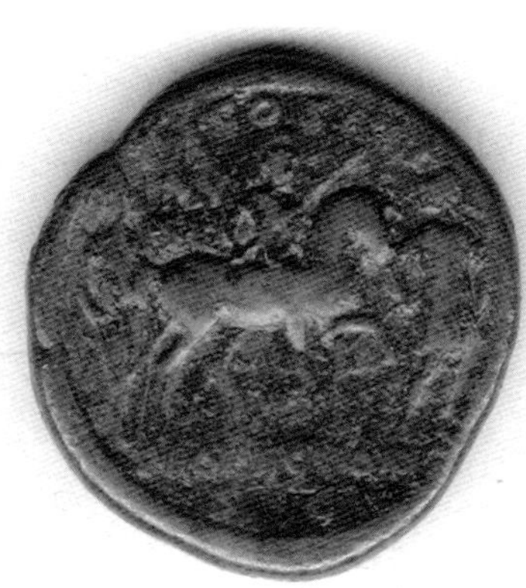

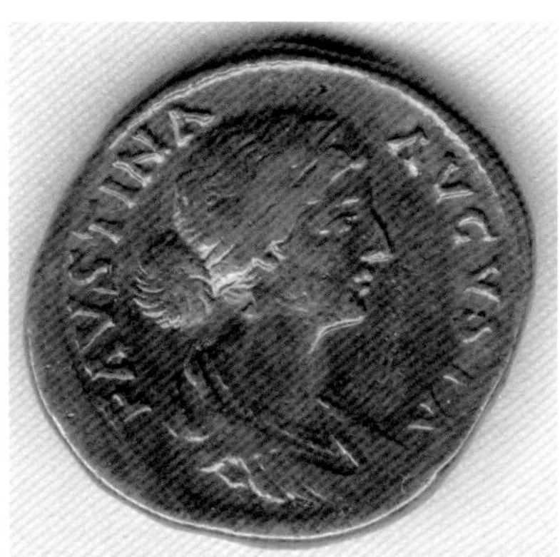

153.
AE sestertius, 32 mm, 28.61 g
Mint: Rome, A.D. 169–170
M. Aurelius, A.D. 161–180
Obverse: draped bust of Faustina II, to right; FAVSTINA AVGVSTA
Reverse: Hilaritas standing, to left, holds cornucopia and palm leaf; HILARITAS S C.
Gift of Mr. and Mrs. Arthur J. Frank, 1977.306

Faustina II was the daughter of Pius and Faustina I. Her coins can be dated by hair styles, seven of which are known before her death in A.D.175.

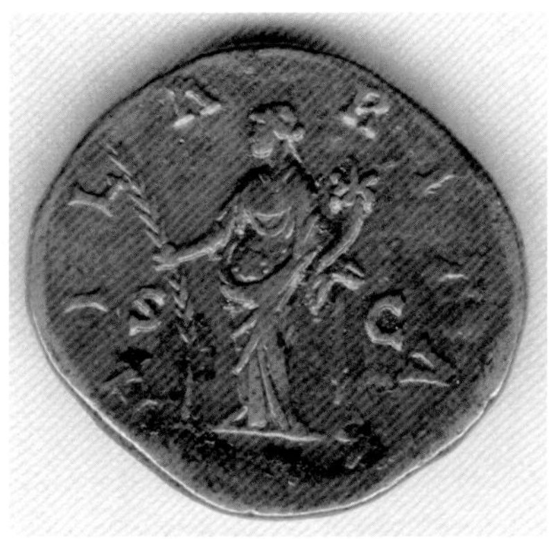

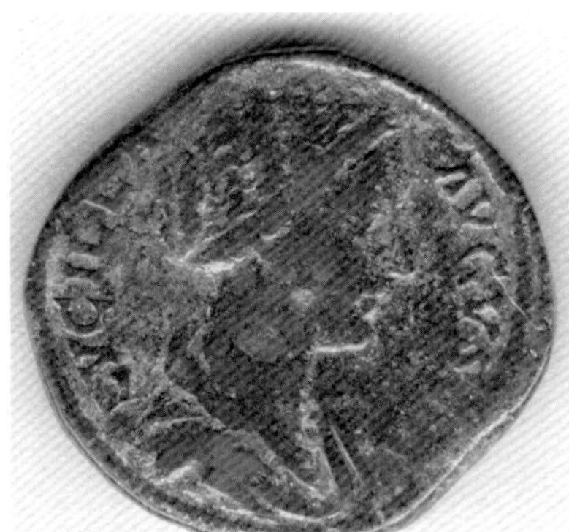

154.
AE sestertius, 26 mm, 27.49 g
Mint: Rome, A.D. 164–169
M. Aurelius, A.D. 161–180
Obverse: draped bust of Lucilla, to right; LVCILLA AVGVSTA
Reverse: Fecunditas (fertility) seated, to right, holding child to her breast, with two other children standing on ground; |FE|CVNDITAS S C
Ref. BMC 1197; Seaby 1477
Gift of Mr. and Mrs. Arthur J. Frank, 1977.307

Annia Lucilla was the daughter of M. Aurelius and Faustina II, and married to L. Verus. In A.D. 182 she was involved in an unsuccessful plot against her brother, the emperor Commodus. She was banished and soon after executed.

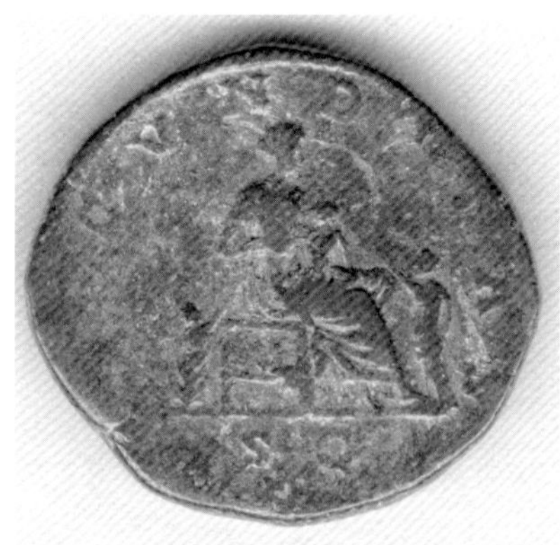

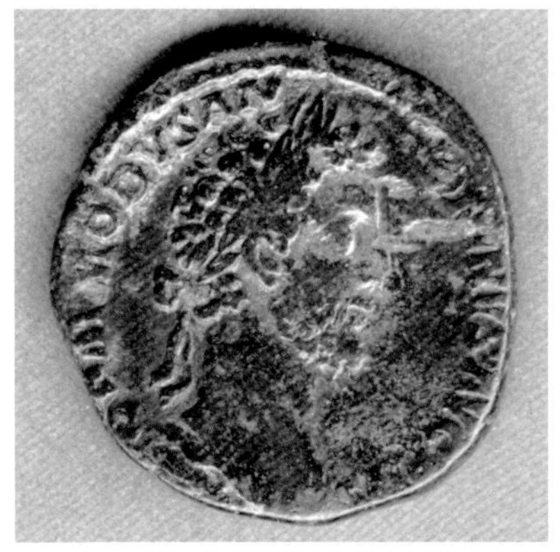

155.
AE sestertius, 30 mm, 20.44 g
Mint: Rome, A.D. 183
Commodus, A.D. 180–192
Obverse: laureate bust of Commodus, to right; IMP COMMODVS ANTONINVS AVG P P
Reverse: Providentia standing, to left; |TR P VIII| IMP VI COS IIII P P
Lent by the State Historical Society of Wisconsin, 1.1990.10

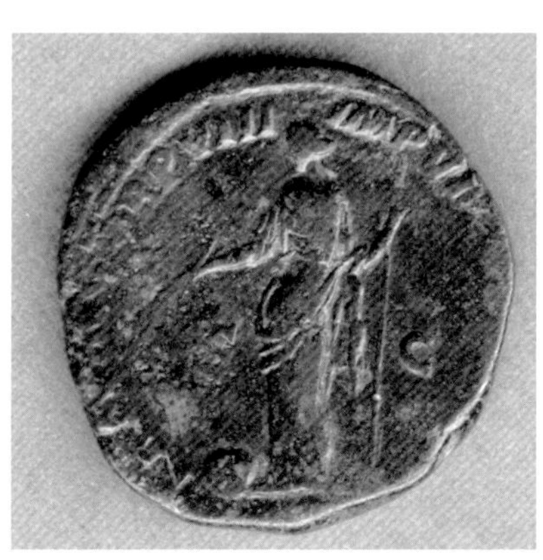

THE SEVERI

Soon after Marcus Aurelius came to the throne in 161 A.D., a series of disasters began that continued for well over a century. Pressure on the frontiers grew with endless barbarian invasions. Plague, perhaps bubonic, carried by rats, invaded the empire from the east. More soldiers were needed to guard the frontiers; they had to be fed, but there were fewer men available to grow food. Taxation, always heavy, became crushing, and needed a huge bureaucracy to administer. Inflation ran wild. Travel, and trade with it, became perilous. The only hope for salvation lay with the military, but the very shape of the empire, with enormously long borders, generated conflict among the generals.

The assassination of Commodus led to a period of rapid turnover of emperors. This turmoil ended with the dynasty of the Severi. The first of them, Septimius, was by birth a Roman from Africa who had risen in the army, married a Syrian woman, Julia Domna, and sired two sons, one of whom was unwilling to share control with his brother. The younger son was murdered, the elder followed him a few years later. But a pair of cousins held the throne for almost twenty years more, most of them peaceful, though hardly prosperous. Then war broke out again, and the last of the Severi, Alexander, was assassinated in A.D. 235.

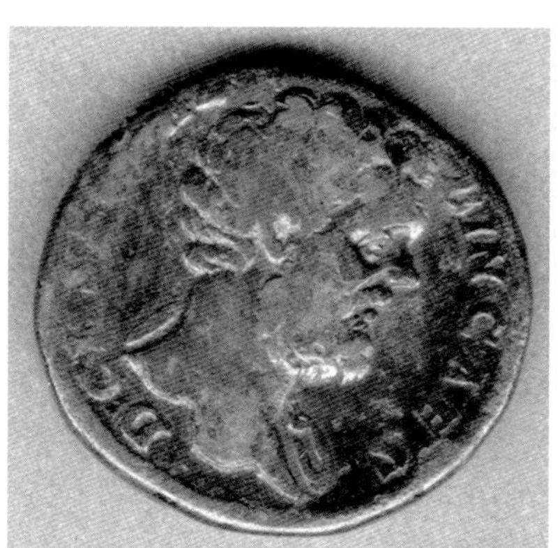

156.
AE sestertius, 30 mm, 26.65 g
Mint: Rome, A.D. 195–196
Clodius Albinus, A.D. 193–196
Obverse: bare head of Albinus, to right; D CLODIVS ALBINVS CAES
Reverse: Felicitas (Happiness) standing, to left; FELICITAS COS II S C
Lent by State Historical Society of Wisconsin, 1.1990.11

Albinus was governor of Britain when Commodus was murdered in A.D. 192. During the next unsettled years he made a truce with Septimius Severus, but they quarreled, and in A.D. 197 Albinus was defeated in battle near Lyons. He committed suicide, his wife and children were killed, and their bodies were thrown into the Rhone.

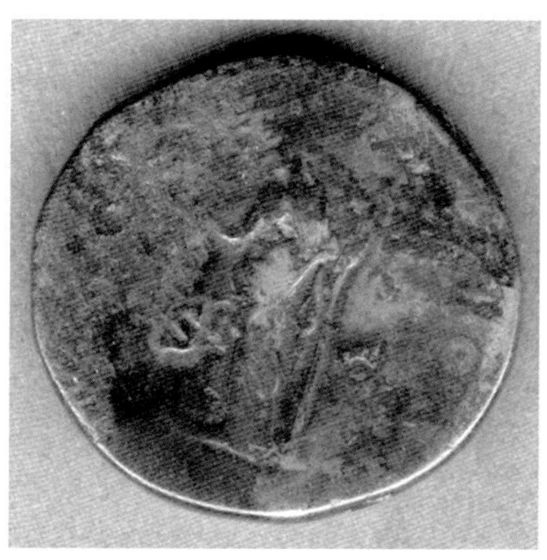

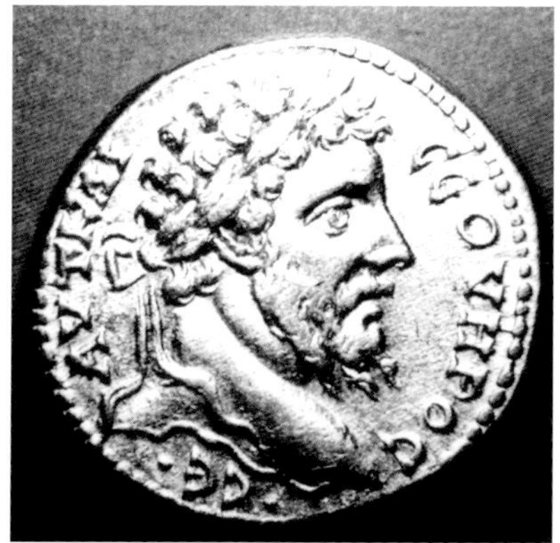

157.
Billon tetradrachm, 25 mm, 13.75 g
Mint: Laodicea ad Mare (Latakia, Syria), A.D. 202–211
Septimius Severus, A.D. 193–211
Obverse: laureate bust of Septimius Severus, to right; AVT KAI CEO GHP CEBACTO [AUTOKRATOR KAISA SEVERES SEBASTOS]
Reverse: eagle with open wings; around
AHNAPXEIV IIATOCT
Gift of Mr. and Mrs. Arthur J. Frank, 1978.336

Severus was a native of Africa, who at the death of Commodus was governor of Pannonia (Hungary). Enraged by the auctioning off of the throne by the Praetorian Guards, he marched on Rome, defeated several rivals, and became emperor.

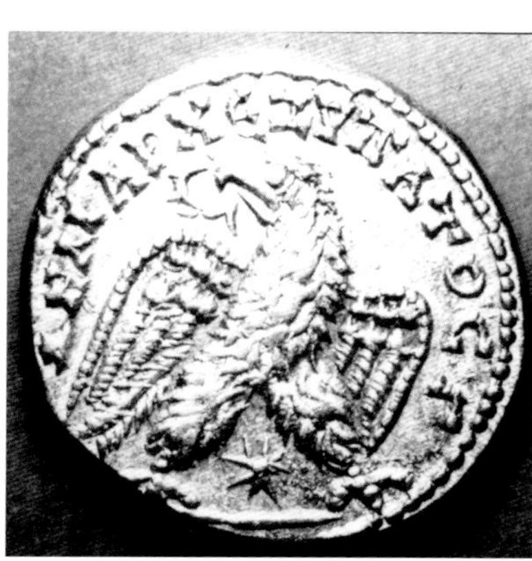

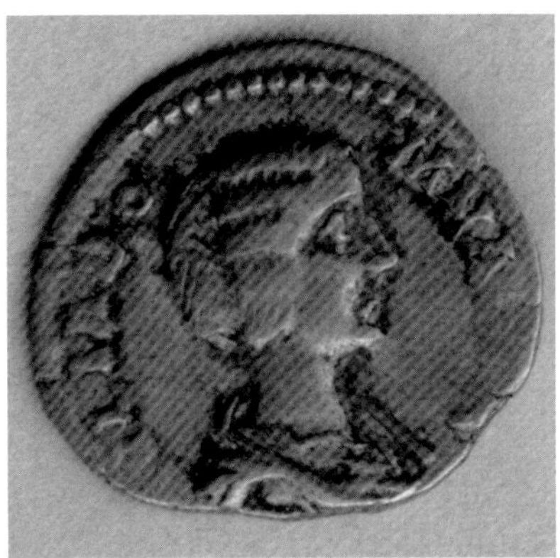

158.
AR denarius, 17.5 mm
Mint: Emesa or Laodicea ad Mare, A.D. 193–197
Septimius Severus, A.D. 193–211
Obverse: draped bust of Julia Domna, to right; IVLIA DOMNA AVG
Reverse: Venus, facing right, leaning on column, holding palm and apple; VENERI VICTR (To Venus, bringer of Victory)
Ref. BMC V 28.51; RIC Jul. Dom. 424
Gift of Herbert M. Howe, 1980.389

Julia Domna, a Syrian by birth, played an important role in the intellectual and political life of her husband's reign. When her son Caracalla was murdered in A.D. 217, she starved herself to death.

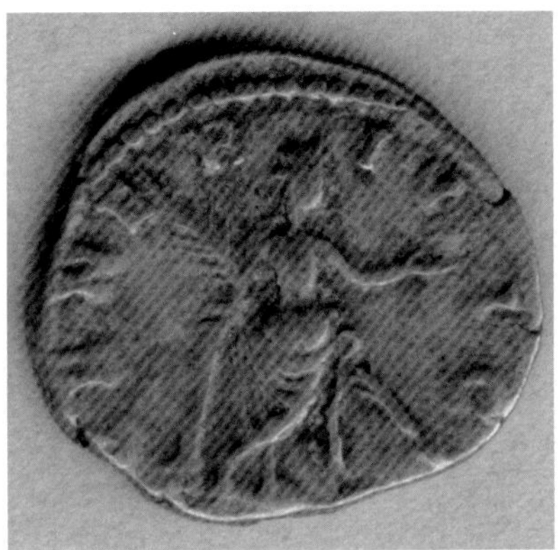

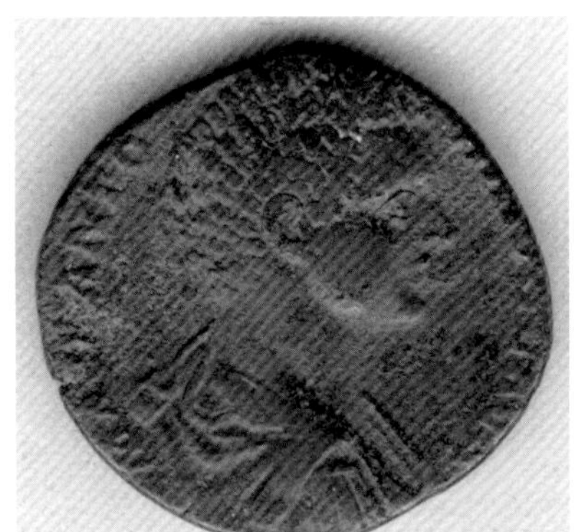

159.
AE sestertius, 28 mm, 18.77 g
Mint: Rome, A.D. 196–198
Caracalla, A.D. 198–217
Obverse: laureate draped bust of Caracalla, to right; M AVR ANTON CAES PONTIF
Reverse: Spes (Hope), advancing, to left; SPEI PERPETVAE (to eternal hope) S C
Lent by State Historical Society of Wisconsin, 1.1990.12

Septimius made his two sons Caesars, expecting them to rule together. In fact the elder, Caracalla, murdered his younger brother Geta (see cat. no. 162) and twenty thousand of his followers and was soon murdered himself. This coin was struck while Caracalla was Caesar. Notice that in the obverse inscription Caracalla calls himself M. Aurelius Antoninus.

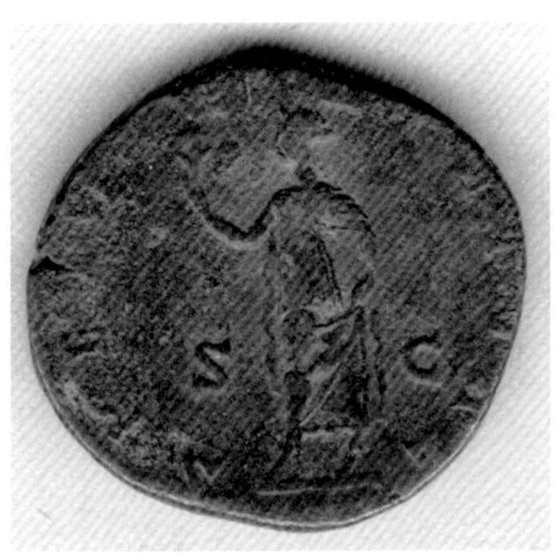

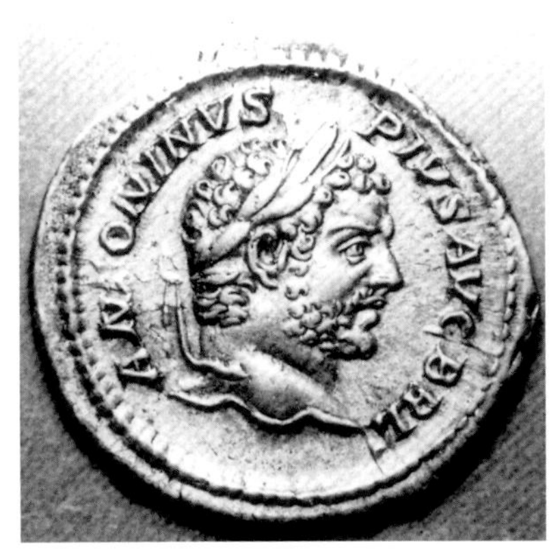

160.
AR denarius, 20.6 mm, 2.92 g
Mint: Rome, A.D. 210–213
Caracalla, A.D. 198–217
Obverse: bearded head of Caracalla, laureate, to right; ANTONINVS PIVS AVG BRIT (adopting the title "victor over the Britons")
Reverse: Mars advancing, to left, carrying spear and trophy; MARTI PROPVGNATORI (to Mars, who fights for [me])
Ref. RIC 223; Cohen 150
Gift of Mr. and Mrs. Arthur J. Frank, 1979.280

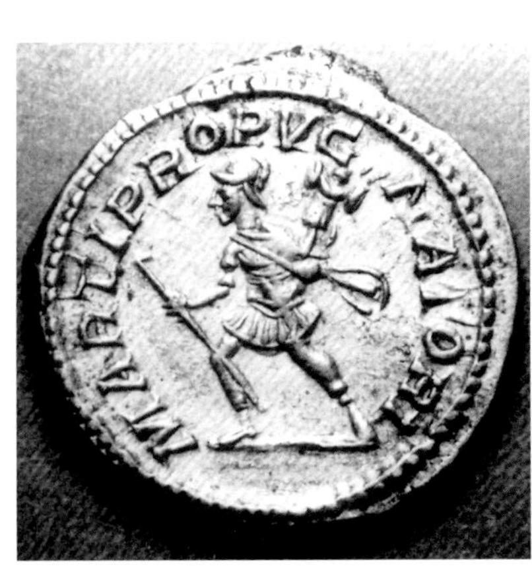

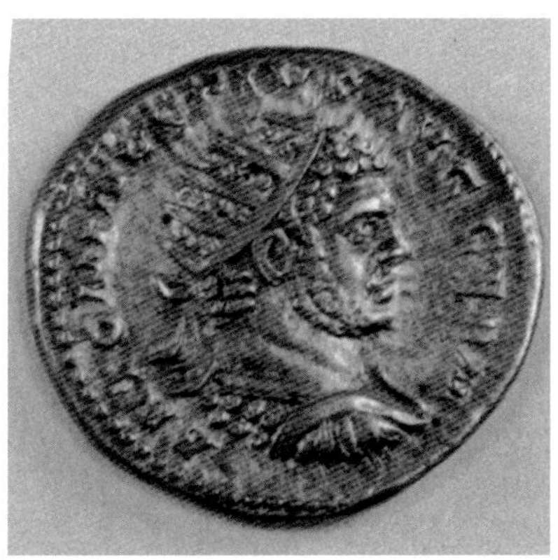

161.
AR antoninianus, 22.2 mm, 5.23 g
Mint: Rome, A.D. 215
Caracalla, A.D. 198–217
Obverse: radiate, draped, cuirassed bust of Caracalla, to right; ANTONINVS PIVS AVG GERM
Reverse: partly nude figure (Sol, the sun) standing, to left; P M TR P XVIII COS IIII P P
Ref. Comp. RIC Carac. 170; BMC V 461.170
Gift of Mr. and Mrs. Arthur J. Frank, 1979.281

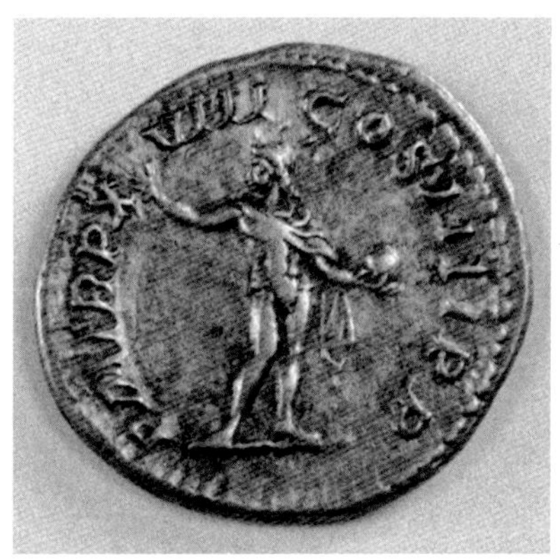

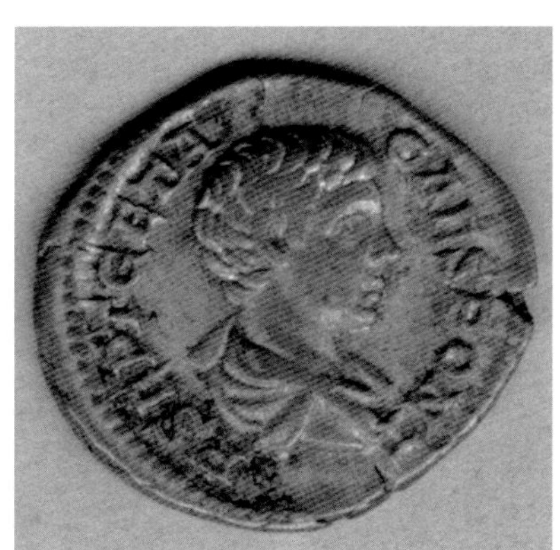

162.
AR denarius, 19.1 mm, 2.94 g
Mint: Rome, A.D. 200–202
Septimius Severus, A.D. 195–211
Obverse: bareheaded bust of Geta draped, to right; P SEPT GETA CAES PONT
Reverse: draped Felicitas, standing front, with caduceus and cornucopia; FELICITAS PVBLICA
Ref. RIC Sep. Sev. 220; BMC V 318.798
Gift of Herbert M. Howe, 1980.393

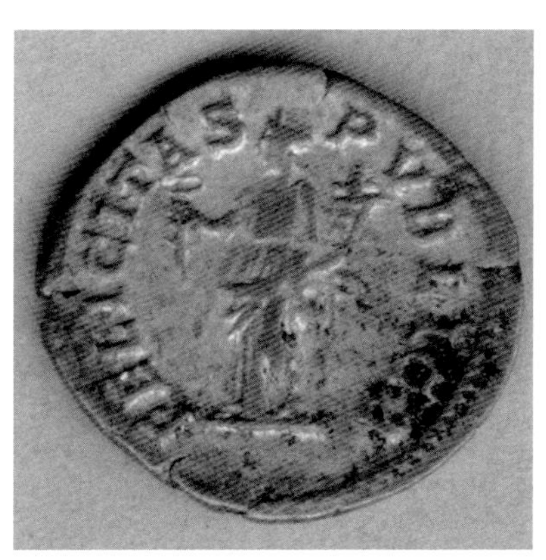

163.
AR denarius, 19.1 mm, 3.45 g
Unknown mint: A.D. 222
Elagabalus, A.D. 218–222
Obverse: draped bust of Julia Maesa, to right; IVLIA MAESA AVG
Reverse: Pudicitia (modesty) sitting, to left, with sceptre; PVDICITIA
Ref. Cohen 36; Seaby 2083
Gift of Mr. and Mrs. Arthur J. Frank, 1978.337

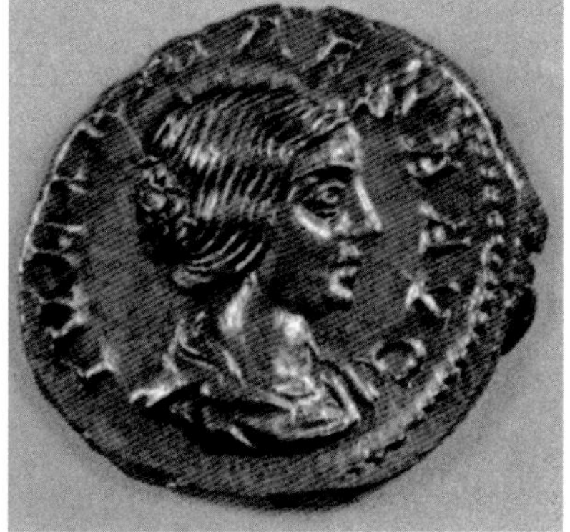

Julia Maesa was the sister of Julia Domna, the mother of Julia Soaemias and Julia Mamaea, and the grandmother of Elagabalus and Severus Alexander; see cat. nos. 164–167. When Caracalla was murdered by the Praetorian Guards, Maesa announced that her grandson Elagabalus, son of her daughter Soaemias, was actually born of the adultery of Soaemias and Caracalla, who had been popular with the soldiery. The Syrian army promptly put Elagabalus on the throne, and Maesa, having publicly demolished her daughter's reputation, struck this coin with its reverse image and inscriptions.

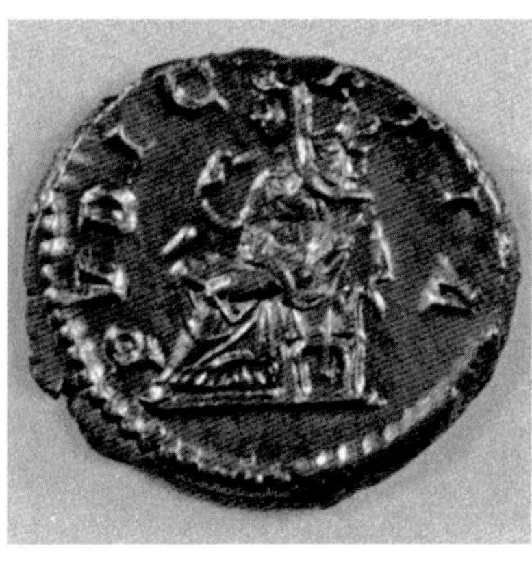

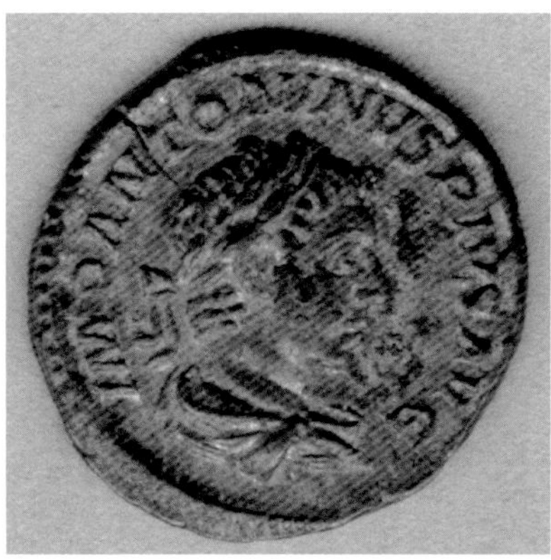

164.

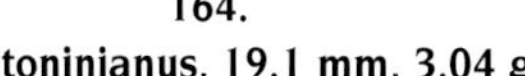

AR antoninianus, 19.1 mm, 3.04 g
Mint: Antioch, A.D. 220
Elagabalus, A.D. 218–222
Obverse: draped laureate bust of Elagabalus, to right; IMP ANTONINVS PIVS AVG
Reverse: Sol standing, to left, with whip; P M TR P III COS III P P
Ref. RIC Elag. 329; BMC V 584.329
Gift of Herbert M. Howe, 1980.272

Elagabalus had been the high priest of Ba'al Shemesh, the sun god of Emesa, whose image appears on the reverse. He mounted the throne at the age of eighteen and tried to syncretize all gods in the cult of the Sun. After four years of astonishing depravity and religious fanaticism, he and his mother, Soaemias, were killed. Their bodies were dragged through the streets and thrown into the Tiber.

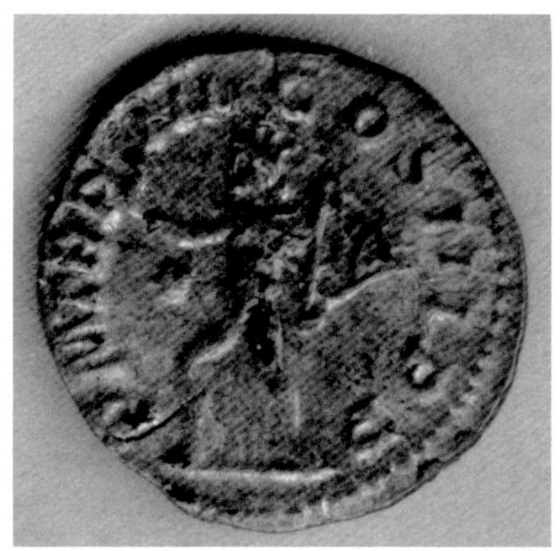

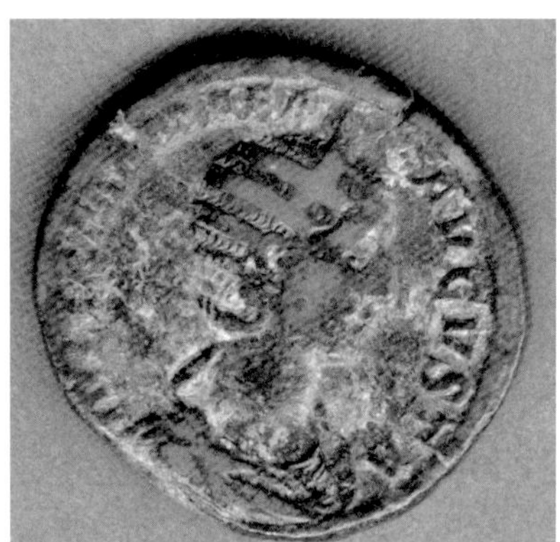

165.
AE sestertius, 30 mm, 23.30 g
Severus Alexander, A.D. 222–235
Obverse: veiled draped bust of Julia Mamaea, to right; IVLIA MAMAEA AVGVSTA
Reverse: Vesta standing, to left, with Palladium and sceptre; VESTA S C
Lent by State Historical Society of Wisconsin, 1.1990.15

Mamaea was the daughter of Julia Maesa, sister of Soaemias, and mother of Alexander.

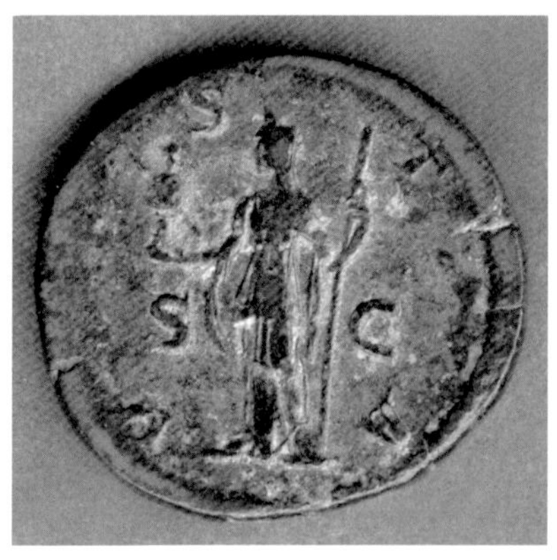

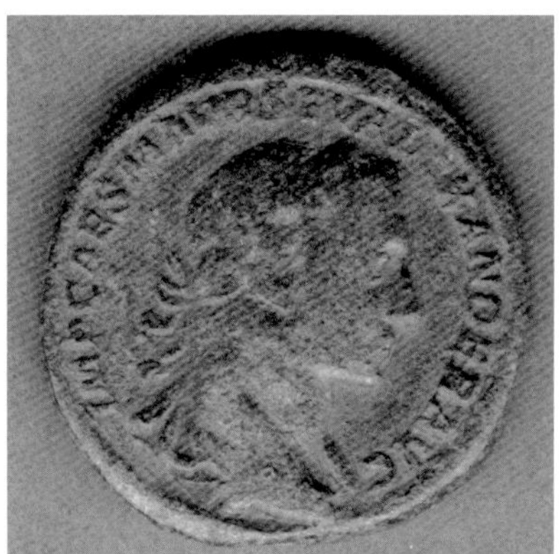

166.
AE sestertius, 32 mm, 21.94 g
Mint: Rome, A.D. 225
Severus Alexander, A.D. 222–235
Obverse: laureate bust of Severus Alexander, to right; IMP CAES M AVR SEV ALEXANDER AVG
Reverse: Mars advancing, to right; P M TR P IIII COS P P S C
Ref. RIC Alex. Sev. 424; BMC VI 138.250
Gift of Herbert M. Howe, 1980.413

Alexander, cousin of Elagabalus, had been adopted by him, and had no trouble with the succession or for ten peaceful years thereafter. But in 232 A.D. Germans and Parthians began making trouble he could not control, and he and his mother were assassinated in 235.

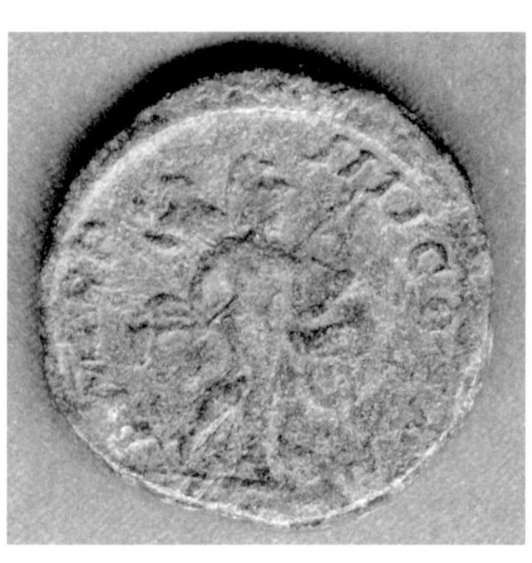

THE EMPIRE'S DARKEST HOURS

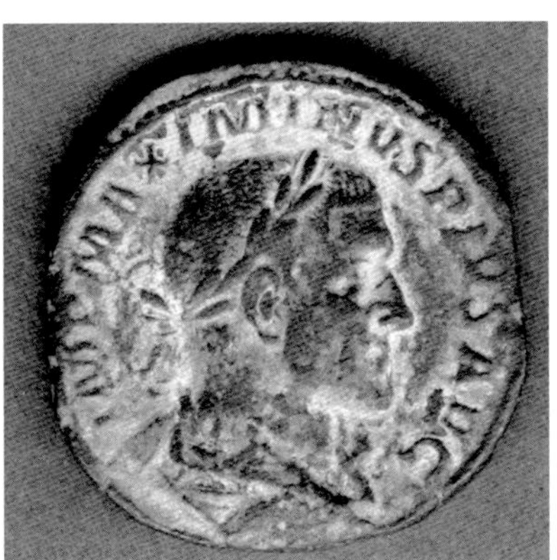

167.
AE sestertius, 28 mm, 19.82 g
Mint: Rome, A.D. 236–237
Maximinus Thrax, A.D. 235–238
Obverse: laureate cuirassed bust, to right; IMP MAXIMINVS PIVS AVG
Reverse: Victoria running, to right, with wreath and palm; VICTORIA AVG; S C
Ref. BMC VI 231.109
Gift of Herbert M. Howe, 1980.333

Maximinus, a gigantic Thracian, was an able general, but unpopular with the upper orders. In A.D. 238 his troops revolted and murdered him and his son.

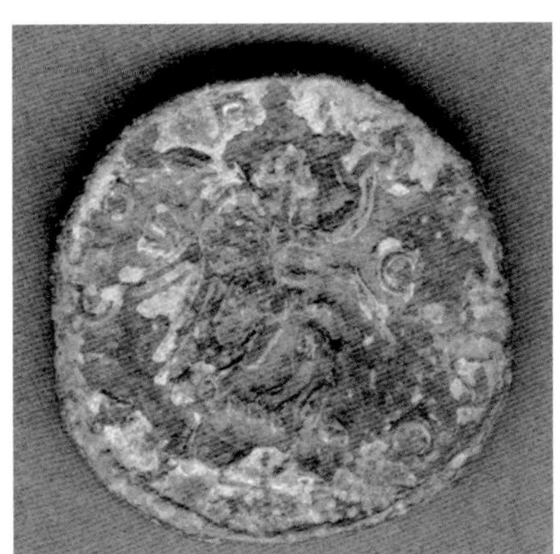

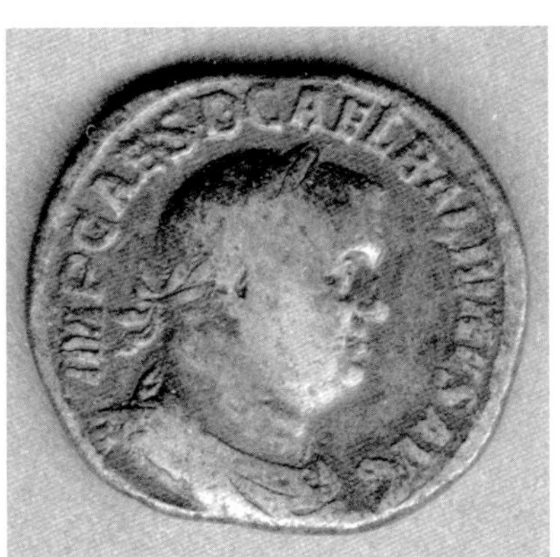

168.
AE sestertius, 30 mm, 16.17 g
Mint: Rome, A.D. 238
Balbinus, A.D. 238
Obverse: laureate, draped, cuirassed bust of Balbinus, to right; IMP CAES D CAEL BALBINVS AVG S C
Reverse: Balbinus, Pupienus, and Gordian III seated, to left, on platform, with Liberalitas and a soldier; to left, citizen mounting the steps; LIBERALITAS (distribution of money to the citizenry) AVGVSTORVM S C
Lent by State Historical Society of Wisconsin, 1.1990.16

After the death of Maximinus, the senate made Balbinus and Pupienus joint Augusti, with Gordian III as Caesar. The first two were murdered after a reign of three months. Gordian III was installed as emperor and reigned until he, too, was assassinated in A.D. 244.

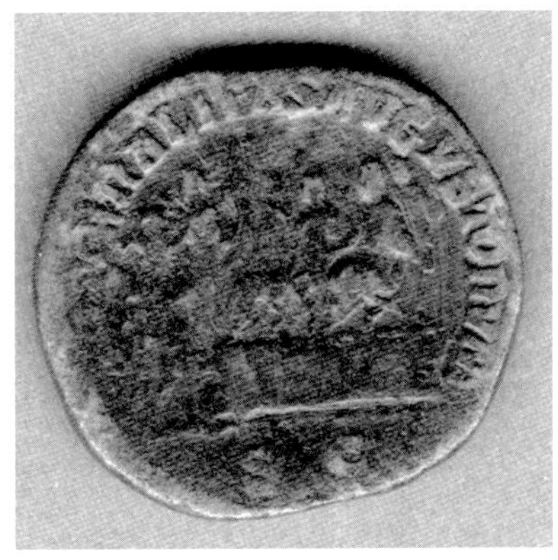

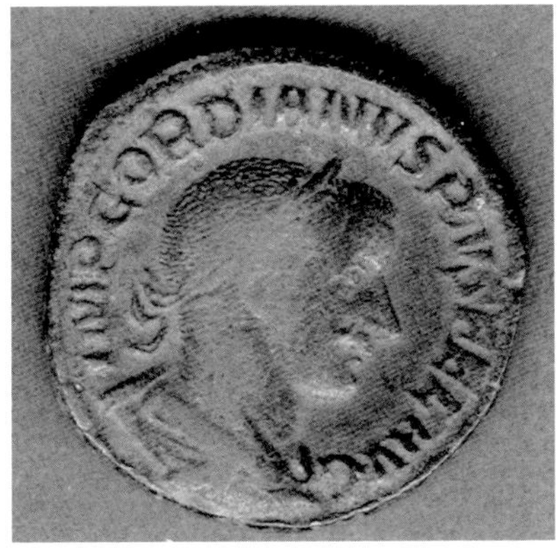

169.
AE sestertius, 30 mm, 19.34 g
Mint: Rome, A.D. 242
Gordian III, A.D. 238–244
Obverse: laureate bust of Gordian III, to right; IMP GORDIANVS PIVS FEL AVG
Reverse: Gordian in military dress standing, to right, with spear and globe; P M TR P V COS II P P S C
Ref. RIC Gord. III 307
Gift of Herbert M. Howe, 1980.287

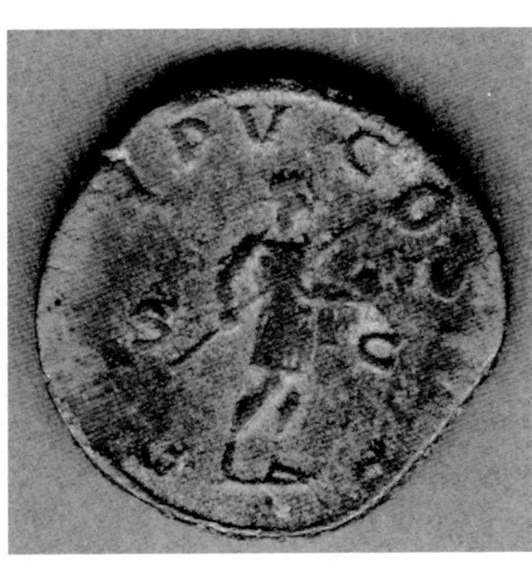

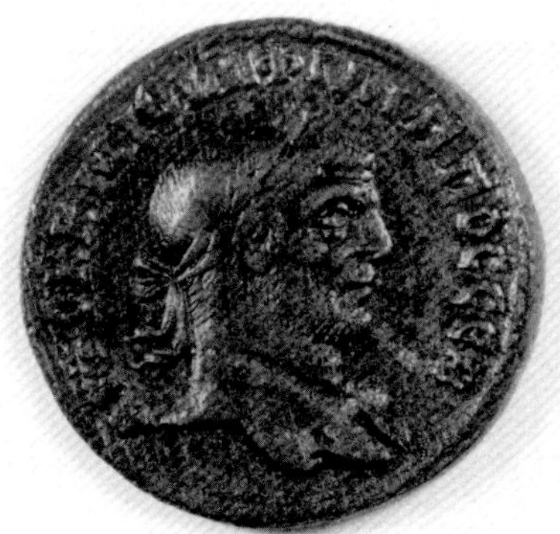

170.
AE, 29 mm
Mint: Antioch
Philip I, A.D. 244–249
Obverse: laureate bust of Philip I laureate; ΑVΤΟΚ Μ ΙΟVΛΙ ΦΙΛΙΠΠΟC CΕΒ
Reverse: Tyche of Antioch, with turreted crown; ΑΝΤΙΟΧΕΩΝ ΜΗΤΡΟΚΟΛΩΝ (of Antioch, mother of colonies)
Ref. BMC 527
Gift of Mr. and Mrs. Arthur J. Frank, 1979.283

Philip, born in Arabia, took the throne after the murder of Gordian III in A.D. 244. The chief event of his reign was the thousandth anniversary of the founding of Rome in 753 B.C., which he celebrated with elaborate games, including hunts of exotic animals, many of which had been gathered by the emperor. He is sometimes claimed, quite falsely, as the first Christian emperor.

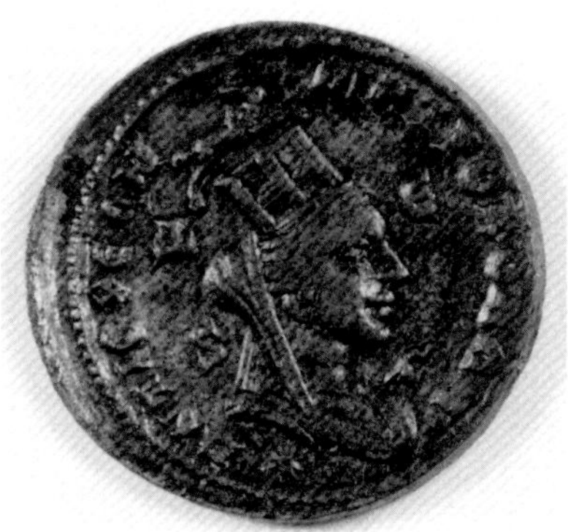

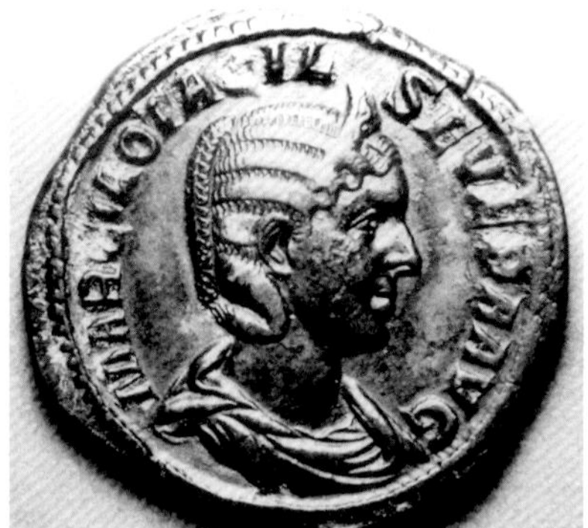

171.
AR sestertius, 32 mm
Mint: Rome, A.D. 247
Philip I, A.D. 244–249
Obverse: diademed and draped bust of Otacilia Severa, Philip's wife, to right; MARCIA OTACILI SEVERA AVG
Reverse: Concordia with patera and cornucopia seated, to left; CONCORDIA AVGG S C
Ref. RIC Phil. I 203b; Seaby 2536
Gift of Mr. and Mrs. Arthur J. Frank, 1979.284, ex Steele collection

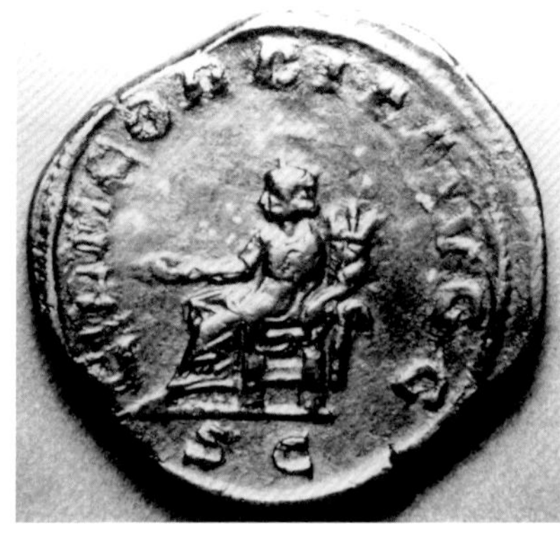

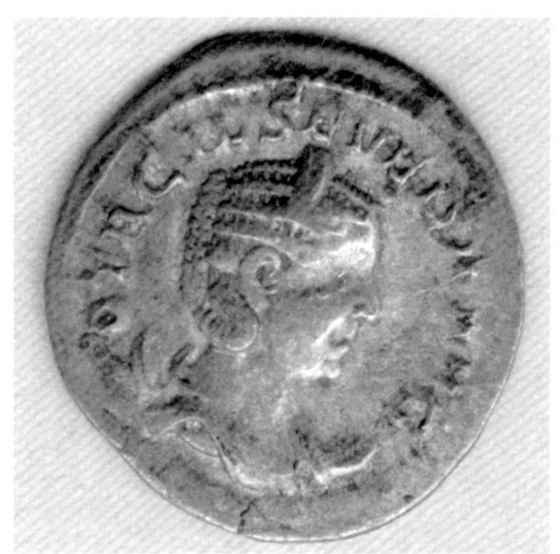

172.
AE antoninianus, 22.2 mm, 3.07 g
Mint: Rome, A.D. 248
Philip I, A.D. 244–249
Obverse: diademed and draped bust of Otacilia Severa, to right; OTACIL SEVERA AVG
Reverse: hippopotamus, to right; SAECVLARES AVGG (centennial games of the emperors)
Ref. RIC Phil. I 116b
Gift of Herbert M. Howe, 1980.358

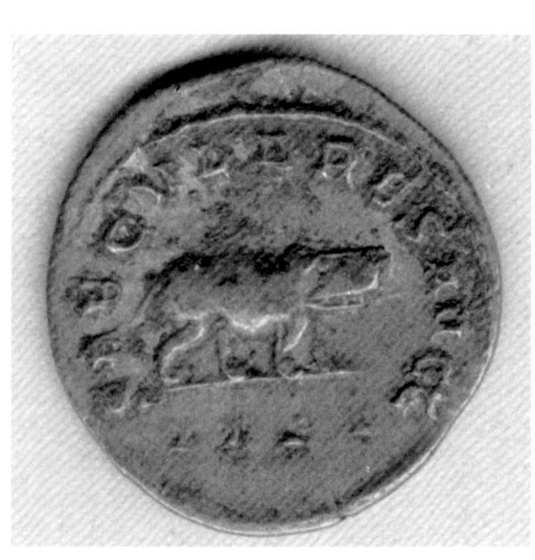

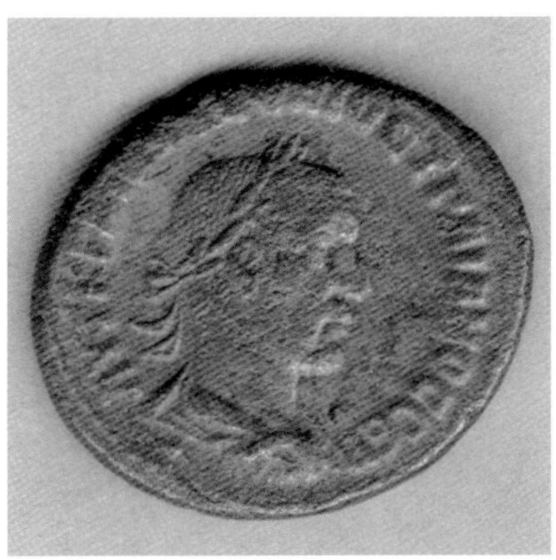

173.
Billon tetradrachm, 26 mm, 11.29 g
Mint: Antioch, A.D. 250–251
Decius, A.D. 249–251.
Obverse: laureate bust of Decius, to right; ΑΥΤ Κ Γ ΜΕ ΚΥ ΔΕΚΙΟϹ ΤΡΑΙΑΝΟϹ ϹΕΒ
Reverse: eagle standing with wreath in beak; ΔΗΜΑΡΧ ΕΞΟΥϹΙΑϹ (Tribuniciae Potestatis); below S.C.
Ref. BMC Galat. 222.296
Gift of Herbert M. Howe, 1980.76

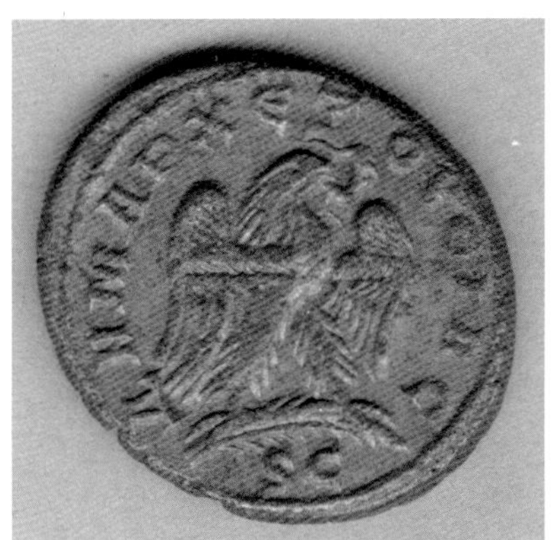

Decius was governor of Moesia (Bulgaria) when revolt broke out against Philip. He marched to his aid, but the troops forced him to take over the throne himself. He is best known for his savage persecution of the Christians: anyone accused of Christianity had to sacrifice to the gods and receive a certificate of the action. About fifty of these papyrus certificates, including one in the University of Wisconsin–Madison Memorial Library, have survived. Decius was killed in battle against the Goths in A.D. 251.

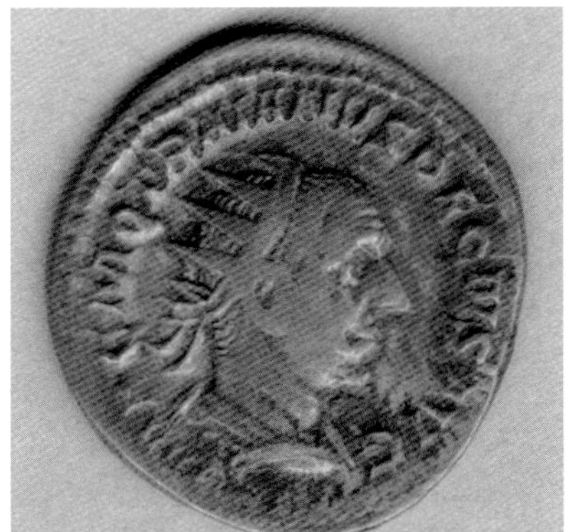

174.
AR antoninianus, 20.6 mm, 4.71 g
Mint: Rome
Decius, A.D. 249–251
Obverse: head of Decius, to right; IMP C M Q TRAIANOS DECIVS AVG
Reverse: Genius (guardian spirit) standing, to left; GENIVS EXERC ILLYRICIANI (the genius of the army of Illyria)
Ref. RIC Decius 16c
Gift of Herbert M. Howe,1980.259

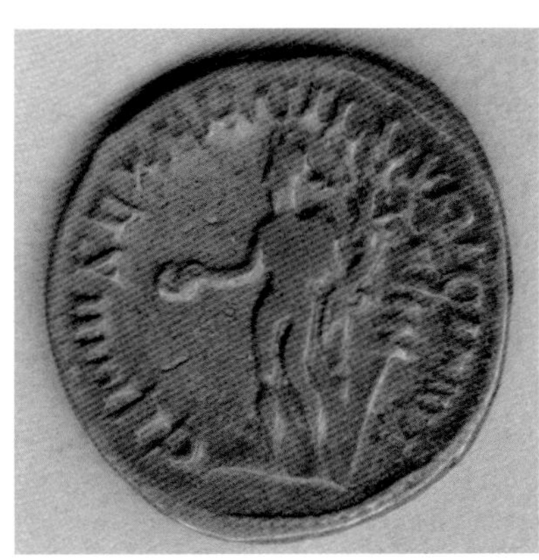

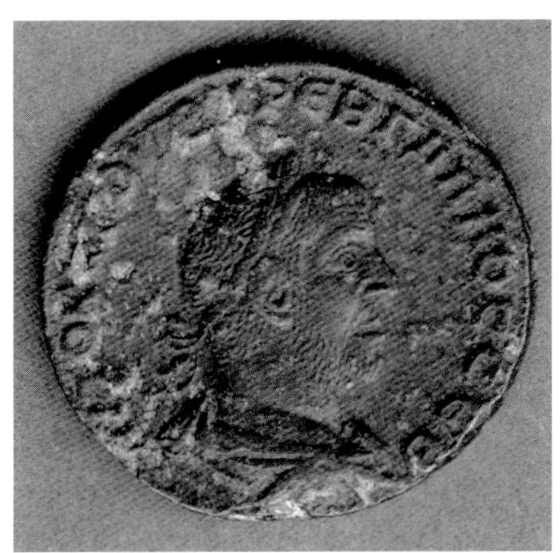

175.
Large bronze, 30 mm, 16.54 g
Mint: Antioch
Trebonianus Gallus, A.D. 251–253
Obverse: laureate bust of Gallus, to right; ΑVΤΟΚ ΚΓ ΟVΙΒ ΤΡΕΒ ΓΑΛΛΟϹ ϹΕΒ
Reverse: tetrastyle shrine containing statue of turret-crowned Tyche of Antioch, with river Orontes beneath her feet; ΑΝΤΙΟΧΕΩΝ ΜΗΤΡΟΚΟΛΩΝ S C
Ref. BMC Galatia 229.653
Gift of Herbert M. Howe, 1980.75

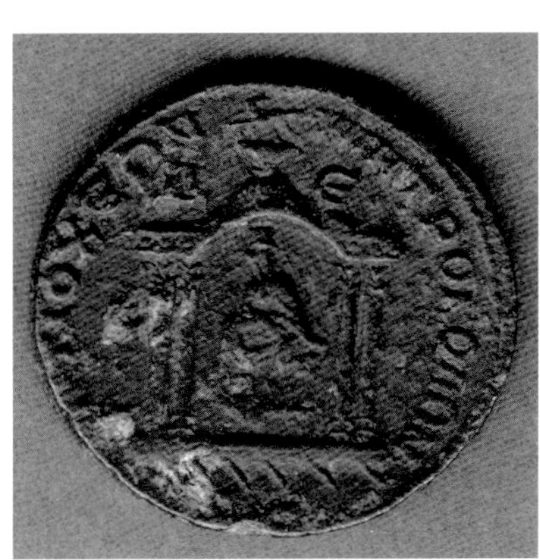

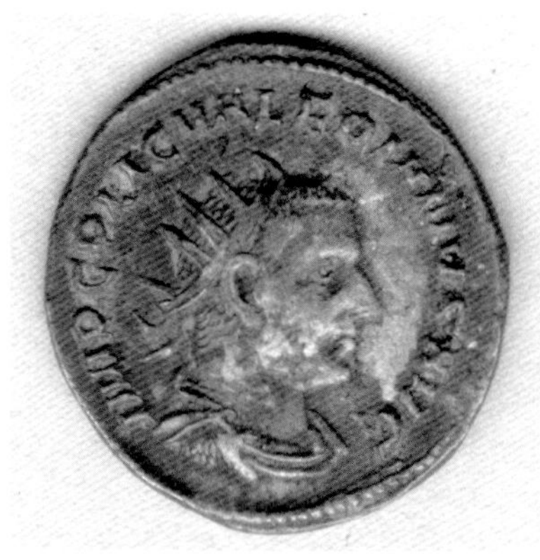

176.
AR antoninianus, 20.6 mm, 2.73 g
Mint: Rome, A.D. 254
Valerian, A.D. 253–260
Obverse: radiate bust of Valerian, to right; IMP C P LIC VALERIANVS AVG
Reverse: Salus (Safety) standing, front, feeding snake; SALVS AVGG (the health of the emperors)
Ref. RIC Val. 121
Gift of Herbert M. Howe, 1980.435

Valerian was a general on the Rhine who came to the aid of Gallus, but too late. He took the power himself, with his son Gallienus as his associate. In A.D. 260 his army was surrounded by that of the Sassanian (Persian) Sapor I, and Valerian was captured, dying (and being skinned, stuffed, and exhibited) soon thereafter. In his reign the antoninianus became a copper-plated coin. Valerian was one of the few emperors of this period to be succeeded by his son.

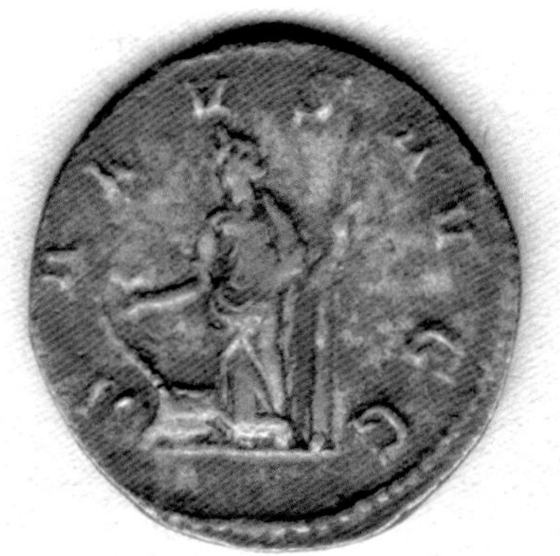

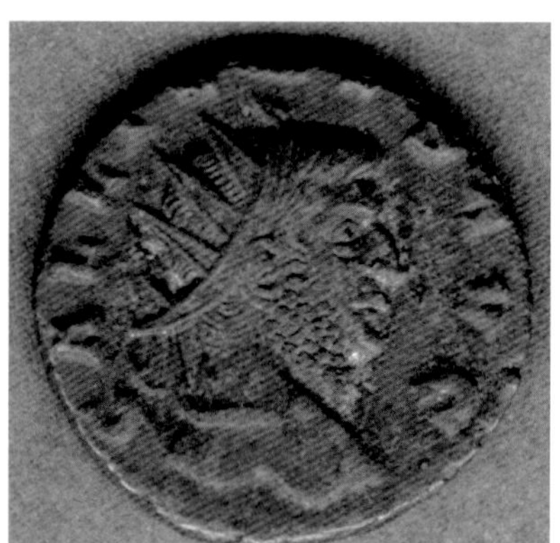

177.
Small bronze, 19.1 mm, 3.28 g
Mint: Milan (?)
Gallienus, A.D. 257–268
Obverse: radiate head of Gallienus to right; GALLIENVS AVG
Reverse: Providentia (Foresight) standing, to left; PROVI AVG
Ref. RIC Gal. 261
Gift of Herbert M. Howe, 1980.285

The reign of Gallienus was probably the low point of the empire, which was racked by plague, famine, frontier wars, and internal discord. Much of the East was lost to Odenathus and Zenobia of Palmyra, and Britain, Gaul, and Spain were lost for a time to Postumus. Gallienus did, however, check the barbarians on several fronts and made concessions to the Christians.

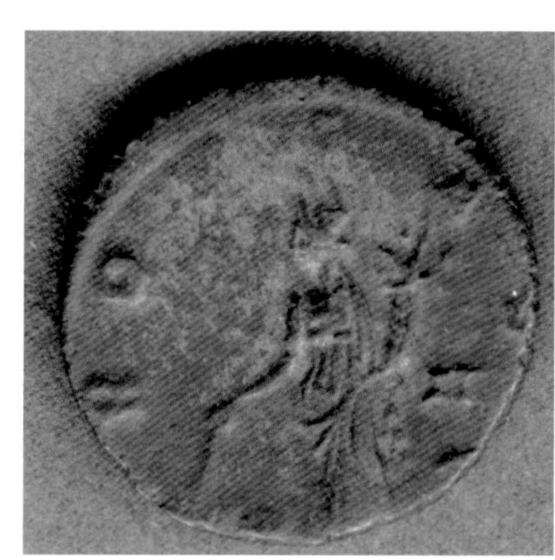

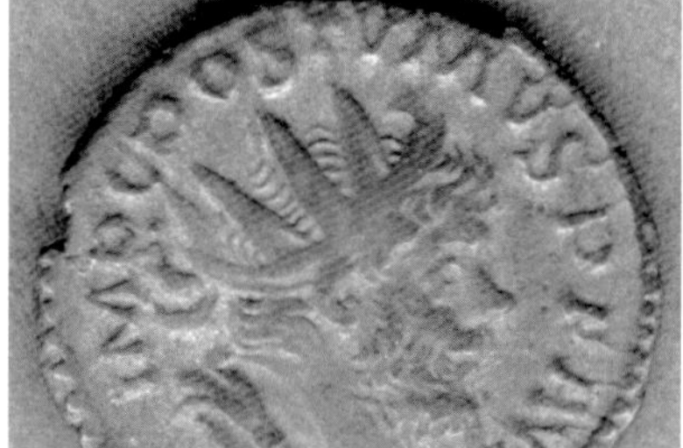

178.
AR antoninianus, 20.6 mm, 2.93 g
Uncertain mint: A.D. 259–268
Postumus, A.D. 260–269
Obverse: radiate draped bust of Postumus, to right; IMP C POSTVMVS P F AVG
Reverse: Providentia facing, with globe and scepter; PROVIDETIA [sic] AVG
Ref. RIC Post. 80
Gift of Herbert M. Howe, 1980.376

Postumus revolted against Gallienus in A.D. 258 and for ten years held back the Germans on the Rhine, establishing himself as emperor in Gaul. He was assassinated by his own troops when he refused to allow them to sack the city of Mainz. He was succeeded by Marius, originally a blacksmith, who in his turn was murdered with a sword he himself had made.

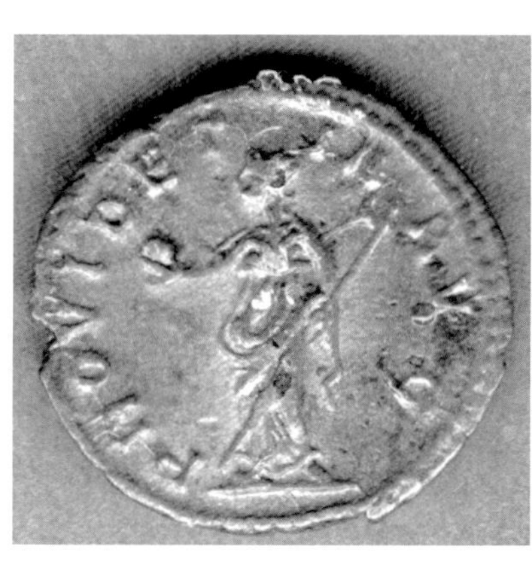

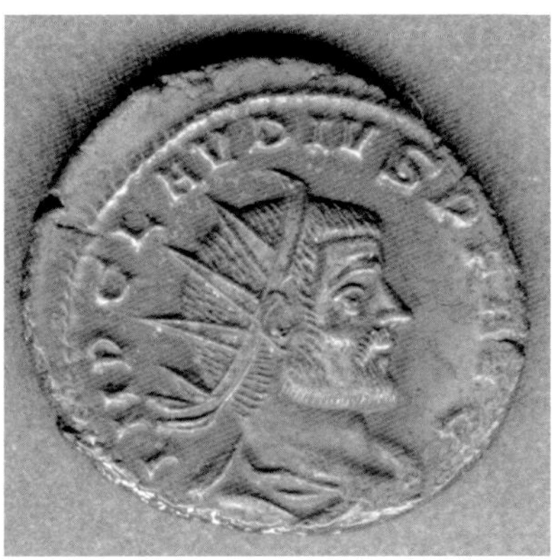

179.
AR antoninianus, 20.6 mm, 3.68 g
Mint: Siscia (Balkans)
Claudius II Gothicus, A.D. 268–270.
Obverse: radiate draped bust of Claudius, to right; IMP CLAVDIVS P F AVG
Reverse: Spes (Hope), standing, to left; SPES PVBLICA
Ref. RIC Claud. II 168
Gift of Herbert M. Howe, 1980.238

Claudius, a general of Gallienus, ruled only two years, but won two crushing victories over the Alemanni and Goths. He died in A.D. 270 of plague caught from captive Germans.

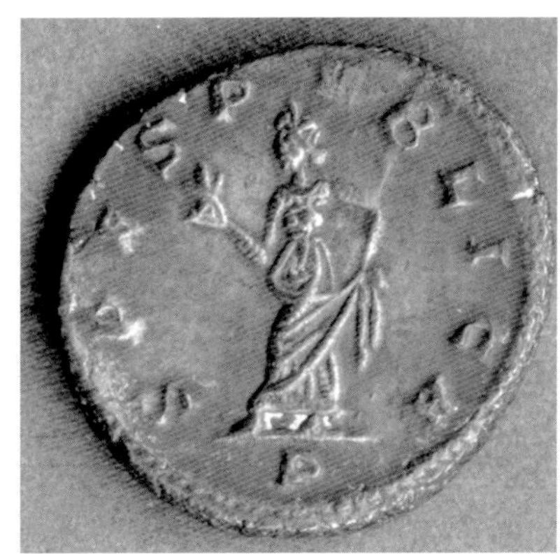

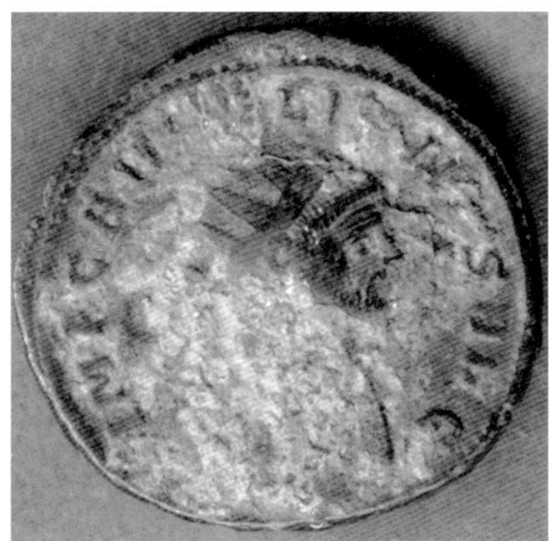

180.
AE as, 20.6 mm, 3.19 g
Mint: Milan or Ticinum
Aurelian, A.D. 270–275
Obverse: radiate bust of Aurelian, to right; IMP AVRELIANVS AVG
Reverse: Aurelian clasping the hand of a woman, presumably his wife Severina; CONCORDIA MILITVM
Ref. RIC Aurel. 82
Gift of Herbert M. Howe, 1980.172

In his short reign, Aurelian won back almost all the lost territory of the empire. He built a new strong wall around the city of Rome, which played an important part in resisting Napoleon III sixteen hundred years later, in 1848. Although this specimen exhibits dramatic deterioration, it represents the condition in which many ancient coins are found.

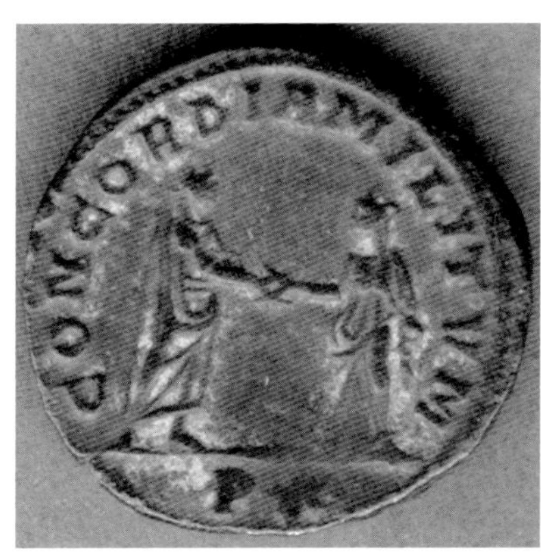

181.
Billon tetradrachm, 20.6 mm, 7.58 g
Mint: Alexandria
Aurelian and Vaballathus, A.D. 270–271
Obverse: draped and cuirassed bust of Aurelian, to right; A K ΔΛOM AYPHΛIANOC CEB
Reverse: draped and cuirassed bust of Vaballathus, to right; IAC OYABAΛΛAΘOC AΘHNOY AY TCPΩ
Ref. BMC Alex. 312.2390
Gift of Herbert M. Howe, 1980.204

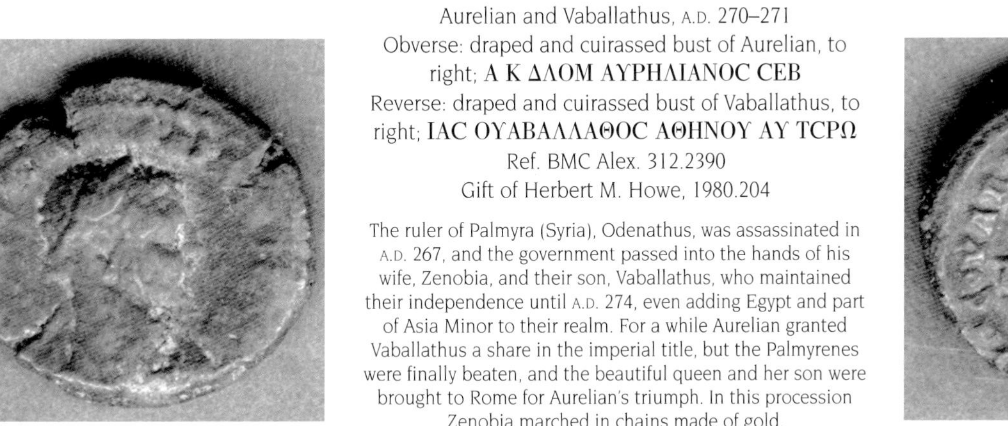

The ruler of Palmyra (Syria), Odenathus, was assassinated in A.D. 267, and the government passed into the hands of his wife, Zenobia, and their son, Vaballathus, who maintained their independence until A.D. 274, even adding Egypt and part of Asia Minor to their realm. For a while Aurelian granted Vaballathus a share in the imperial title, but the Palmyrenes were finally beaten, and the beautiful queen and her son were brought to Rome for Aurelian's triumph. In this procession Zenobia marched in chains made of gold.

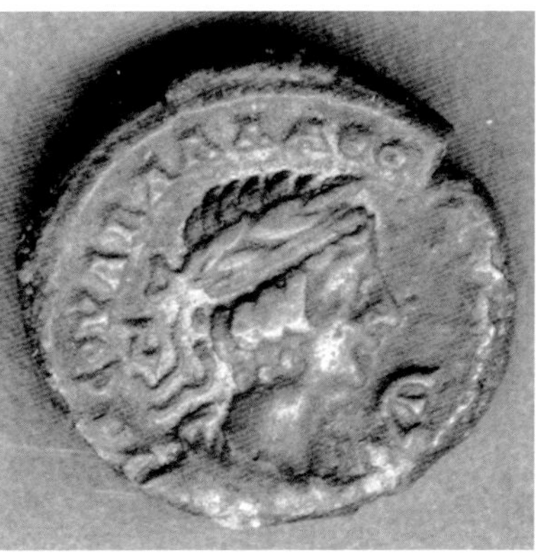

FROM DIOCLETIAN TO THEODOSIUS

From the time of Marcus Aurelius to that of Diocletian the empire had been on the verge of collapse. But it survived for over a hundred more years, though often divided. The western empire continued to have an emperor, at least in name, until A.D. 476. The eastern, Byzantine, empire continued, with one sixty-year interruption from 1204, until the Turks took Constantinople in 1453.

During this period the coinage suffered from debasement of the metals used and–at least to modern eyes–from changes in taste. The Severi could not solve the economic problems of the state, and Caracalla was forced to issue a new coin, the antoninianus, nominally worth two denarii, but in fact worth one and a half. This too was debased and soon became a copper core with a steadily thinner silvering, which finally became virtually worthless, until it was replaced by a new coinage under Diocletian. Of course, good and handsome coins were struck in this period, but the general picture is that of a flood of mean little copper pieces which, by "Gresham's Law"–"bad money drives out good"–drove good money into hoards. From about A.D. 270 onward a series of Roman victories and a renewal of the supply of precious metals gave the empire a respite. But Diocletian even felt it necessary to issue an edict, though unsuccessfully, for fixing prices.

The coin types of the two centuries of this period varied greatly, but a few matters should be noticed. First, as early as the time of Hadrian separate provinces had been honored by representation on coins. Second, family continuity was sometimes denied, but usually asserted. The Severi, who had no family connection with Marcus Aurelius, all took the name of Antoninus. Third, the importance of the army was recognized: see, for example, the coin of Decius (cat. no. 174) of A.D. 250, whose reverse legends read "to the genius of the army of Illyria" [former Yugoslavia]. Finally, a number of eastern cults were recognized on imperial coins, especially after the Severi. The most important was the Syrian sun-god, whose image appears from the time of Elagabalus (A.D. 218–222) to that of Constantine. Sol, the sun, served as a sort of rallying point for different monotheisms, eventually including Christianity, the cult of the "Sun of Righteousness," foretold by the prophet (Malachi 4:2).

Diocletian, who came to the throne in A.D. 284, made several important changes in the structure and institutions of the empire. He abandoned the old coinage, striking a new and sound one. This included a new bronze coin, the **follis**, of about the same weight and fineness of the as of Nero's time, and a silver coin worth about five folles. There was further tinkering in the reigns of Constantine (A.D. 307–337) and Constantius II (A.D. 337–361). Diocletian divided the empire in two parts, each ruled by an Augustus—Diocletian himself in the East, Maximian in the West. Under each Augustus was a Caesar, whose designated heirs were Galerius in the East and Constantius in the West. But the system broke down after the abdication of the first Augusti in A.D. 305. Not until A.D. 324 was peace restored, with Constantine (son of Constantius I) as sole emperor. About A.D. 303 Diocletian began a last and savage persecution of the Christians, continued by his successors Galerius and Maximinus Daia. At least partly for political reasons, Constantine took the Christian side, and in A.D. 312 proclaimed toleration for them. A succession of privileges was granted the new religion, until by the end of the century, it was the only cult recognized. But Constantine's coins kept the familiar types, and he was not baptized until his deathbed. He was succeeded by several members of his family, the last of whom, Julian (A.D. 360–363), reverted to paganism. The last of the coins displayed here is one of Theodosius (A.D. 379–395), at whose death the empire was divided, never to be reunited, and at whose death the Christian church was firmly established.

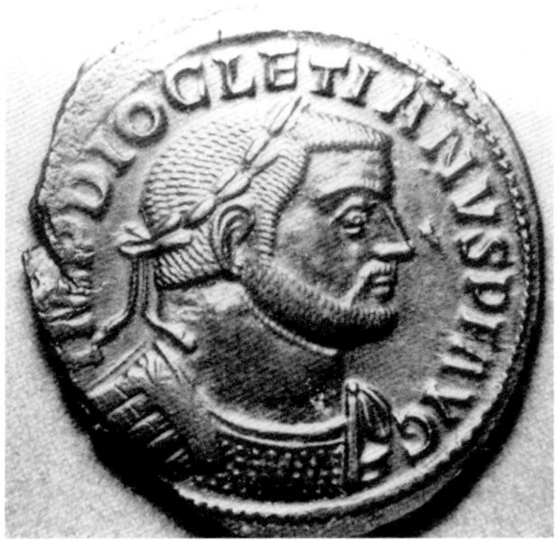

182.
AE follis, 28 mm
Mint: Lugdunum, A.D. 295–305
Diocletian, A.D. 284–305
Obverse: laureate bust of Diocletian, to right; DIOCLETIANVS P AVG
Reverse: Genius standing, to left; GENIO POPVLI ROMANI; in exergue PLG
Ref. Cohen 125
Gift of Mr. and Mrs. Arthur J. Frank, 1977.310

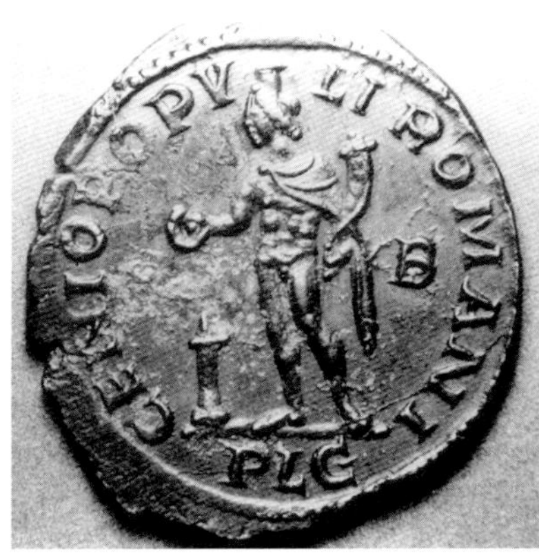

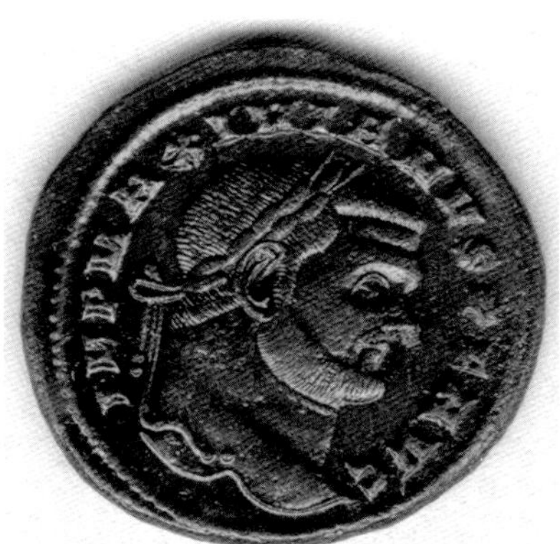

183.
AE follis, 28 mm
Mint: Carthage
Maximian, A.D. 295–305.
Obverse: laureate head of Maximian, to right; IMP MAXIMIANVS P F AVG
Reverse: Africa standing, to left, with elephant tusk; lion and antelope skull at feet; FELIX ADVENT AVGG NN (The luck bringing arrival of the emperors)
Ref. RIC 19b; Seaby 3530
Gift of Mr. and Mrs. Arthur J. Frank, 1979.297

Carthage was in Maximian's half of the empire.

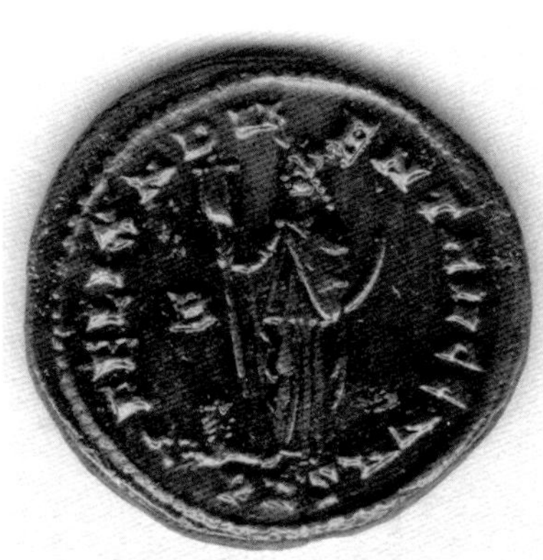

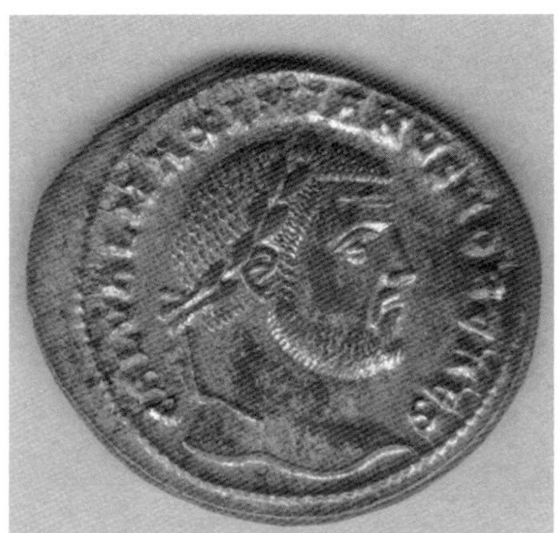

184.
AE (silvered) follis, 28 mm, 9.38 g
Mint: Cyzicus (Asia Minor), A.D. 295–296
Galerius, A.D. 293–305
Obverse: laureate head of Galerius, to right; GAL VAL MAXIMIANVS NOB CAES
Reverse: Genius standing, to left, holding cornucopia and paterna. GENIO AVGG ET CAESARVM N N; in exergue K A
Ref. Seaby 3607; BMC 11b
Gift of Mr. and Mrs. Arthur J. Frank, 1979.298

Galerius was the eastern Caesar. After the abdication of Diocletian and Maximian, he became Augustus and pressed on with the persecution of the Christians. He came down with a painful disease, possibly stomach or colon cancer, and one of his last acts was calling off the persecution and asking the prayers of the Christians. He died in A.D. 312.

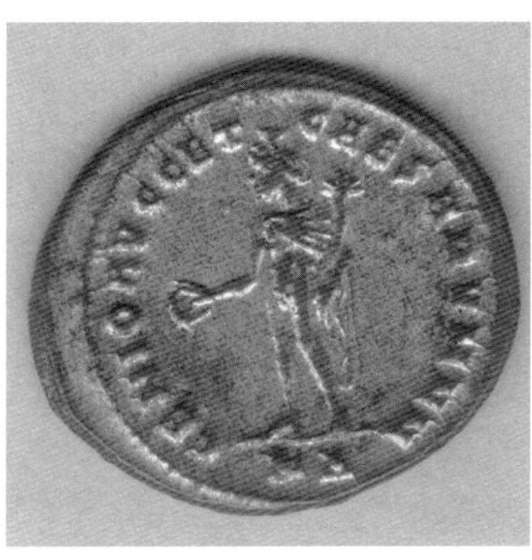

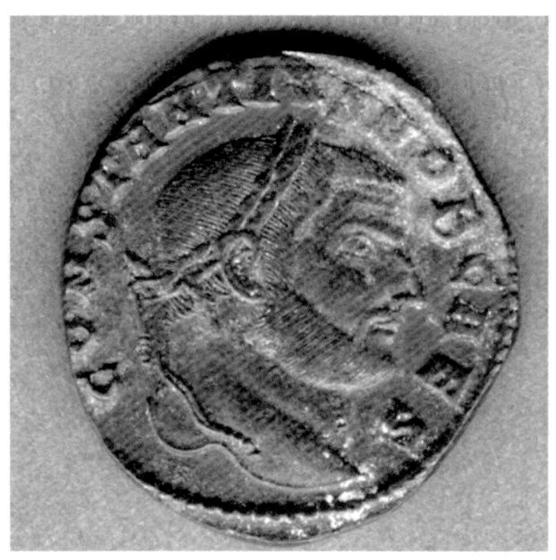

185.
AE follis, 25 mm, 8.83 g
Mint: Rome, A.D. 293–305
Constantius I Chlorus, A.D. 292–305
Obverse: laureate head of Constantius I, to right; CONSTANTIVS NOB CAES
Reverse: Moneta standing, to left, with scales and cornucopia; SAC MON VRB AVGG ET CAESS (The Sacred Mint of the Augusti and the Caesars)
Ref. Cohen 261
Gift of Herbert M. Howe, 1980.248

Constantius died soon after the abdication. His son, Constantine I, was acclaimed emperor by the troops in the West. The double "S" of CAESS indicates there were two of each.

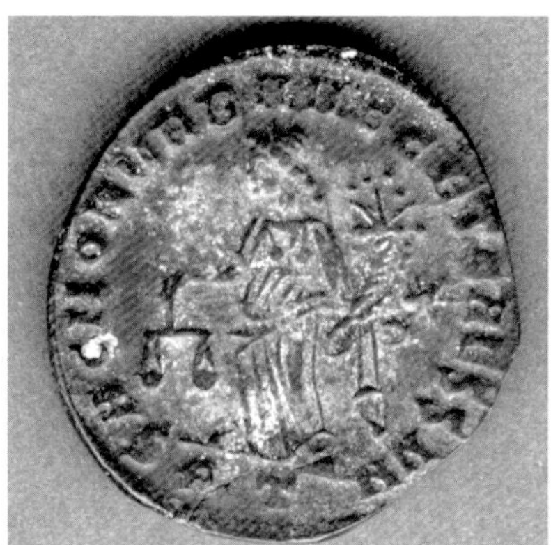

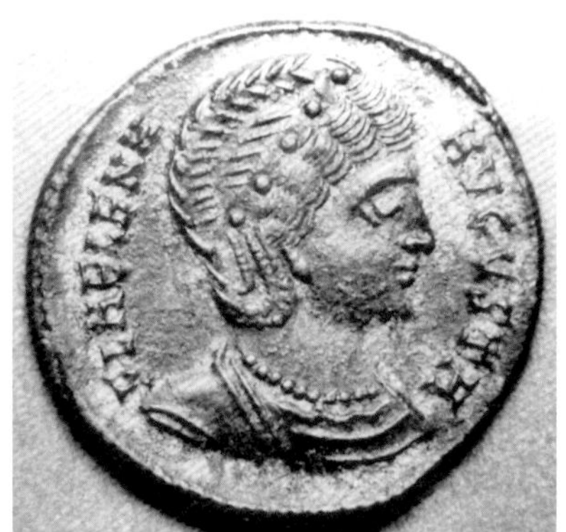

186.
AE follis, 19.1 mm, 2.62 g
Uncertain mint: A.D. 337–339
Helena (wife of Constantius I, mother of Constantine I),
Obverse: diademed bust of Helena, to right; FL HELENA AVGVSTa
Reverse: Helena standing, to left, holding branch; SECVRITAS REIPVBLICE; in exergue SMHΣ
Ref. RIC 95
Gift of Mr. and Mrs. Arthur J. Frank, 1980.27

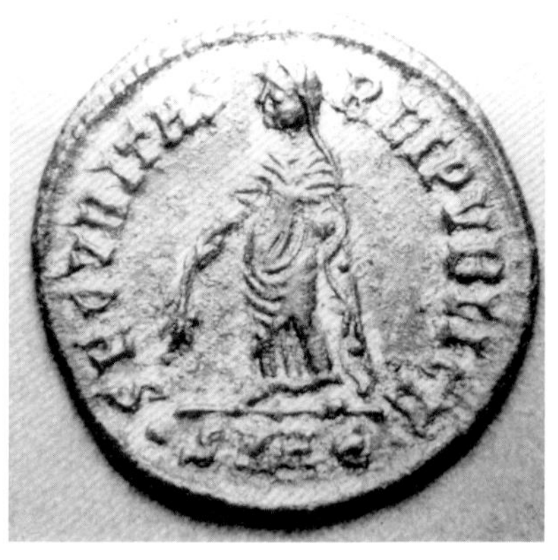

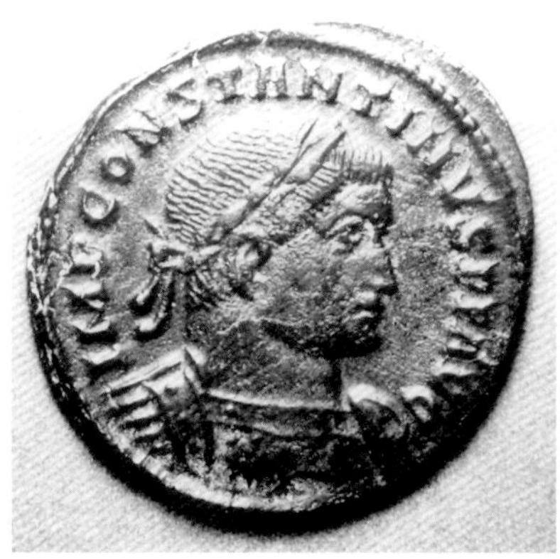

187.
AE follis, 25 mm, 7.43 g
Mint: Trier
Constantine I, A.D. 307–337
Obverse: laureate bust of Constantine, to right; IMP CONSTANTINVS P F AVG
Reverse: Mars advancing, to right; MARTI PATRI PROPVGNATORI (to father Mars, [my] ally); in exergue PTR
Ref. Seaby 3764
Gift of Mr. and Mrs. Arthur J. Frank, 1978.339

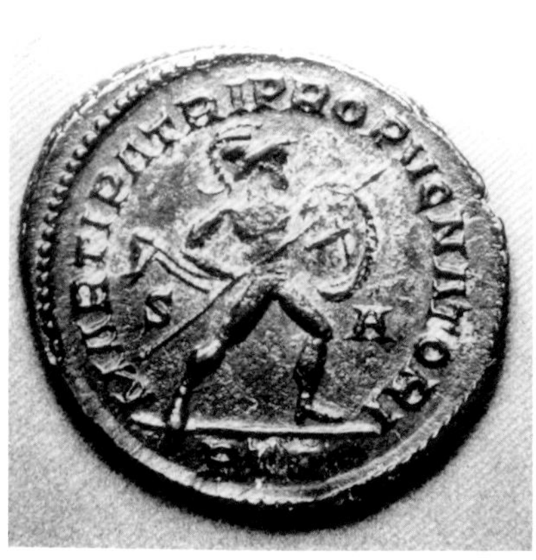

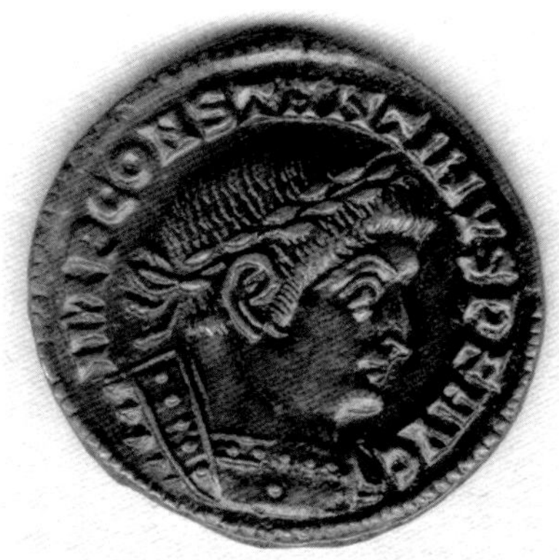

188.
AE follis, 22.2 mm, 4.66 g
Mint: Lugdunum (Lyons)
Constantine I, A.D. 307–337
Obverse: laureate bust of Constantine, to right; IMP CONSTANTINVS AVG
Reverse: Sol, to left, with globe; SOLI INVICTO COMITI F T (to [my] comrade, the unconquered Sun); in exergue PLG
Ref. RIC 17 var; Seaby 3768
Gift of Mr. and Mrs. Arthur J. Frank, 1978.340, ex Little Orme's Head hoard

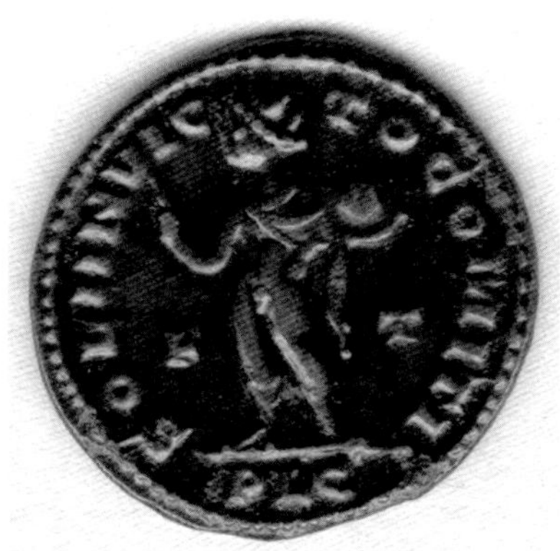

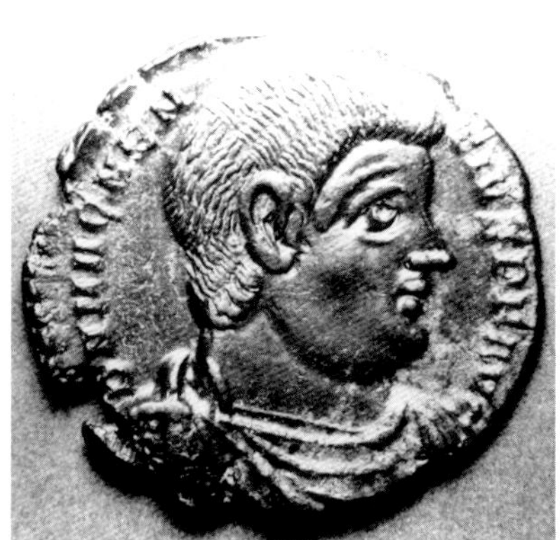

189.
Large bronze, 25 mm, 7.82 g
Mint: Trier
Magnentius, A.D. 350–353
Obverse: draped bust of Magnentius, to right; MAGNENTIVS P F AVG
Reverse: Christogram, the Greek letter X superimposed on P, for ChRistos; at sides, A (alpha) and W (omega); SALVS DD NN AVG ET CAES (DD NN stands for two Nostri Domini; our lords), in exergue TR P
Ref. comp. Seaby 3917
Gift of Mr. and Mrs. Arthur J. Frank, 1979.305

Magnentius rebelled against Constantius II in A.D. 350 and was killed in 354. This coin represents one of the earliest uses of a specifically Christian symbol.

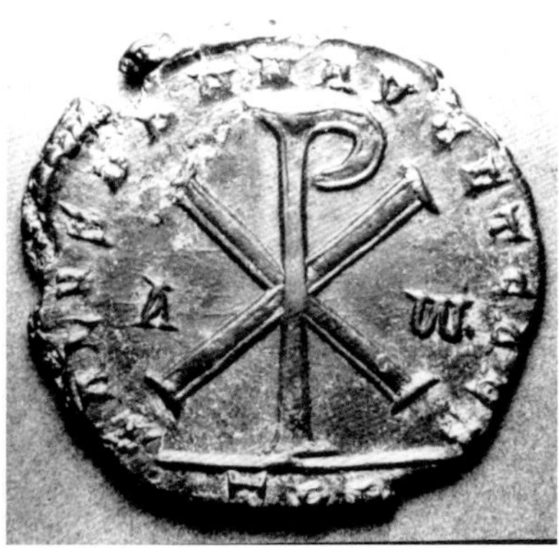

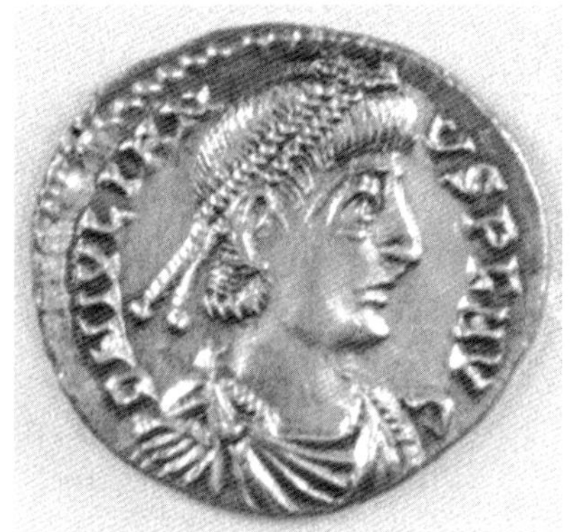

190.
AR siliqua, 17.5 mm, 2.30 g
Mint: Constantinople
Julian II (the Apostate), A.D. 360–363
Obverse: beardless bust of Julian II, to right; D N IVLIANVS P F AVG
Reverse: VOTIS V MVLTIS X (vows [for his safety, to be paid if he survives for] five years, and many [more vows if he survives for] ten); in exergue SCON
Ref. comp. Seaby 3971
Gift of Mr. and Mrs. Arthur J. Frank, 1979.306

Julian, a deist rather than an anti-Christian, was a great-nephew of Constantine I. In an expedition against the Parthians, he was shot in the eye by an arrow.

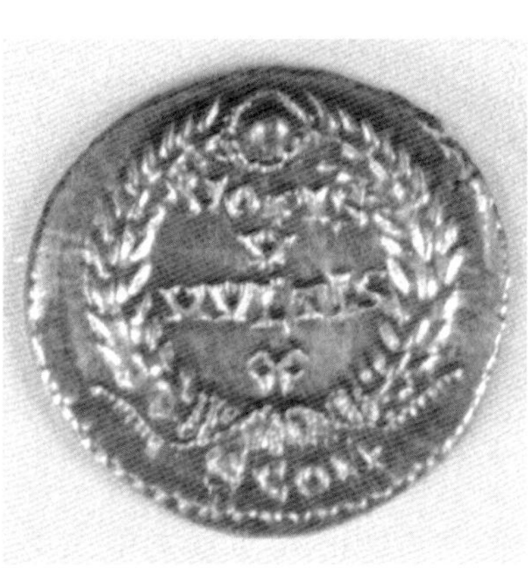

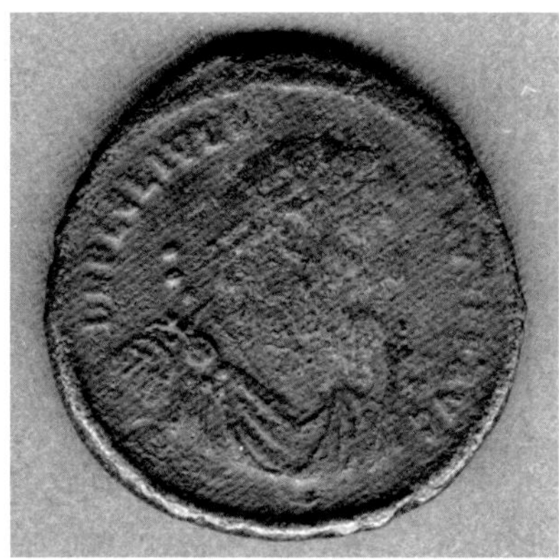

191.
Large bronze, 28 mm, 7.64 g
Mint: Rome
Julian II (the Apostate), A.D. 360–363
Obverse: laureate draped bust of Julian II, to right; D N FL CL IVLIANVS P F AVG
Reverse: Egyptian Apis, or bull, standing, to left; SECVRITAS REIPVB. Julian tried to renew the vitality of the pagan cults
Ref. Cohen 38
Gift of Herbert M. Howe, 1980.305

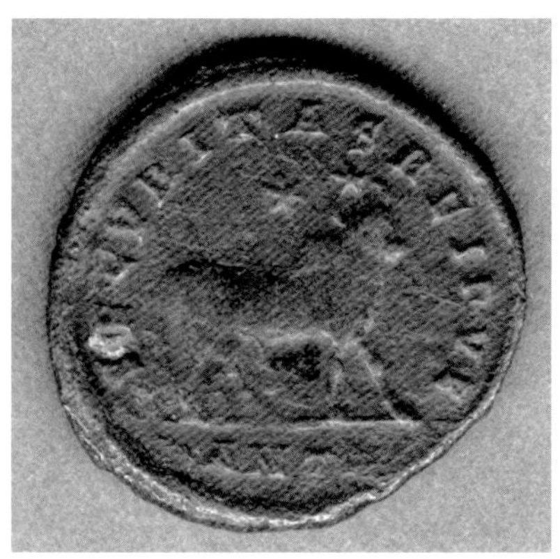

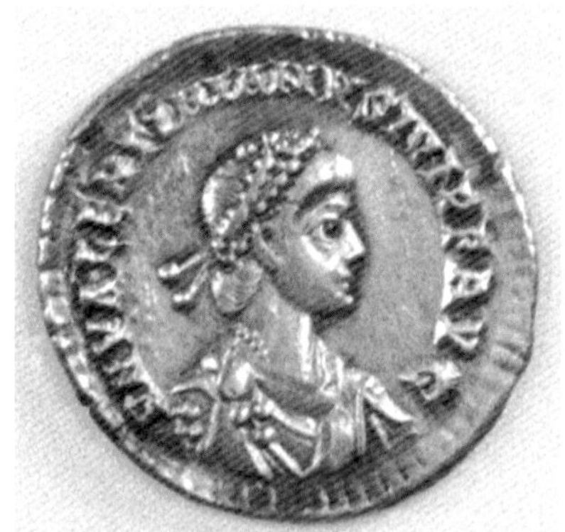

192.
AR siliqua, 17.5 mm, 1.78 g
Mint: Trier
Valentinian II, A.D. 375–392
Obverse: diademed bust of Valentinian II, to right; Dominus Noster VALENTINIANVS IVN [the younger] P F AVG
Reverse: Roma, seated left, holding Victory and spear; VRBS ROMA; TRPS
Ref. RIC 46c; Seaby 4058
Gift of Mr. and Mrs. Arthur J. Frank, 1979.307

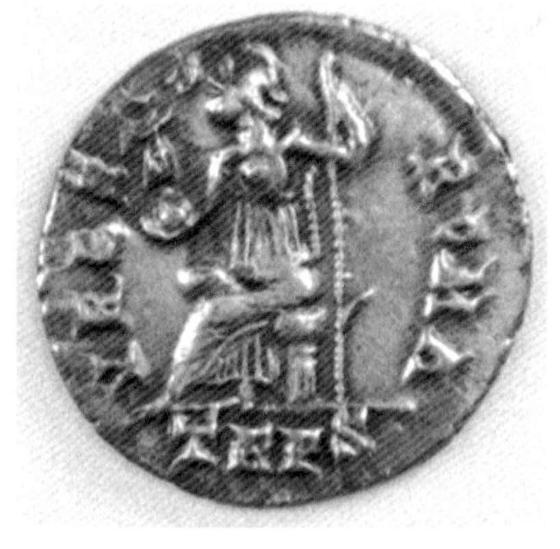

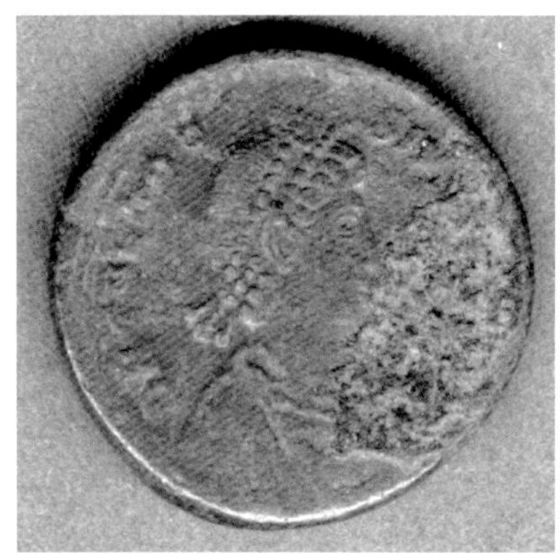

193.
Medium bronze, 23.8 mm, 6.30 g
Mint: Constantinople, A.D. 383–388
Theodosius I
Obverse: diademed bust of Theodosius, to right; D N THEODOSIVS P F AVG
Reverse: emperor standing, to right, with standard and globe, and left foot on captive; VIRTVS EXERCITI
Ref. RIC2 IX 233.83b
Gift of Herbert M. Howe, 1980.404

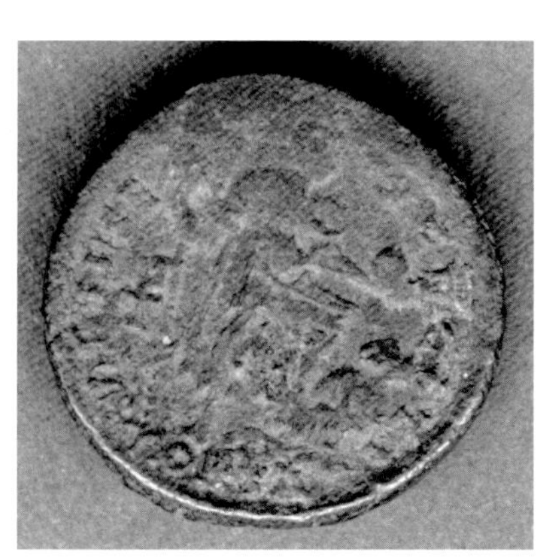

BRIEF GLOSSARY

Biga a chariot drawn by two animals, usually horses

Billon alloy of gold or silver with greater proportion of tin or copper

Diadem a band worn around the head and tied at the back, symbol of sovereignty

Drachm the fundamental unit of coinage for many Greek cities

EL (electrum) a natural alloy of gold and silver in Asian river sands

Exergue the space between the horizontal line under the design and the edge of the coin

Incuse punched-in

Janiform looking in two directions, after Janus, Roman god of gates and doorways, giving rise to the name January, which looks back to the previous year and forward to the coming year

Laureate with a crown of laurel leaves

Moneyers those licensed to issue coins

Nike the Greek goddess of victory, often winged and bearing a wreath

Obverse the side of the coin where the profile is convex, the "heads" side

Omphalos "navel," a stone at Delphi

Protome front half

Quadriga four-horse chariot

Radiate a crown of rays

Reverse the side of the coin where the profile is concave, the "tails" side

Rostral crown showing beaks of ships

Scyphate cup-shaped

Triskele three legs, joined at the top, radiating, emblem of Sicily

Tyche the goddess of fortune, often a patron goddess of a particular city

COMMON ABBREVIATIONS ON ROMAN COINS

AVG	Augustus, granted to Octavius in 27 B.C. and to subsequent Roman emperors
AVTO or **AVTOK**	Autokrator, single ruler
CAES or **CAESS**	Caesar, Caesars
CENS	Censor , Roman magistrate responsible, among other things, for the census
COS	consul, chief magistrates (two elected annually)
D, DD	dominus, domini, lord(s), master(s)
DICT	dictator
DIVI	deified, made a god by the act of the senate
F	Filius, son
IMP	Imperator, commander, later emperor
KAI, KAISA	Caesar on coins from Greek-speaking east
N	Nepos, grandson
NOB	nobilis, of noble birth
OB CIVES SERVATOS	(for having saved citizens)
P F	pius felix , dutiful and lucky
P M, PON M, PONTIF MAX	Pontifex Maximus, chief priest
POT	potestate, power, authority
P P	pater patriae, father of the fatherland
PRAE	praetor, magistrate
PRAEF	praefectus, prefect
Q	quaestor, treasurer
S C	Senatus Consultum, degree of the senate
SPQR	Senatus Populus Que Romanus, senate and people of Rome, issued by the senate
SEB	sebastos, augustus
TR	Tribunicia, tribune, an officer (usually TR POT, with the power of a tribune)
V	five
VIR	man, III VIR, triumvirate

ABBREVIATIONS FOR REFERENCES CITED

Bab. Babelon, Ernest. *Monnaies de la Republique Romaine*. 2 vols. Paris 1885. Reprint Bologna 1974.

Blanchet Blanchet, Adrien. *Traite des monnaies gauloises*. Bologna 1970.

BM *Catalogue of Greek Coins in the British Museum*. 27 vols. London, 1873–1927.

BMC *Catalogue of Coins of the Roman Empire in the British Museum*, I-VI. London, 1923–62; reprinted London 1976. with suffix denoting area

BMCRR Grueber, Herbert A. *Coins of the Roman Republic in the British Museum*. 3 vols. London 1910. Reprint London 1969.

BN Bibliothèque Nationale de France, Paris

Cohen Cohen, H. *Description historique des Monnaies frappées sous l'Empire Romain*. 8 vols. Paris, 1880–92. Reprinted London 1956.

Crawford Crawford, Michael. *Roman Republican Coinage*. 2 vols. Cambridge 1974.

Head Head, Barclay V. *Historia Numorum*. New edition. Chicago 1947.

Mac. Macdonald, G. *Coin Types*. Glasgow 1905.

Newell Newell, Edward T. *Royal Greek Portrait Coins*. Racine, Wis. 1937.

RIC Mattingly, Harold and E.A. Sydenham, E.A. *The Roman Imperial Coinage*. London 1923.

RIC2 Mattingly, H., E.A. Sydenham, R.A.G. Carson. *The Roman Imperial Coinage*. Rev. ed. London 1984.

Seaby Seaby, H. A. *Roman Silver Coinage, Vol. I, The Republic to Augustus*. 3rd ed. London 1978.

Sellwood Sellwood, David. *The Coinage of Parthia*. 2nd ed. London 1980.

Seltman Seltman, Charles T. *Greek Coins: A History of Metallic Currency and Coinage*. London 1960.

Svor. (1904) Svoronos, J. N. *Ta nomismata tou kratour ton Polemain*. Athens 1904–8.

CRR Sydenham, Edward A. *The Coinage of the Roman Republic*. Rev. G. C. Haines, ed. L. Forrer and C.A. Hersh. London 1952.

Private Collections

Forrer L. Forrer, *Descriptive Catalogue of the collection of Greek Coins formed by Sir Hermann Weber*. London 1922–19.

Grose Grose, S. W. *Catalogue of the McClean Collection of Greek Coins*. 3 vols. Cambridge 1923–29.

Jameson Collection R. Jameson: *Monnaies grecques antiques*. 4 vols. Paris 1913–32.

Lockett *Sylloge Nummorum Graecorum*. Great Britain: III (1938–49) *Lockett Collection*

Pozzi *Monnaies grecques antiques provenantes de la collection de feu le Prof. S. Pozzi*. Sale catalogue by Naville Geneva, 4 April 1921.

SNG *Sylloge Nummorum Graecorum*. American Numismatic Society

Syll. Lloyd *Sylloge Nummorum Graecorum*. Great Britain: II (1933–37) *Lloyd Collection*

INDEX